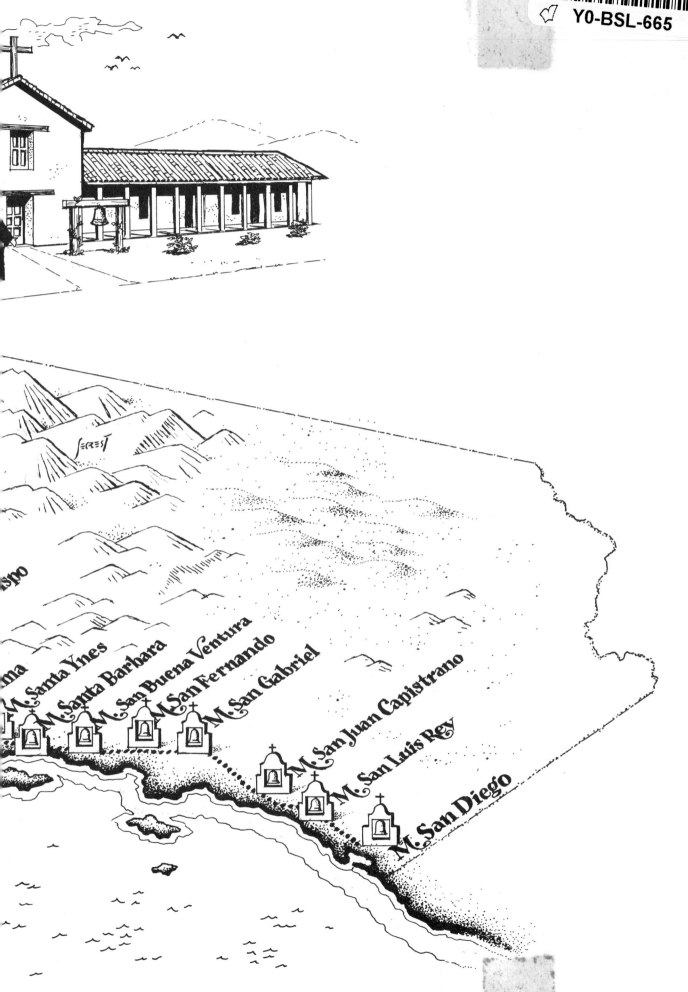

THE SONOMA MISSION

SAN FRANCISCO SOLANO DE SONOMA

Endorsed by
The American Revolution Bicentennial Commission
of California and the
Bicentennial '76 Commission of Sonoma

LIBRO

SEGUNDO DE PARTIDAS

DE

BAUTISMOS

ADMINISTRADOS EN ESTA IGLESIA

DE

S.ᴺ FRAN.ᶜᵒ

SOLANO

DE

SONOMA, EN LA ALTA CALIFORNIA.

DÁ PRINCIPIO

EN EL AÑO DEL SEÑOR

DE

MDCCCXL.

POR

El P. F. J. L. Q.   R. M.º Del C. A. D. P. F. D. N, S. D. G. D. Z.

La Rosa Fecit.

Baptismal Book Tome #2 Frontispiece   *Courtesy St. Francis Solano Church Archives.*

THE
SONOMA MISSION

SAN FRANCISCO SOLANO
DE SONOMA

by

Robert S. Smilie

*The Founding, Ruin and Restoration of
California's 21st Mission*

VALLEY PUBLISHERS • FRESNO • 1975

Library of Congress Catalogue Card No. 74-81641

ISBN 0-913548-24-3

First Edition

DEDICATION

To the memory of
Fray Buenaventura Fortuny
the forgotten Father of
Mission San Francisco Solano
who accepted a demoralized embryo
mission and in his quiet,
efficient manner developed
it into an outstanding and
wealthy part of the
California Mission Realm.

Contents

Cover Photograph:
SONOMA MISSION by the camera of Wm. Frohmader.

Mission day weights and measures used in this volume.

Vara	33 inches
League	2.6 miles
League square	4,340 acres
League square	6.76 square miles
Fanega	1.6 bushels
Almud	1/12 *fanega*
Arroba	25 pounds

Acknowledgments

A small grass fire, started in June 1896 beside the first St. Francis Solano Catholic Church on Napa Street which ultimately destroyed the church, is about forgotten. But in the preparation of this history of Mission San Francisco Solano, the little fire created a serious obstacle to the necessary research as all the mission records and documents, except four small books, were destroyed. They, with all the church properties and vestments had been moved to the new church from the 1841 chapel after it had been sold in 1881.

The search for other copies of the records and information on the mission was far and wide and the gracious help of many persons allowed the writer to piece together, bit by bit, the many missing parts so that an authentic history and readable story could be offered.

Among those who assisted, I wish to mention and thank especially the following:

Mrs. Maud K. Swingle, Reference Librarian, California Historical Society, for her unstinting help and encouragement in producing this volume; and Mr. Jay Williar, of the same staff, who repeatedly produced my dimly described items — pronto.

Dr. John Barr Tompkins, of the Bancroft Library, who offered so much help and advice from his vast knowledge of early Californiana; and his fine reference staff who deciphered my vague requests for relevant materials.

Mr. Harry Downie of Carmel, who furnished the major part of the present interior items of the Mission Chapel, for his advice and review of the plan of the early buildings and their furnishings.

Rt. Rev. Monsignor John P. Farrell, Pastor, St. Francis Solano Church, for the use of the early records available and his interest in the mission's history; also Fr. Patrick Moriarty, Assistant Pastor.

Rev. Arthur D. Spearman, S.J., Archivist, University of Santa Clara, for supplying permission to use the de la Rosa early Spanish multiplication table.

Rev. Thomas I. Kennedy, Pastor, Mission San Rafael Arcangel, San Rafael, who opened up his early mission records of the Fr. Quijas period for my inspection.

Rt. Rev. Monsignor Clyde Tillman, Pastor, St. Vincent de Paul, Petaluma, whose staff supplied records of early "circuit rider" padres of the area.

His Excellency Mark J. Hurley, Bishop of Santa Rosa diocese for use of valuable items from their archives; and Sister Alecia Whalen, O.P. for kind help with above material.

Rt. Rev. Monsignor Donnell Walsh, Chancellor, Archdiocese of San Francisco, who supplied early records from their archives relating to San Francisco Solano Mission.

Reuben Woodworth, Archivist, Sonoma Valley Historical Society, whose memory and advice of early Sonoma were invaluable, as also were his stock of photographs.

Staff of the Sonoma County Recorder's Office, Santa Rosa, who could locate just about everything legal that was asked for.

The Sonoma Valley Historical Society for use of their book *Saga of Sonoma* and many photographs of old Sonoma.

The staff of the Sonoma Public Library who pleasantly cared for the many requests for elusive books, Mrs. Polly Meyers, Mrs. Elizabeth Field, and Mrs. Leroy Barr (retired).

California Department of Parks and Recreation, John H. Knight (Chief, Division of Operations), Norman Wilson, Mrs. Eletha Rea — Sacramento; also Sonoma Area Manager Richard L. Menefee for use of photos and much relevant data on the Sonoma Mission; and the helpful cooperation of his assistant, Richard Beach Alexander, Ranger #1.

Wm. Getchey, Historian and Ranger, Sonoma State Historic Park, whose knowledge of and research of the early history of Mission San Francisco Solano have been a great help and graciously shared with the writer.

Robert Lynch, Publisher of the *Index-Tribune,* Sonoma's weekly, and the use of his early files; also data from *People of the Pueblo,* Celeste Granice Murphy.

Wm. Frohmader for his fine photographic work and reproductions and use of the Sonoma Mission photo.

Richard Douglas, Historian-Ranger, Sonoma State Historic Park, for information and discussions on early phases of mission and pueblo subjects.

J.S. Holliday, Executive Director, California Historical Society, for the privilege of quoting relevant Sonoma items from their excellent files and Quarterly publications, as indicated in the chapter notes.

Stanford University Press for permission to quote from their two publications, *Historic Spots in California* and *The Lives of Wm. Hartnell.*

The Society of California Pioneers whose early annual publications supplied numerous items listed in the notes.

The story of John A. Sutter's visit to Sonoma in 1839 by Julian Dana is acknowledged.

The Huntington Library and Art Gallery for permission to quote from their *Franciscan Missionaries in Hispanic California,* Maynard Geiger, O.F.M., Huntington Library Publications, San Marino, California 1969.

William F. Knowland, *Oakland Tribune,* for permission to quote from his father's publication *California, a Landmark History,* 1941.

Marguerite Eyer Wilbur who granted permission to quote from her translation of *Duflot de Mofras' Travels on the Pacific Coast* — on his visit to Sonoma.

Marie Walsh Harrington who traced the Sonoma Mission bells and recorded their history in her volume *Mission Bells of California,* as noted, and who graciously sent permission to use the information.

Mrs. W.B. McKittrick for allowing information from her volume *Vallejo, Son of California* to be used.

The *Press Democrat* of Santa Rosa for permission to quote from their *History of Sonoma County,* E.L. Finley, editor and Mrs. Ruth W. Finley, owner and publisher.

The Department of Anthropology, University of California, for allowing the use of information on the excavations of Mission San Francisco Solano by J.A. Bennyhoff and Albert B. Elsasser in 1953; and Dr. Adan E. Treganza in 1954.

The Macmillan Company for permission to quote from *History of California, The Spanish Period* by Charles E. Chapman. (Copyright 1920 by The Macmillan Company, renewed 1949 by Aimee F. Chapman).

Smithsonian Institution, Washington, D.C. for allowing use of the items from *Indians of California,* A.L. Kroeber, 1925.

Peabody Museum, Harvard University, Cambridge, Mass. for use of Lt. George Gibb's sketch of Sonoma 1851.

Howell-North Books which graciously granted use of data from their book *Redwood Railways* by Gilbert H. Kness.

C.E. Mannion for permission to use old mission photos.

Francis L. Cross who allowed quotes from the excellent book *Early Inns of California.*

One source of information on the early years of the Sonoma Mission and the Contra Costa del Norte Este, that was found to be indispensable, is the Bancroft Library of the

University of California and Hubert H. Bancroft's *History of California* published in 1886-90. Many of the "nuggets of history" are deeply buried but diligent digging with the help of the efficient reference staff, under Dr. John B. Tompkins, brings them to light; and we are pleased to thank the Director of the Library for permission to use valuable written material and photograph prints supplied from their archives.

Also thanks to Paul C. Johnson, formerly Director of Publications, California Historical Society, for his kind help and valuable advice.

Whitney T. Genns, the well-known bibliopole of De la Guerra Street, Santa Barbara, for his gracious and valuable advice in publishing this volume.

Robert D. Parmelee, Sonoma historian, for our many talks on early Sonoma and his confirmation of many historic items.

And there are two other persons who are responsible for this volume — and without either I feel it never would have seen the light of day (or desk lamp). One is acknowledged as today's authority on California Missions and their Padres, Father Maynard Geiger, O.F.M., Ph.D., Archivist and Historian, Santa Barbara Mission Archive-Library, Santa Barbara.

Father Geiger became interested in the story of San Francisco Solano when he answered my letter a few years ago regarding early documents of the mission and their whereabouts. Since then, he has been untiring in his help, supplying information and material from his vast Mission Archives, offering advice, correcting many of my errors, encouraging, and guiding the author along a path to producing a readable yet authentic volume of local history. Words of thanks are inadequate to express my appreciation.

And the second person is Lilla Bell Smilie, my wife, who should be named as co-author, but refuses that title. There is not a sentence or subject in these pages that she has not studied, discussed, and edited, and often improved upon. The entire manuscript has been typed and corrected at least three times, at this writing, on her busy typewriter; then proofread repeatedly. She joins me in presenting this volume — the story of Mission San Francisco Solano de Sonoma.

As publication nears completion, my thanks and congratulations to Charles Clough and his enthusiastic staff at Valley Publishers who have so pleasantly and efficiently produced a beautiful and entertaining volume from my oft puzzling manuscript.

R.S.S.

Introduction

It has been the general impression that Mission San Francisco Solano de Sonoma was just a small church or chapel, with a priests' house and enclosed quadrangle and, perhaps, a few adobe houses and some Indian huts made of poles and thatch scattered around nearby.

Because it is not to be seen today, people cannot conceive that this mission was a large settlement, with a wide quadrangle completely surrounded by permanent adobe buildings with tile roofs. The main church of adobe, now completely obliterated, was as large or larger than the church edifices at half or more of the other 20 California Missions.

The other essential buildings were built or under construction, and the well-stocked ranchos extended far and wide over the surrounding territory at the time secularization was ordered.

The spiritual results over the first twelve years (until secularization) were far above the average of the other missions for their initial periods and were evidence of the earnest work of the lone padres of San Francisco Solano.

After secularization, the mission affairs became closely interwoven with those of the pueblo and the Contra Costa del Norte Este for the next hundred years.

As the story unfolds, the struggle for survival of Mission San Francisco Solano de Sonoma through secularization, military occupation, dismantling, revolution, neglect, and final restoration, is here recorded for the reader — a section of California Mission history long overdue.

R.S.S.

Meadowlark Ranchito
Sonoma — 1974

S. Franciscus Solanus

PART I

SAN FRANCISCO SOLANO
DE SONOMA — THE BEGINNING

I

Contra Costa del Norte Este
Mission San Francisco de Asis

Forty years after Mission San Francisco de Asís was founded on Lagunda de los Dolores, the Mission Fathers became more and more interested in extending their chain of missions northward into the vast areas of the Contra Costa del Norte Este. The Indian tribes were large and numerous and occupied each valley and the vast plains of the interior Rio Sacramento and its many branches.

Many explorations had been made into this area. In August of 1775 Don José Cañizares, sailing master of the *San Carlos*, the survey vessel of Don José Manuel de Ayala, sailed up into Bahio Redondo (San Pablo Bay) and Bahia Junta de los Quatro Evangelistas (Suisun Bay). During the two trips the bays were surveyed and the shores examined.[1]

The following year, 1776, the *San Carlos* returned to the harbor. Captain Fernando Quiros, Pilot José Cañizares, Fr. Pedro Cambón, surgeon, and sailors left in the ship's launch to further explore the upper Bay on September 26, 1776. Lieutenant Moraga left by land along the eastern Contra Costa (East Bay) and planned to meet Quiros' party at Carquinez Strait but did not make it in time.

Captain Quiros' party discovered a large "harbor" which he called Puerto de la Asunción de Nuestra Señora (Vallejo Bay or Suisun) with many estuaries. They followed a wide estuary north for a day and night to its end in a couple of streams -- thinking it might lead to Bahia Bodega. They called the estuary Nuestra Senora de la Merced (Petaluma Creek) and its head Punta de los Esteros (head of the estuary). The party returned to Cantil Blanco (San Francisco) on the 29th.[2]

For 30 years the Contra Costa del Norte Este was not active. However, the native Indians from the tribes in the eastern plains and the great river valley to the northeast had become more bold and stolen cattle and horses, and attacked mission Indians of the San Francisco Bay area.

In May 1810, Lieutenant Gabriel Moraga with 17 men traveled via Carquinez Strait and engaged 120 natives of the Suisuns. The battle occurred on a large plain about 10 miles north of Suisun Bay (near Rockville). Here, nearly all the Suisun warriors were killed.[3]

In September of the same year Moraga, now a brevet lieutenant, made a trip up San Pablo Bay and towards Bodega Harbor checking on Russian expansion. After visiting Estero de San Juan Francisco (Tomales Bay) and Bodega Harbor, he returned via the wide plain and Arroyo de Santa Rosa and upper Russian River. He continued south by way of Sonoma Valley to San Francisco. (First mention of entering Sonoma Valley.)[4]

The year 1811 found Sergeant José Sánchez, with Fr. Abella and Fr. Buenaventura Fortuny, on a voyage in October up the Bay and to Suisun Creek. They ascended the creek one league to a wide plain near the 1810 battleground. After contacting the local Indian tribes from *Rancherías* Malaka, Suisun and nearby Ululatto, the party returned to San Francisco.[5]

Lieutenant Moraga made a trip into Sonoma Valley during 1817 but there is little data available as to purpose, extent, or results obtained.

In July of 1819, Lieutenant Luís Argüello with Fr. R. Abella of Mission San Francisco de Asís and Fr. Narciso Durán of Mission San Jose left San Francisco by boat via Isla de Los Angeles and Carquinez Strait. They traveled to the junction of the two great rivers, Sacramento and San Joaquin, then proceeded for 40 leagues up the Rio Sacramento. Here, they carved a cross on a tree before returning down the river and to San Francisco.[6]

Captain Luís Argüello, on October 18, 1821, left with De Haro, Sanchez, Estudillo,

Navaretto, Fr. Blaz Ordaz, 35 leather soldiers and 20 infantrymen. Via San Rafael, they traveled to the Sacramento Valley.

Following up the west side of Río Jesús María Valley (Sacramento Valley) for nine days, the party could see two mountains (Shasta and perhaps Lassen) beyond which was the river of the Columbia. Turning west, they entered the mountains and marched southward, passing numerous Indian *rancherías* in the valleys. Finally, they arrived at the upper Russian River Valley, the Arroyo de San Ignacio (Russian River at approximately Cloverdale). Continuing south, they passed the *Ranchería* Libantiloyomi (near Santa Rosa) and on to *Ranchería* Olompali, arriving at the *asistencia* (submission without resident priest) of San Rafael on November 12th.[7]

During the years, things at Mission San Francisco de Asís were becoming critical. The cold foggy weather was not very healthy for the Indians living there, especially those from the warmer interior areas. Many Indian neophytes were sick and deaths were far above normal. Land for the cultivated crops was short and the cooler coastal weather restricted the kinds grown and harvested. The missions to the south, Santa Clara and San Jose, blocked any expansion in that direction and the latter, any additional land on the eastern shore.

The experiment at San Rafael had succeeded beyond expectations, both in health of the Indian converts and the crop and grazing situation. It was at the suggestion of Governor G. Paplo Vicente de Solá that some sick converts had been sent over to this area where a small building was erected. Now, as they wished to enlarge the settlement, a padre was located temporarily and building started. The establishment dated from December 14, 1817, and Fr. Luís Gil y Taboada agreed to take charge -- with 230 neophytes transferred from Mission Dolores.

The *asistencia*, San Rafael Arcangel, was built at the base of a high hill on the south side with good land around it and in many nearby sheltered *cañadas* (valleys). An embarcadero on a short arm of the Bay of San Francisco was half a league away. Soon, early in 1818, they had their first adobe building, 15 *varas* by 31½ *varas* -- 6½ *varas* high (42' x 80' -- 18' high), with tule covered corridor finished. It housed their chapel, living quarters and storerooms. Crops were planted and cattle pastured in the lush fields.[8]

In May 1818,[9] Fr. Commissary Prefect Mariano Payeras was on a visit to San Rafael *asistencia*. While there, he traveled east to a high hill where he saw far to the north at six leagues Cañada de los Olompalis and on

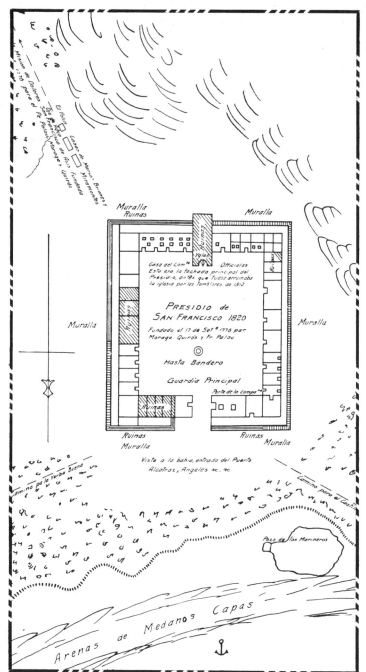

Presidio of San Francisco, 1820 [from Beginnings of San Francisco], *copied from a tracing in possession of George Davison, certified by General M.G. Vallejo. Zoeth S. Edlredge, December 25, 1908*

beyond, at about twelve leagues, Llano de los Petalumas. Off to the northeast was a great river and mountain range on the horizon. He suggested a presidio between the Bahía Bodega and Cañada de los Olompalis and a mission in the area of the Petalumas and another farther east in the land of the Suisuns. Missions farther east into the great valley could follow after further explorations.[9]

With the plight of Mission San Francisco de

2

Mission San Francisco de Asǐs or Dolores.
Etching by Borein in Missions and Missionaries, *Englehardt.*

Asís becoming serious, a conference was held between Canon Agustín Fernández de San Vicente, Fr. Commissary Prefect Mariano Payeras and Governor Luís Argüello in 1822. It was decided to move the Mission San Francisco de Asís from the peninsula below the Presidio of San Francisco to the "northeastern Contra Costa on the gentile frontier." The reasons for the move were given as: insalubrity of the peninsula climate; the success of the experimental founding of San Rafael *asistencia.* No action was taken at this time by the padres.[10]

The imperial commissioner, Rev. Agustín Fernández de San Vicente, now determined to visit the Russian Settlement at Fort Ross, which the Spaniards from its founder called Coscoff, for the purpose of gathering as much information as possible for his government. Fr. Commissary Prefect Mariano Payeras, who consented to accompany him, kept a journal of the expedition from which we extract the most interesting points. Leaving Monterey on October 11th (1822), the two dignitaries with their attendants went by way of the Rancho del Rey, through the Cañada de Natividad northeast to Mission San Juan Bautista where they passed Sunday, October 13th. Next day they arrived at Mission Santa Clara, and in the evening of the 15th they reached Mission San Francisco by way of San Francisquito, Rancho de las Pulgas, San Mateo, and El Portezuelo. "On the 19th," Fr. Payeras writes, "we set out at seven in the morning for the presidio, which is one good league distant. There Captain Luís Argüello and Lieutenant Antonio del Valle

with some troops and servants joined us. At ten o'clock we embarked in the launch, but for want of wind we had to row. We reached the Estero of San Rafael, seven leagues distant, at three in the afternoon. Fr. Juan Amoros, the missionary, with the sergeant and the neophytes, received us amid the ringing of bells and extraordinary rejoicing." The horses had been sent hither before.

On Sunday October 20th, Fr. Payeras celebrated holy Mass in honor of the angelic patron San Rafael for the success of the journey. Then "in the name of God" they went five leagues north to the place called Santa Lucía de Olompali, thence northwestwardly two leagues to Arroyo San Antonio. Leaving the arroyo to the left, they travelled laboriously over hills without water or wood and through a cañada for six leagues, until they arrived at two springs which were named San Vicente, probably in honor of the comisionado. Next day the little party continued toward the northwest over steep hills, rounded the Estero del Americano, and at noon descried the port of Bodega to the south. Descending they stood at the bayshore eleven leagues from San Vicente. Four leagues more of painful travel towards the northwest brought them to Salmon Creek, which the comisionado for reasons of his own named Arroyo Verde. Two leagues farther on the travellers reached the Russian River, which Captain Argüello the year previous had seen about thirteen leagues higher up and had christened San Ignacio. One and a half leagues beyond, they passed Arroyo Santa María, and four leagues more of hard riding brought the imperial comisionado and his following to the Russian fort. The commander, Captain Carlos Schmidt, received him cordially with a salute of four guns, and treated all with the kindest hospitality. The Spaniards remained there two days. Fr. Payeras drew up a very long description of the fort and vicinity which it would be tedious to reproduce here. On October 24th the two Fathers with a few attendants were rowed down to Bodega Bay, ten leagues south, by fifteen oarsmen. After a lunch there the comisionado and companions crossed over to the other side and camped at the point. Next day they made their way over the hills, came back to the so-called Estero del Americano, thence went for a league and a half over hills to another estero which received the name Herrera, because Sergeant Herrera had the misfortune to fall into it without more harm to himself, however. "We passed it," says Fr. Payeras, "and after two leagues of travel we came to a grand estero eleven leagues long and six hundred yards wide, which the Indians called Tamales, but which the Spaniards named San Juan Francisco Regis. On the left bank were two springs."

Leaving the estero to the right, they went southeast three leagues to the two springs of Fr. J. Amoros where they took dinner. Continuing in the same direction they reached the Arroyo of San Antonio, where they had been on the 20th, and after having travelled six leagues they pitched camp once more on its left bank. October 26th saw them leave the arroyo to the left. They traversed the Sierra de Santa Lucía, passed through the Valley of Lobato, and after eight leagues of wandering returned to San Rafael. On Monday 28th, after holy Mass, both priests with their attendants embarked half a league from San Rafael, crossed San Pedro and San Pablo Points, and after coursing over the water towards the southeast for five leagues disembarked in the Estero of San Pablo to camp for the night. Next day, partly on horseback and partly in a carriage, passing the Ranchos of San Leandro and San Lorenzo, they made the eleven leagues to Mission San Jose. On October 31st, after holy Mass, accompanied by Fr. Durán of San Jose and Fr. Viader of Santa Clara, the party proceeded in a carreta to Mission Santa Clara, five leagues to the west. All Saints Day was celebrated with splendor at Mission Santa Clara, and next day the comisionado with Fr. Payeras set out for Mission San Juan Bautista, where they finished the journey shortly after noon.[11]

On this same trip, on October 19, 1822, Fr. Payeras while visiting San Rafael *asistencia* decreed that San Rafael was now an independent mission and that, as Mission San Rafael Arcangel, it was independent of Mission San Francisco de Asís in everything.[12] Padre Juan Amoros was padre at San Rafael Arcangel, having relieved the founder Padre Gil y Taboada in the summer of 1819.

The following year, 1823, the transfer of Mission San Francisco de Asís to the northern frontier had the attention of Fr. Payeras but no further action was taken before his February sickness and death on April 28th of that year. He had, in this last month, appointed Fr. José Francisco de Paula Señán to succeed him on his death. The decision on moving Mission San Francisco de Asís was now in Fr. Señán's hands.[12]

II

Fr. Altimira's Explorations
Founding of New Mission San Francisco

At Mission San Francisco de Asís, or Dolores, Fr. José Altimira, a 36-year-old Spanish priest from Barcelona was in charge. He had been in California three years at this mission. He was zealous, eager to convert the heathen and expand the missions. The state of affairs at Mission Dolores was restricting his efforts and the pace of the older padres was too slow for his young energies and ideas.[1] In the move of his mission north to the new lands of Contra Costa del Norte Este and its potential for growth and survival, as discussed in the Conference of 1822, Fr. Altimira saw the opportunity to accomplish his goals.

When there was no word of the hoped for move from Fr. Commissary Prefect Payeras, who happened to be critically ill at his home Mission Purisima in the south, Fr. Altimira prepared a memorial under date of March 23, 1823, advocating the transfer of Mission San Francisco de Asís from its present location at Laguna de los Dolores to one located in the Contra Costa del Norte Este, as discussed at the Conference. It was generally assumed that Governor Argüello, who was eager to expand Mexican settlements to the north frontier, encouraged Fr. Altimira in his preparation and presentation of the memorial. They had become close friends while they were serving, one at the Presidio de San Francisco and the other at Mission San Francisco de Asís.

This memorial was presented in early April to the new *diputación*, the six-man territorial legislature organized in Monterey the previous April, 1822. The *diputación* did not take long to deliberate. On April 9, 1823, they acted in favor of the memorial. They ordered that: Mission San Rafael Arcangel be again joined to Mission (Dolores) San Francisco de Asís and transferred with it to the Contra Costa and suggested new sites in the country of the Petalumas or in that of Canicaimos.

Immediately, Governor Argüello forwarded copies of the *diputación's* orders to the government in Mexico on the 10th of April. Fr. Altimira forwarded copies to the new Fr. Commissary Prefect Señán at the end of the month, April 30, 1823. Fr. Señán had assumed these duties when Fr. Payeras became seriously ill.[2]

Over at Mission San Rafael Arcangel, Fr. Juan Amoros had heard of the proposed transfer of Mission San Francisco de Asís and his mission and became very much concerned. He had worked very hard and produced a fine operating mission station with 800 Indians being well-cared-for and self-supporting. He addressed a letter on May 17, 1823, to Governor Argüello protesting the suppression of his mission and stating these facts, and emphasized that the action was unjust and unreasonable.

Fr. Payeras had passed away and no word was received from his successor Fr. José Señán. Fr. Altimira decided to go ahead with an expedition to thoroughly explore the lands and valleys of the Contra Costa del Norte Este where the new mission was to be located.

On June 25, 1823, Fr. José Altimira, with *Deputado* Francisco Castro and 19 armed men under Lieutenant José Sánchez, left San Francisco in launches with supplies for the trip. Both Fr. Altimira and Lieutenant Sánchez kept diaries, practically the same. However, it appears Sánchez' diary was taken in substance from Fr. Altimira's detailed descriptions.

"Diario de la expedición verificada con objecto de reconocer terrenos para la nueva planta de la Misión de Nuestro Padre San Francisco principiada le dia 25 de Junio de 1823." - heading Fr. Altimira diary.

"Diario de la expedición verificada con objecto de reconocer terrenos para la nueva planta de la Misión de San Francisco." - heading Lieutenant Sánchez diary.

5

DIARY OF THE EXPEDITION
WITH THE OBJECT OF EXAMINING TERRITORY
FOR THE NEW SITE FOR THE MISION
OF
OUR PADRE SAN FRANCISCO
BEGINNING ON THE 25TH OF JUNE 1823

(Translated from the original Spanish script copy of his diary, signed by Fr. José Altimira, in the archives of the Bancroft Library, Berkeley, California - by Robert S. Smilie, Sonoma, California - 1970-71. NOTE - Co-ordinated with and supplemented from early translation by Alex S. Taylor, 1860. Sentences in brackets are added from the Taylor translation and were not in the above script copy. Taylor had access to another more detailed copy in the Archbishop's archives.)[3] [4]

Day 1

25th June. Departed from the embarcadero of the Presidio at 9:30 of the morning for the *Asistencia* of San Rafael, situated in the Contra Costa del Norte about four leagues distant. Left with a fresh breeze and arrived at said *asistencia* about one and a half hours of the afternoon. Besides, some new explorations of the said *asistencia* took up all the afternoon of this day.

2

The 26th. Departed San Rafael at 5½ of the break of day for land leading in this manner to the north, and without change proceeded to the place called *Olompali*, distant from San Rafael approximately 5 leagues, to 9 of the morning where we camped until 3 of the afternoon the same day; left from this reported place and followed the same course (north) then turning by the point of the *estero* named *Chocuay*, and arrived at 7 of the night at an *arroyito* of the plain of the *Petalumas* called Lema, on which bank we encamped to pass the night in company with some 8 or 10 Petaluma Indians, who were wandering warriors and were hiding from the fury of the Indians of the *Ranchería* of the *Libantiloyomi*, distant from this place 3½ leagues to the northwest.

Nothing happened of more novelty than the men of the party saw close by a bear with cubs which they killed.

3

The 27th. Departed from this point about 6 of the break of day and went exploring the part of the plain which leads also to the east, which expanse is extensive, its land very fertile and covered with grass, but of scant use for plants which need irrigating in the dry summer season since their creeks have then little water, neither has the large *arroyo* on the plain, called *Choquiomi*.

Leaving in the same manner, explored each of the hills which, with this plain, extend to the northeast for a distance of 2 leagues without discovering anything of great utility except some small oaks in the *cañadas* near the summits.

Nevertheless we entered these hills, found a small lagoon covered with tules, its expanse maybe is 50 *varas* wide and 100 long; in another *cañada* more to the east, the large *Laguna de Tolay*, so named for the chief of the Indians who formerly populated this vicinity *(Ranchería Tolay)*. The extent in parts to be with small difference 150 *varas*, at other 200 *varas*, at other ¼ league; the length about ¼ of a league. In this and other *laguna* the water is sweet, which circumstance with the hills referred to provide sufficient for the population of the pastures and offer the convenience and capacity to raise enough cattle in this place.

Following the direction northeast we reached the plain of the place called *Sonoma* by the Indians who in other times dwelt there, about by the 11 of the morning. And we camped on the bank of an *arroyo* with the intention of stopping over for time needed to reconnoitre well this place and its vicinities, since it offers then a point of observation, about which we speak successively.

By the afternoon approximately at 3, maintaining the camp in the same place, we set out to explore (leaving for custody of horses, tents and other equipment, a soldier with some Indians who came in our company of San Francisco; and firmly anchored our launch in the *estero*, which arrived this same day very near the place of our temporary dwelling).

We went over the plain of the spoken *Sonoma* toward the northwest. We discovered an *arroyo* which flows 500 *plumas* of water, both very clear and appetizing to drink, under a good luxuriant thicket of various trees pleasing to the sight and of various uses. This *arroyo* descended from the range of hills which serves as a wall to the plain by the same bearing and ending thus to the north. We passed through an extensive oak grove (trees very high and vigorous) which contribute an eternal utility thus for firewood, also for making *carretas* and other works. These oak trees which are in the plain extend eastward 3-10 of a league and north and south a league and a half, though in some parts narrower.

Bordering this same plain, another *arroyo* still more copious and agreeable than the one formerly referred to descends from west to east to about the middle of the plain then turns for the north. The first named *arroyo* does not flow beyond the border of the hills but the second does not cease to run until, following the last named direction, it joins with the *Arroyo de Sonoma* which flows west to east to the *estero*.

Inspected this afternoon all of the site which the day permitted us. The multitude of permanent small waters, according to the declarations of the Indians who observed during more extreme years, are innumerable. The most of which we observed this afternoon.

The ridge of mountains which wall in the plain on the north are heavily wooded with firewood and some timber; the redwood, pines and in parts these latter are abundant, though some measure small trunks for the reason this plain is exposed to fresh gales, especially from the northwest.

All the hills which encircle the plain measures in the abundant good building timbers, numerous expanses bare of timber but, above that tribute, with utility for man for they are merely in place to the hand diverse stones of the greatest abundance for

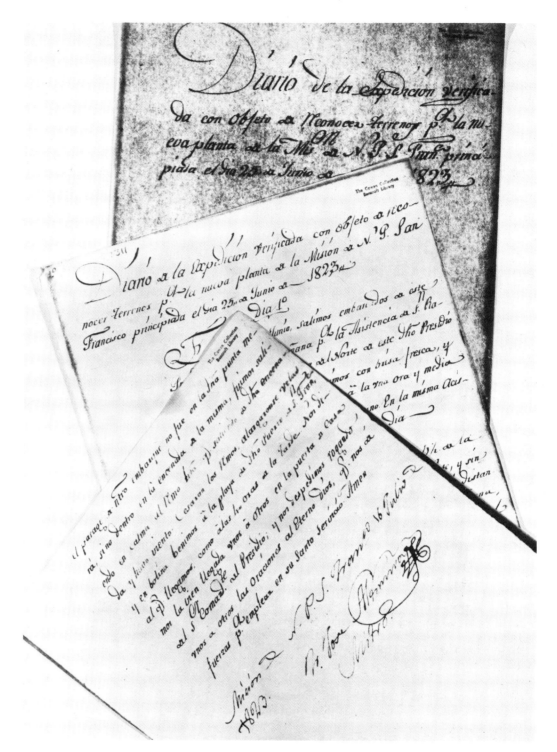

Pages from Fr. Altimira's Diary, 1823. Courtesy Bancroft Library.

making the cement, and building as well the magnificent buildings.

We singled out the hills that ran north to east, the stone was without defect for the aforesaid utility. Another stone, named *malpais*, used for making *metates* was there, also a white stone which no one who had seen it doubted but that it was limestone.

The soil of this plain is not all of the best, but fertile for all purposes. Explored all the plain with some superficiality as gently upon ourselves softly pressed the night. We retired to the point where we had rested and arrived about 8 hours of the same with

courage to continue the discovery the day following in this same and other places. This afternoon the men with our company killed many bears, animals offensive to humans.

4

The 28th. After taking our breakfast, we started in the same manner at 7 of the morning (keeping always the encampment at this same place, and the launch in the *estero* a ¼ league distant) for some places of the above mentioned plain which the day before we were unable to explore.

Climbed a small hill which is situated in the plain to

7

the east, distant from the *estero* ½ - ¼ league, since from which place we could see with much ease all the plain; the *estero*, all the coves of the Bay and hills which circle to the east and west, and the entrance of the harbour of San Francisco. Observed per the thermometer 11 degrees more heat than that at the *Misión* of San Francisco. No one can doubt the mildness of the climate of *Sonoma* after observing the plants, the very tall trees, their delicate foliage according to their species: sycamore, cottonwood, ash, laurels and others. Above all the abundance and vigor of the wild grapes, the tall grass and other wild plants, we cannot vacillate of the kindness of the climate.

We explored the borders of the *estero* and found large spaces of land very good for sowing corn, and where the launch can enter until where it meets the point end of the *estero*, this is also where we can build a town.

We asked of the Indians of that named *estero* if it produces fish or not and we were assured there was enough, especially salmon.

Taking this and other circumstances into consideration, *Sonoma* is a place well fitted for founding a *misión* here, that was searched. With all desire to improve our knowledge, we decided to withdraw to our point approximately by the 11 of the morning with the will of resting. For the afternoon we set out traveling approximately at one hour, leaving the launch in the *Estero of Sonoma*, and we went thus to the northeast by one range of hills (which without delay were to be burned of the long grass by the Indians whom we encountered) we knew very well. Their soil good for pasturing cattle, horses and sheep, by distributing the places, then above them on said named hills are good pastures having waters sufficient and permanent as we know. And without losing sight that the place is bare of thick woods which favor the straying of the above mentioned cattle.

About 2 leagues from the point of starting, we encountered in a small *cañada* a spring approximately of 25 *plumas* of water, said to be hot. It is more probable because of no shade and only the tall grass on this border.

There is a white ground, very poor and sticky. This condition which is no doubt to be the same quality as the lands which are found in the Mountain of *Monjui* in Barcelona, which is of good value for work on copper kitchen utensils, beaters of brass, on marble and other uses for which services are consumed in the named city some dozens of loads of the same soil.

Continuing on and at the end of this spoken of small *cañada*, and on climbing a hill, saw another *cañada* more extensive and in that place from a low point saw 2 or 300 head of female elk. This species is much in abundance in all this land past the *Olompali* and beyond as are also the antelope and deer.

Presently we arrived at an *arroyo* which was said to be the entrance to *Napa*. This measures very little flowing current, of not much abundance are their waters, but we observed by measuring some places

there are small permanent ponds with clear, sweet, abundant and pleasing water, sufficient to water some cattle.

Continuing our course, we arrived about at the 6 of the afternoon at another *arroyo* of the same size as the grand *Arroyo de Sonoma*, which served the belt to the beautiful plain of the aforesaid *Napa*, so called by the Indians who formerly lived here.

A special site for certain the one which was explored except we did not find as much water as was in *Sonoma*. Excepting this item, *Napa* is all as a picture, equal to *Sonoma* for its certain resemblance.

We camped finally on the bank of the named *arroyo*. Came the night, we rested - and we without more happening awaited the happiness of the Sunday, the *Day of St. Peter*.

5

The 29th. Which starts the sun after the dawn, the more serene and brilliant, we said mass and concluding, we gave to the *arroyo* the name of *San Pedro* for to be the honor of the day; we breakfasted and approximately at the 7 of the morning started, following the same bearing N.E. We observed that the Indians of the neighborhood, by one some distance from us, were setting prearranged fires for warning.

We observed in the plains and hills large oak groves; tramped over long, bare pieces of land much adapted for vines; and ascended a slope of a mountain which, with their hills nearby, could furnish the stone for making a new Rome. Descending then the named slope, we saw near us the famous Plain of *Suisun* which was the name of the Indians previously settling at this place, and with no particular exploring, arrived approximately of the one hour of the afternoon at the stream of named site. (Said place is distant about 5 leagues from the starting point, 10 leagues from *Sonoma*. Inferring that the distance from *Sonoma* to *Napa* be 5 leagues (15 miles) and from *Napa* to *Suisun* also 5 leagues).

The temperature of the *Napa*, and which continued until coming down off the referred slope of the mountain for the spoken of *Suisun*, was with small difference, believe it to be the same as in *Sonoma*. We observed more temperature in *Suisun*, good to be hotter.

When we finally arrived at this place, we camped on the bank of the *arroyo* which runs in its plain from north to south to its outlet in the *estero*, bearing to the east. This is a plain which is verdant and which measures good soil for the planting of each seeds but it is not as abundant as that which we considered in the past. It is equally well known that the soil, chiefly which is close to the *arroyo*, needs little or no irrigation. This in this season is green and very luxuriant; the pastures and other plants which we saw the afternoon of this day. The soil more distant is already scarce of these peculiarities and it is not proper to sow always in the same soil and do not offer much opportunity for varying. Neither is sufficient for the support of a large town. There is sufficient firewood on hand but no timber for manufacturing. There is land and pastures from north to the

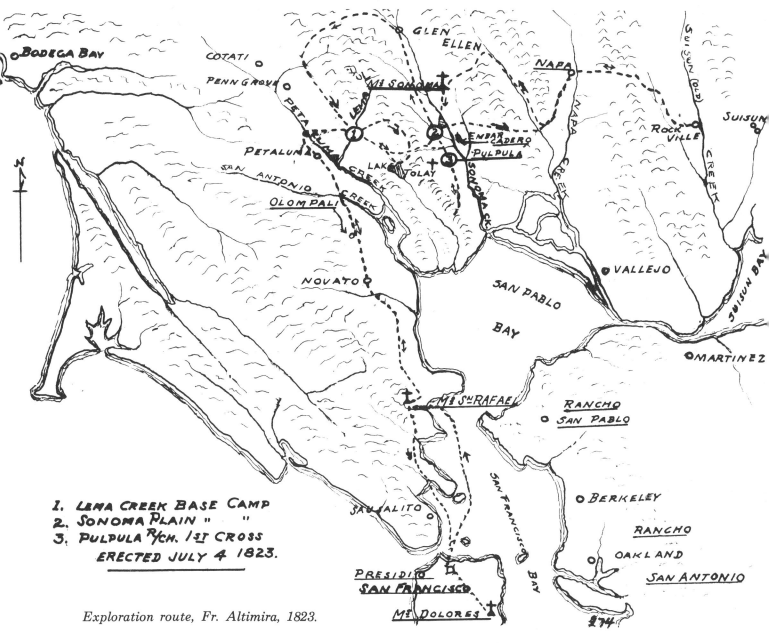

Exploration route, Fr. Altimira, 1823.

1. LEMA CREEK BASE CAMP
2. SONOMA PLAIN " "
3. PULPULA R/CH. 1ST CROSS
   ERECTED JULY 4 1823.

east for pasturing cattle, but lack of waters for which to drink.

All this was considered this afternoon, and also the excessive distance for communicating a lone *misiòn* with the Presidio of San Francisco, (we convinced ourselves that this locality was not proper for our interest.)

We were desirous to communicate to the Indians from the north the reason that we must come here and to finish with a preparation for a smooth conquest, dispatched to the *Rancherías* of the Hulatos, 5 Christian Indians of the San Francisco *Misión*, for which they invited them to come to the place where we were plaining (camping).

Then the night came on and we went to the resting, expected that the day following some gentile Indians would arrive to visit with peace.

6

The 30th. Destined for rest. We remained in this place but not without reward as we then obtained 10 bears and finally by the 3 hour of the afternoon willing came to us 19 Indians of the *Ranchería* of the

Libaytos, 5 chiefs or captains; they came with peace as we desired to the calling of our neophyte invitation. So thus these gentlemen arrived, some with lances, others with bow and arrows; one after the other in file formed their circle and sat down. We perceived at first some mistrust which was soon removed by the following operations. With kindness the friendly ones were asked how they had been during the trip, and if there had been changes in their lands, etc. To them we offered at the same time a grand quantity of *pinole* (ground parched corn) which they ate and soon satisfied the hunger which they felt. Afterwards in the day, a bale of dried meat of 5 or 6 *arrobas* (*arroba* equals 25 pounds) was given to them. We also gave fresh meat of elk and deer which we ourselves had kept for our eating at dinner.

We distributed to them cotton shirts, striped cloths, and a good portion of glass beads to each one. The tallow and fat of an elk recently killed was given them also, as they relish it.

Came the night, we laid down until dawned the day.

1st of July. This day, before the rise of the sun, we arose with intention to take leave of this place and to return to where we had come from. We breakfasted; we took leave of the Indian gentiles, using up, to complete the work with giving a bag of *pinole* and more dried meat, also the skin of the bear which they prize highly; and the exhortation of the peace with the Christians and other fellow men, and not to fear us since already we have not harmed them, etc.

And afterward we started by the same road thus to *Napa* where we arrived approximately with the 10 hour of the morning. We have not explored anything particular and nothing has occurred except the killing of 3 bears by our men. We took shelter on the bank of the *arroyo* in the shade of these trees and in that place rested.

At 2:30 of the afternoon we followed our route of return to *Sonoma*. Approximately a league before the arrival at its plain, we passed by some hills a little more to the north that were passed traveling from *Sonoma* towards *Napa*, and we discovered one white rock which looks like limestone; observation and all others declared for certain that it actually was limestone. Passing the front of this, we arrived at the plain of *Sonoma*; exploring for a league the road, a hill which was not searched before, we saw land good for planting of vines; we climbed to a point of the mountains which formerly were spoken of as having lime rock for more exploring and were convinced with what it was.

We descended to the plain, went exploring and in less than ¼ league we found 6 or 7 ponds of water, one between willows and others amidst tules and covered, but with waters clear, sweet, fresh and appetizing; and the best which we well know to be of permanent springs.

We went, continuing in the night toward our place of residence where in former times we had camped, to which we arrived approximately to the 8 hour of the night, to rest until the dawn of the day.

The 2nd. To the beginning we breakfasted and started with direction to the northwest, followed entirely the plain of *Sonoma* for the flat plain of the grand *arroyo*; we fell more in love with the tree grove which bordered this named *arroyo*, and as our object was to go to the *Petalumas* to explore, and being already informed of the particularities of *Sonoma*, little we detained this morning; only continuous traveling and looking along the route.

Before the plain ended, we noticed it narrowed and the mountain ridge of north and south which make the wall of the *cañada* are well covered with trees fit for the lumber for workers of a pueblo; and as this is a road between *Sonoma* and *Petalumas*, then we thought it an opportunity and more advantageous to situate the *misión* at this place or whether at the other; always with others we have assistance and for it we exult with the good rewards found on this road.

Traveling approximately 4 leagues and after covering the flat part, we fell in between hills with the second *arroyo* which flows toward *Sonoma* and u-

Tolay Gap, named for the chief of the Indians who formerly populated this vicinity.

nites there with the grand one.

Here we rested and found (on a barren hill adjoining the *arroyo*) other stone, which to all of us resembles limestone. With leaving approximately to the 3 of the afternoon we followed the hills, and a league before arriving at the plain of the *Petalumas* we encountered a lagoon which appeared approximately 200 *varas* long and 70 or 80 the width. The water is sweet, and is between tules, so can only serve for cattle and they lose themselves easily in the nearby woods so the laguna does not offer much utility.

Following and to the arrival at the point of the hills where we descended down to the plain, we found between some oaks other limestone of the same quality as found before.

Descending to the plain and after following with the *arroyo* or stream which we heard as most copious between the Indians and other men of our company who had seen it on various occasions, found only a small pond and coming out on the plain it dries up and nothing more promising.

Superior is the plain (which is most extensive) favored by timber and good soil to the distance from where we may place the *misión*, has only a few small ponds. But this is not sufficient except for some livestock which can be pastured on this plain because of the lack of water. This offers with all its emissions one point of view more desirable except it is all dry.

Now we saw that at best there is no guarantee in this place and as it is now growing late, we began searching between the hills for a little water for the horses of the drove and for ourselves to drink. It is night but all are found dry until the small water of the *rancheria* of the *Petalumas* who in former times lived there, and having to hurry our campers to reach the small *Arroyo* of *Lema* in the same place occupied on the night of the 2nd day of our expedition, close by to find some small water for ourselves and the drove of horses.

Arriving at this place approximately to the 8 of the night, we rested and with the intention of returning

Rancheria Pupula - site of the first mission cross, July 4, 1823; also known as Yenni Ranch, Salt Ranch, and Poppe Ranch.

One of the warm springs of the Ranchería Pupula.

to *Sonoma* the day following to seek the small place of its plain in which to place the Holy Cross, first sign of the *Misión*.

9

The day 3 with the same. As at the 6 of the morning we started proceeding straight for *Sonoma* which is distant from *Lema* 2 leagues and before 8 we were now in its plain. On arrival, we went straight toward some hills which by the south guards the plain to the point of its *estero* from the winds.

We had been told that from the hills passed a middling spring, the water of which descended toward the *estero*.

(A quarter of a league distant (before) we came to said rill (spring) and on the plain, we discovered a small lagoon, covered with tules and full of fresh water, good to drink, yet with the defect of being muddy. This lagoon maybe 50 *varas* square. Some 500 *varas* further, there is another pond of fresh water, good to drink.)

(We noted all this and traveled all along the hills and towards the *arroyo* when we soon came to the spring we were told of; but instead of descending (from) the hills) we found at the base of the hill a flowing spring of water very fine and which united with a little excavation could hold 70 *plumas* of sweet water, good for irrigating, washing, tanning, etc. though not agreeable to the palate for drinking for being luke warm at all times. Questioning an Indian of our *Misión* who was formerly of this place if at any former time the spring ran dry, he informed us that never had they seen it dry; (he ought to know it well) and how his *ranchería* it "was settled at a distance of 20 *varas* from this same source." When it was gentiles they used the same water and still we in the 24 hours which we remained there used no other for cooking or drinking.

This place for more water needs a good felling of reeds. At a short distance there is a small tule lake with ample sweet water good and fresh for drinking, which in passing is at present destined to be filling up with mud; with preparation a small ditch can join it with the other small pond distant from it approximately 300 *varas*. We will lead this to the site where we place the *Misión* and have here in this place water in abundance for drinking.

For more of this in the back of the same place, for 500 *varas* of distance, there are other small ponds with small permanent springs of sweet water, abundant and very clear which come out between rocks. And there are 2 or 3 *Zapos* who agree to its excellence, which is reasonable proof. Finally we wearied of seeing permanent springs and others around this place.

This particularity with that of having the launch anchored unattended a distance of 600 *varas*, a point of view which offers timber most handy 2 leagues with level road, the firewood at hand and in much abundance, the limestone one short league away, the proposition of raising cattle on the plain of the *Petalumas*, with a rancho on which we have Indian servant, and provides the steps for subduing the

11

gentiles of the northwest; the advantage of being able to raise also cattle and sheep at *Napa* another small rancho, for softening the roughness of the gentiles of the northeast and all the other circumstances; we agreed without opposition the opinions and decisions between myself the S. Minister, Sr. Don Francisco Castro, Deputy of this Province, who with us came on the discovery, and the graduated *Alférez Brevet* Don José Sanchez, who commands the troop escort, to place the *Misión* in this place. So we resolved this same morning and we went to the bank of the small *arroyo* on the plain, ½ league distant approximately the 10 and half of the morning where we stayed in encampment to siesta.

By the afternoon, approximately to the 3, we arose and transported all of the referred encampment to the place where we have agreed to place the *Misión*; and we went so thus to the south and followed the range of hills which are at one's back, from this place and extend to the end of the *estero* for this route. (The hills form a point towards San Rafael whose top) serves to put a lookout and with good distance discover who goes or comes by water.

Contingent is a cove of ground adapted for pasture for horses and some small flats for planting corn, watermelon, squash, etc.

This finished, we returned in the afternoon of this day and as to us came the night we retired to the place of our rest with spirit and *prebencia* (enjoyment) for fixing at that place the Holy Cross.

10

The day 4. Have for this day ourselves a festival. We arose the people as to the 6 of the morning and breakfasted. We prepared a camp Altar. We blessed the Holy Cross made from redwood provisionally, its length 7 *varas* and 3 *varas* wide from the arms. We blessed the place and within the site at where the gentile Indians of *Sonoma* formerly lived in their *ranchería*, we planted the Holy Cross and at the moment of raising high this image, this instrument of *nuestra* salvation, the troops discharged a volley and at the same time the padre and with 2 neophytes sang the verses of the *Pangue Lingua y Cruz Fidelis* which we sang in the adoration of the Holy Cross. We celebrated the sacrifice of the Mass in action of gratitude to which all of our retinue assisted.

About the 8 of the morning, although we had concluded the function, we advised those present that in the future the place we named the New San Francisco.

We dined there at that same place and about 2 of the afternoon started to return and we arrived at *Olompali*, distant from New San Francisco approximately 6 leagues, not long, at where we arrived approximately to the 6 hour and half of the afternoon. Here passed the night and rested until the dawn.

11

The day 5. As at 6 and half of the dawn, we started from this site and we continued to San Rafael at where we arrived without trouble approximately at 9 and half of the morning. Here we passed all of this day, expecting our launch which had sailed from New San Francisco at the same hour as we ourselves did. On account of opposing the northwest wind, which is contrary here, the launch anchored at the point of *San Pedro* (3 leagues distant to the east of San Rafael) and we continued here until the morning of the day.

12

The day 6. Approximately by the 5 hour of the dawn, the launch rowed past in sight of San Rafael steering toward the point of Tiburon (one of those which form a circle to the waters of the Port of San Francisco). In the meantime, the P. M. Fra José Altimira said low mass and divine service at *Misión* San Rafael (at which all the companions of the expedition assisted; at the conclusion of same we breakfasted and started from San Rafael at) approximately the 7 and half of the morning, arriving at the said point of Tiburon approximately at 11 of the same morning.

We embarked approximately by 11 and half despite having to walk by land 5 leagues, which is the distance from San Rafael to the mentioned point, and as the place of our embarking did not take place at the said named point Tiburon but within the bay of this same place. Started and took to the oars in the calm until we sailed out of the Bay and had the wind. Ceasing with the oars, and extending the sails, we continued on favoarable winds to the beach of the said named Port of San Francisco arriving approximately about 4 hour of the afternoon.

We gave the welcome arrival one to another at the door of the house of Sr. Commandante of the Presidio; and we took leave begging one to another the prayers to the Eternal God, which gives us with fortitude for serving in his Holy Service - Amen.

MISIÓN OF OUR PADRE SAN FRANCISCO
16 July of 1823
(signed) Fr. José Altimira
Minister[3]

Exploration Trip - Fr. Altimira
Route, June 25-July 6, 1823.

1. Day 25th.
Left San Francisco Presidio Embarcadero.
Arrived San Rafael Embarcadero (2nd & C Sts.) and Mission. Obtained horses.
2. Day 26th.
North via las Gallinas, Ignacio, Novato (old town) to Olompali (Burdell R.R. Station & Hiway 101).
After resting (3 p.m.) continued N. thru Petaluma; 1 mile north of Petaluma turned E. across plain to Lema Camp (present Adobe Creek below Vallejo Adobe).
3. Day 27th.
Explored flat to east and hills east Adobe Road, SE to Lake Tolay (now dry), ½ mile SW junction Adobe and Stage Gulch Roads.
NE to enter Sonoma Plain.
Base Camp - along a small stream west of Big Bend.
Junction Hiways No. 121 and 116 (Arnold Drive).

Boat arrived above embarcadero, Schellville Bridge area. Explored NW Felder Creek - oaks - west side of Sonoma Creek.
Second stream - (Carriger) - Fowler Creek - Valley to north - Hannah Boys Center area.
4. Day 28th.
Explored lower valley - hill - Hydes' Road area; Townsite area; above embarcadero, approx. foot of Broadway.
Afternoon - to Napa; Hot Spring, etc. - Stornetta Dairy area; Elk in Huichica Creek Valley.
Arroyo - lower Caneros Creek) Approx. route
Congress Valley) Old Sonoma Road.
Camp - Napa Creek approx. town Napa.
5. Day 29th.
Named Napa Creek San Pedro - continued east up Tulucay Creek - old Indian trail - across Green Valley through low pass on Indian trail to Rockville area. Camped on Suisun Creek.
6. Day 30th.
Remained in camp.
7. Day 1st July.
Returned via same route to Napa. Rested at old camp, Napa Creek. Resumed trip towards Sonoma. At Carneros Valley turned NW up valley and by mountain trail (probably along Patrick Road) then SW on old Indian trail (Grant boundary) - over summit to Lac Rancho and Sonoma area - springs - ponds. Arrived back at former camp at Big Bend area.
8. Day 2nd. July
Up west side Sonoma Valley - Arnold Drive, El Verano, Eldridge, Glen Ellen. Rested Bare Hill, north junction Sonoma-Calabasas Creeks.
3 p.m. Along Warm Springs Road area, Bennett Valley; pond ½ mile east of junction with Sonoma Mt. Road; south on Sonoma Mt. Road on to Pressley Road summit route on to Roberts Road route to north of Penngrove - then SE Adobe Road general.
Indian *Rancheria* north of Waugh School corner (Adobe Road and Hardin Lane); on to Adobe Creek (Lema) campsite for night camp.
9. Day 3rd.
To Sonoma Plain via Stage Gulch to previous camp at Big Bend.
Leaving camp - going south towards Sear's Point.
Tular Lagoon - pond and spring ¼ mile north of Meadowlark Lane and Farm Road junction (now two ponds).
2nd small lagoon - spring - swamp - south end Farm Road.
Rill and spring - spring base of hill - old Poppe Ranch to the south. (Ranchería Pulpula)
Note above on USGS quad. "Sears point."
Anchorage - Launch at Poppe's Landing.
Wood lot - hills in rear to west.
Mission site - Poppe Ranch site -
explored hills towards Sears Point.
Lookout - Summit - or Wildcat Mt.
Inlet - Horses' pasture - Flying Arrow Ranch Valley, lower Tolay Creek.
10. Day 4th.
Festival - Altar.
Raised Cross - above site, Poppe Ranch. Bath House.
Mission site - dined. Camped night Olompali, early

rest site.
11. Day 5th.
To San Rafael Mission - retrace early route.
Spent night. Returned horses.
12. Day 6th.
To Tiburon - on foot.
Embarked - Richardson's Bay.
By boat - Embarcadero - Presidio San Francisco.[4]

NOTE - The camp sites chosen by Fr. Altimira were, no doubt, in the open plain with the only shade the trees along the creeks. This was usual in strange country. One reason was the ability to see any approaching or lurking hostile Indians, and another was so that the animals of the party could have ample grazing close to the camp.

As the expedition camped on the Sonoma Valley plain during the summer, they, no doubt, experienced the strong west winds that blow each afternoon and evening during Summer and Fall. The padre noted (9th day) that the range of hills (South Sonoma Mountain Range - Wildcat Mountain area to Sears Point) sheltered the valley from these winds and so located his cross in a sheltered area - on their east slope near an estero anchorage. (Approximately Poppe's Landing).[10]

On his return to Mission San Francisco from his exploratory trip, Fr. Altimira addressed a letter to his superior, Fr. Senán on July 10th, advising what had been done so far on the project and that a foundation of the new San Francisco de Asís had been made on July 4th in the Valley of the Sonomans. He brought out that the Mission at Dolores was on its last legs and a change was necessary and that Mission San Rafael Arcangel could not subsist alone. Fr. Altimira cited as his authority the consent given by Fr. Payeras entrusting him with the transfer and choice of the new site.[5] He hoped for an early approval but that, if no change was made, he would leave the missions here in California and return to Europe at the first opportunity. Further, he charged that the authorities at Mission San Jose were forcibly seizing gentiles of the Contra Costa del Norte Este and taking them against their will to their mission, which was contrary to an agreement made when Mission San Rafael Arcangel was made an independent mission, and that these former inhabitants be returned to the new mission establishment.

On July 16, 1823, Fr. Altimira sent his official report of the exploration expedition to Fr. Senán.[6]

The native Indians or gentiles of the immediate area of the Valley of the Sonomans, as Fr. Altimira found them, were of the coast Miwok race which extended west and southwest to the Pacific Ocean. They were not an aggressive people though they retained their area intact against the more warlike tribes to the north and east.

They were of medium size and heavy build with long black hair. Red and black stripes were painted on their cheeks and chins. For dress, a loin cloth and beads sufficed for the men, and the women wore a short skirt or double apron of tules, grass, or skins. For cold weather, skins of rabbit or deer made into a robe were sometimes used. Some mission blankets or clothing was used by the gentiles, having been brought or traded by members who had lived or worked at the earlier Bay area missions in recent years.

Their food was obtained from the large areas of oaks which supplied the basic acorns, seeds from the many grasses, roots and bulbs from the hills and extensive tule marshes along their southern boundary. They made their usual trips to the coast for salt and mussels, shells, and for trade with coast tribes. Meat was obtained from the small game, as well as rodents and insects. Large game, deer, elk and bears were abundant but were seldom killed with their small arrows and spears. Some fish were caught in the streams and sloughs. Clams were found in some sections of the Bay side.

Arrowheads, cutting and scraping tools were made from obsidian located at a few places in the surrounding mountains. Stone for grinding mortars was in all the creeks. Their baskets were well made and were used for carrying and storing seeds, acorns and food. Cooking baskets were closely woven and hot rocks were used in them for boiling.

Housing was a simple matter. With a circular pit as a base, small willow or other tree shoots were pushed in the ground around the circle and then brought together at the top. Some branches were woven around the circle, then the frame was covered with tules, making a fairly weatherproof thatched roof. A small hole at the side was the crawl-in entrance and one at the top let the smoke out from the fire burning in the center. Their rancherías looked like an assembly of large rough beehives.

Each ranchería had its sweathouse which was used by the men folk. It was their meeting place as well as ceremonial center. It was usually half in the ground with a small entrance and controlled smoke exit. The covering of tules over a willow frame was covered with earth. It was usually near a stream or pond so the men could plunge into the water after a period in the sweathouse. Other times it was a warm place for the idle men, especially during cold weather.

In some sections their rancherías were close together but, in the Valley of the Sonomans,

they were well separated - each with a large area of its own - plain, hills, creeks and springs. At some seasons the rancherías were not used as the gentiles en masse would move to acorn areas, fish areas, or to the coast on their annual trip. Sometimes they had more than one location and would abandon a ranchería for a new one when adjacent food, diminishing wood, or filth, made the move imperative.

The main Miwok rancherías of the Valley were:

Pulpula - west side of Arroyo Sonoma near Embarcadero (Poppe's Landing and Ranch - Yenni Ranch).

Temblek - springs - two miles southwest of Mission Sonoma (Temelec area).

Tuli - Carriger Creek and Yulupa Spring - 2½ miles west of Mission.

Huchi - general area of Mission site.

Wugilwa - Agua Caliente Road east of Arroyo Sonoma - three miles northwest of Mission.

In the upper end of the Valley in Wappo country was:

Ranchería Wilikos - east side of Arroyo Sonoma - 11 miles north of the Mission (Mount Road, south of Kenwood).

To the west, the Ranchería Petaluma on Tolay Lake was on the divide and many Miwok rancherías were farther west along Arroyo Petaluma and to the north.

Over in the Valley of the Napas were the rancherías - all of Wintun race:

Teimenukas - at the Arroyo Napa.
Tulukal - to the southeast.
Suscol - on Arroyo Suscol to the south.
and on further east in the Valley of the Suisuns -
Suisun - on the west side (Rockville).
Yulyul - on the east side beside slough (Suisun).
Ulato (Ulalatto) - near by Yulyul, north side Suisun Valley.
Hesala - near and west of Suisun.
Malaka - above old Suisun area.

Suisun Ranchería was the center of the gentiles of that area. The Chief, Sen-Yeto, an unusually large man - six feet seven tall, became friendly with the padre.[7]

By the end of July, Governor Argüello was concerned that no further action was being taken in the matter of transferring the mission to Sonoma. He was advised by Fr. Altimira that more people than those at Mission Dolores would be required and the people at Mission San Rafael Arcangel were needed also. Fr. Altimira made a trip to Monterey and the Governor instructed him to go ahead with the transfer of both Mission San Francisco de Asís and Mission San Rafael Arcangel to the new site in the Valley of the Sonomans which he had dedicated on July 4th.

Lower Sonoma Valley, traveled by Fr. Altimira July 2, 1823, is sheltered from the strong west winds of summer by the South Sonoma Mountain Range.

Llano de Sonoma [flats of Sonoma], chosen as a campsite by Fr. Altimira so that the party would be aware of any possible attacks by hostile Indians.

Confirming the above, Governor Argüello on August 4th wrote to Fr. Commissary Prefect Señán, Fr. Amoros at Mission San Rafael Arcangel, Fr. Altimira at Mission San Francisco de Asís, and Lieutenant Martínez, Presidio de San Francisco.[8] With the authority of the Governor's letter, Fr. Altimira with Lieutenant Martínez left on August 12th and took possession of Mission San Rafael Arcangel and inventoried the mission property.

On the 23rd of August, Fr. Altimira left Mission San Francisco de Asís with a force of 12 men, one artillery man for the cannon, and a group of neophyte laborers for New San Francisco. They arrived at the new Sonoma site on August 25th and commenced work on the "New Mission San Francisco." Construction of a granary, corrals, irrigation ditch, and temporary housing was soon in full swing.[8]

In a letter to Governor Argüello, August 31, 1823, Fr. José Altimira stated:

The 23rd of the same march toward this place (Sonoma) with some people whom I obtained from the Rancho of San Pablo, and the 25th we arrived and *selected the site* and began the work. In 4 days we have cut 100 beams of redwood in order to build the granary; we have built a ditch for water which already we have running in the place were we are living. We are establishing a farm and corral and tomorrow with the favor of God we will receive the cattle in the morning.

All persons endorse the *site which we have discovered* and all say that it offers more good fortune than any place this side of San Diego.[9] (Emphasis added).

This selected new site for the mission buildings was on the large oak studded Sonoma plain on the east side of the Valley, two leagues north of the former Pulpul *Ranchería* location where the foundation Cross had been planted July 4th - on the tenth day of the exploration trip. Around this new site were many permanent springs and extensive level grounds for the large quadrangle, adobe brick yards, orchards and gardens. Also, the summer winds were mild and not destructive. However, it was a league and a half away from the proposed mission's embarcadero.[10]

III

Political vs. Church Control
Controversial Delay—Compromise

The missions in California were under the strict rule of the Franciscan Order and long established procedures and customs governed their establishment and operation. The civil governors and military were under separate jurisdiction from the capital in Mexico - and the missions under their Franciscan College of San Fernando in Mexico.

In California, the missions were governed by the Franciscan Father Presidente and Father Commissary Prefect - and the civil and military were under the appointed governor. Any agreements between the two departments were made between these two offices or by their superiors in Mexico.

The Franciscan College and the Fathers had absolute control of the padres and any change in their assignments. They also passed on any new missions, their sites, and assigned the priests to them. They controlled the funds of the church available for each mission and its work and were the only authorities who could discipline an erring padre, but they consulted with the governor as to the protection and areas given to each new mission.[1]

The Pious Fund of the Californias was the financial backbone of the Spanish and, later, Mexican missions in Baja and Alta California from their beginning in the early 1700's until the middle of 1800.

Early gifts of moneys and lands were offered, often for separate missions and, eventually, the entire capital, moneys and lands were combined into one fund - called the Pious Fund of the Californias. Assets were invested mostly in operating large *haciendas* and the income used for the establishment and support of missions in Baja California and, later, Alta California. Donations amounted to $120,000 by 1731 and, subsequently, many large contributions swelled its coffers.

The Jesuits became administrators of the holdings, having the most extensive mission domain. When the King expelled them from the Spanish dominions in 1767, he assumed charge of the fund.

The grants were then made by the King to the Dominican and Franciscan "Colleges" in Mexico, which controlled and administered their various units of missions. The usual payment was $1,000 for founding of each new mission and $400 a year to each padre. The latter was to be used for church goods, furniture, implements, seeds, raw materials and food supplies. The padres drew on their balance, sending orders to the College *sindicio* (treasurer) who shipped the supplies to them. This worked out very well, though shipping costs were high.

After the Mexican Revolution, the new government took over administration of the fund. But in 1842, the government sold the assets and added the moneys to the national treasury. Six per cent annually was allowed for California religious purposes -- but it was often unpaid.

The U.S.-Mexican War stopped all payments and it was only when Bishop Alemany made claim for payment that the Claims Commission, in 1875, awarded the northern California missions $900,000 back payment. A later claim before the Hague Tribunal in 1902 resulted in U.S. winning an annual payment to the Archbishop of California of $43,050 from the Republic of Mexico -- being income from Pious Funds still held by the Republic.

The situation at the new San Francisco Mission was critical. Fr. Altimira, in his zeal to develop new territory and abandon the old, had far overstepped his bounds. He by-passed his Franciscan Superiors, the Father Presidente as well as the Father Commissary Prefect, in going to the governor with his complaints - even complaining about the lack of cooperation of his superiors. He reported repeatedly to the governor rather than through his own organization. Then he proceeded to establish a new mission site, prepared to close and transfer an old well established one, as well as close and transfer the new independent prosperous Mission San Rafael Arcangel to a site only he had examined and explored and chosen.

All of this was done without any permission or approval of his own superiors but with the approval and encouragement of the governor in civil authority only. Even the order of the *diputacíon* was illegal because they had no power to establish or move missions.

At this period the mission administration was in a difficult period. Fr. Commissary Prefect Payeras, a strong administrator, was critically ill in February 1823 and had died on April 28th. Fr. Señán took over the duties and he was very upset at the events at Sonoma and the actions of the young Fr. Altimira in proceeding without permission or consultation. However, he was also in poor health and he soon followed Fr. Payeras, passing away August 25, 1823, at Mission San Buenaventura.

Fr. Señán had transferred his duties to Fr. Vicente Francisco de Sarría and, in a letter of August 14th, stated he considered the transfer of Mission San Francisco de Asís as striking at the authority of the church. He was opposed to the suppression of the flourishing San Rafael Arcangel. He was astounded at the illegal way that the new *diputacíon* had acted without consulting the Mexican Government. He did not altogether disapprove the transfer of Mission San Francisco de Asís.[2]

Fr. Presidente Sarría, in his new office, had to take over the critical situation. On August 23rd he wrote a letter to Fr. Altimira explaining the decision of the mission authorities as to the founding of the new mission at the Sonoma site and the transfer of the two existing missions and the church laws that had been violated. He refused him permission to proceed further.

This letter and subsequent correspondence are here related by Fr. Z. Engelhardt.

After consulting with Fr. Estévan Tápis and Narciso Durán at San Juan Bautista, Fr. Vicente de Sarría accordingly wrote to Fr. Altimira as follows: "I have learned with regret what Your Reverence has done in attempting to found the new Mission of San Francisco. By order of the Rev. Fr. Presidente José Señán, who is now so grievously ill that he is incapacitated to govern the missions, I shall have to act in his place in accordance with his circular which has made the rounds of the missions. Nevertheless I have not wished to take any steps until the subject was discussed in keeping with our regulations. For this purpose various Fathers and myself have assembled to-day at this mission. According to their judgment as well as mine, I have to say that Your Reverence is not lawfully authorized to undertake said founding of a mission, and that consequently you expose the spiritual functions of your ministry to nullification, because the faculties which we have are in *locis a suis superioribus assignatis* (for places assigned by their Superiors.) Such is the declaration of the Bull of Pius V. on this point. Your Reverence cannot defend your actions with the alleged will of the Rev. Fr. Prefecto, God rest his soul, which did not touch the present transaction of designating time and place, nor did it extend to the topographical site of the found, or the sending of Your Reverence to such a distance without an associate contrary to canonical and civil laws and in opposition to the statutes of our Apostolic College. I do not know that there is among the Fathers one who approves of your way of proceeding. It will cause much grief at our College when it is informed about the matter. My dear Father, no one perhaps will surpass me in zeal for extending the glory of the Holy Name of the Lord by means of the light of His Holy Gospel; but Your Reverence knows that this zeal must be *secundum scientiam* (according to wisdom). If it must be against charity and its sweet fruit - peace, then let us put it aside or at least postpone it, the former for the sake of the latter which is more necessary."[3]

Fr. Altimira received the letter August 31st and was furious but stopped all work on the new Mission San Francisco which had begun one week before. He wrote a blistering letter of complaint to Governor Argüello on the 31st.

Recounting what had occurred, and that he was obliged to interrupt the work, he complained most bitterly of the way in which he had been treated, and of the "frivolous difficulties" put in the way by the missionary of an unprofitable *asistencia*[13] through "underhand efforts," and the aid of "confederate padres." The Fr. Presidente[14] he goes on, had obstinately kept silent, though not worse in health than usual and perfectly able[15] to confirm the orders of his predecessor. The confederates were all blind to the circumstances and had exerted themselves in the office of Satan by throwing obstacles in the way of a great enterprise, especially Fr. Durán.[16] The new presidente, too, seemed to be one of the plotters, inasmuch as he had complained that his permission should have been awaited, though all might have died before it came. The angry young friar then concluded in substance as follows: "I wish to know whether the *diputacíon* has any authority in this province, and if these men can overthrow Your Honor's wise provision.[17] I came here to convert gentiles and to establish new missions. If I cannot do it here, where as we all agree is the best spot in California for the purpose, I will leave the country."[18]

(Notes 13-18 by Fr. Englehardt on above.)

13 He was wrong; San Rafael was a mission at this date.

14 Bancroft has "prefect." There was no prefect at this time.

15 When Fr. Altimira wrote Fr. Senán had already expired.

16 He was the missionary of Mission San Jose.

17 A right "liberal" view of State authority. It would seem from this, and the charges Fr. Altimira

makes against Fathers Durán and Amorós, that untamed passion and baffled vanity had deprived the young man of his reason temporarily. He showed that the "glory of the Holy Name" had not been the prime motive for wanting to start a mission.

18 Fr. Altimira to Argüello, August 31st, 1823. We use Bancroft's version very much because Fr. Altimira's communications were written on the poorest paper and in places almost illegible when we examined them. Archb. Arch., no. 1464; Bancroft, II, 501-502.[4]

Fr. Presidente Sarría wrote a letter to Governor Argüello on the Sonoma Mission subject explaining why the Church did not approve of the proposed transfer, and citing the lack of authority under which Fr. Altimira had proceeded on his own initiative.

His letter of September 5, 1823, covered 11 main points as follows:

The main points are the following. After explaining that as presidente *ad interim* he disliked to give positive orders, he insists 1st, that the New Constitution of Mexico does not change the old laws and usages which intrusted the whole matter of founding, suppressing, or moving of missions and the appointment of missionaries to the respective prelate, and that therefore the *diputación* had no authority on the subject. - 2nd. The original decree of the *diputación* provided that Mission San Francisco along with San Rafael should be transferred to the country of the Petalumas or of the Canicaimos, whereas now without consulting the Superior of the missions another locality is selected at the word of one friar. What would Captain Argüello say if in military matters at the dictates of a private soldier, and he a visionary, the location of a fortification settled by the military authorities were changed? - 3rd. Through the transfer a wrong is committed against the neophytes of San Rafael, who, now under the new order of things being citizens and on an equality with white men, are forced to leave their birthplace, their lands, their houses, and the missionary whom they love, though unanimously opposed to the removal. - 4th. There is a great lack of missionaries which makes it impossible to assign two Fathers to so distant a place where it is unsafe for a friar to live alone. - 5th. Even if Fr. Payéras had approved of the transfer on general principles, it would be an insult to his memory to suppose that he would have approved of such violent ways of effecting it. - 6th. Neither Fr. Payéras nor Canónigo Fernández ever approved the transfer of San Rafael; on the contrary both had promised the neophytes a new church. - 7th. Fr. Presidente Senán, the representative of the bishop, had entertained the same views as the writer, and was much astounded at the proceedings. "What a labyrinth! Political authorities assuming the functions of a bishop." - 8th. It may be said that application was made to the prelate. So did Henry VIII apply to the Pope for approval of his unholy union, but he obtained no favorable reply; neither did Fr. Altimira. - 9th. Nevertheless, Fr. Altimira is not accused of bad faith because letters are known to have been delayed on the way. - 10th. Too much weight should not be laid upon the representations of one friar unsupported by his prelate and associates. - 11th. All the Fathers are zealous for the conversion of the pagan Indians, but they wish it to be accomplished in an orderly manner.[19]

19 Fr. Sarría to Argüello, September 5th 1823. Archb. Arch. No. 1465. The document is in the hand of Fr. Tapis; Fr. Sarría signed it. See also Bancroft II, 502-503.[5]

Governor Argüello replied on September 17th and passed over the arguments of Fr. Presidente Sarría's letter. He declared that now the establishment at Sonoma was a fact, it would continue as a military post. If Fr. Altimira was refused permission to continue the mission, the matter would be referred to the Mexican authorities.

During September, other correspondence passed between the two leaders in Alta California and finally a compromise was reached - satisfactory to both parties. The main provisions were:

That Mission San Francisco de Asís was to remain at its present location on Laguna de los Dolores.

Mission San Rafael Arcangel was to retain its independence and remain at its present location - San Rafael.

The new mission at Sonoma, New San Francisco, was to be built as a separate and independent mission; that Padre Altimira was to be in charge but still associated with Mission San Francisco de Asís - subject to the approval of the Franciscan College.

Also, neophytes may come to the new mission from old San Francisco, San Rafael, or San Jose missions if they were originally from the Contra Costa del Norte Este. In the case of Mission San Rafael Arcangel, they might return if they wished at any time within a year.

New converts may choose their own mission but no force was to be used in convincing them.

On September 30th, Fr. President Sarría sent a copy of the agreement with an appointment and instructions to Padre Altimira for the new mission at Sonoma. Copies were sent to Governor Argüello as well.[6]

An extract of the appointment follows: *"I designate your Reverence and I give you the faculties for founding of that mission of which you treat and in which you are involved so that I constitute you minister in the same form and with the same authority as the rest with regard to their missions and conversions."*[7]

So, for the present, the situation was clarified and work could start again in the Valley of the Sonomans.

IV

Mission San Francisco Solano de Sonoma
The First Years

Now in October 1823, Fr. Altimira returning to Sonoma had, with his appointment and instructions, a fine opportunity to build his great new mission establishment in the Contra Costa del Norte Este. Buildings started before were completed, foundations for a *palizada* church were laid, and logs brought in from the mountains were hewed and split into timbers and boards. Adobe brick yards were laid out and clay beds were found nearby for the making of roof and floor tiles. The kilns were built so that the buildings could be roofed with fired tile as soon as possible, replacing the temporary roofs. These industries were located just north and west of the mission where a spring fed stream supplied ample water for their operation. Crop land was laid out and prepared for sowing. Cattle, horse, and sheep pasturage was staked out

in adjacent valleys ready for the livestock being received from the other nearby missions as a start for their herds of the future.

With this new activity at New San Francisco keeping Fr. Altimira busy, he still found time in October to write letters of complaint against padres of other nearby missions. The complaints were that the padres were using their influence -- and false statements -- to keep their neophytes from moving to his new mission; that his new mission had received less aid and cooperation from the nearby older establishments than was customary when new missions were founded; that the padre at San Francisco de Asís retained anything of value; that more military power was needed for show against the gentile frontier; and that the Indians had too much liberty. However, he stated that he was

Mission San Francisco Solano de Sonoma, circa 1826.

19

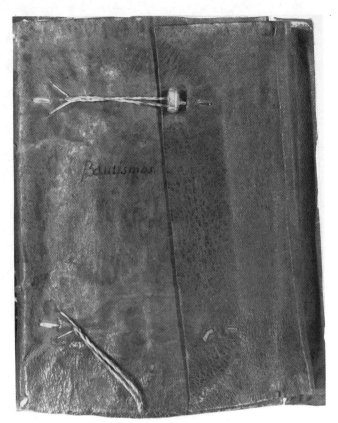

Bautismos Tome No. 1 [Baptismal record of Mission San Francisco Solano]. Courtesy Bancroft Library.

making progress in founding the new mission.[1] He made his letter of complaint to Governor Argüello instead of to Fr. Presidente Sarría, again stepping out of line for a Franciscan padre.

At the end of his first year, 1823, Fr. Altimira's annual report included:

Baptisms	0
Marriages	1
Deaths	1
Total Indians at mission	482

The animals included:

Horned stock	180
Sheep	1100
Tame horses	46
Mules	15

No crops were harvested the first year.[2]

In the spring of the following year, the mission at Sonoma had begun to take shape. There was a large granary, a house for the padres and seven houses for the *escolta*, or guards, and their families, as well as the necessary guardhouse or *cuartel*. All were built of wood of the *palizada* type with thatched roofs.

And, on April 4, 1824, Passion Sunday, the new church was dedicated. The building was 10 *varas* wide and 34 *varas* long, built of boards and whitewashed inside and out. A small sacristy was built on the patio side. The interior was well furnished for the dedication. Three candle-lit crosses were on the walls and in the sanctuary was the sacred altar. Above, hung a large canvas painting of San Francisco Solano, a gift of the Father Presidente. A pack train had arrived from the Russian settlement at Porto Bodega with many gifts of altar cloths, vestments, candlesticks, mirrors, holy pictures, and other religious articles. That, with donations from the other missions, made the mission church quite complete. The padre was hoping to receive a mission bell also.

Fr. Altimira conducted the dedication services with all the soldiers, workers, and many Indians in attendance. The mission was dedicated to SAN FRANCISCO SOLANO, the great Franciscan apostle of the Indies and Peru. Thus, the designation New San Francisco was discarded and the confusion with San Francisco de Asís was eliminated. To complete the dedication, Fr. Altimira baptized the first persons on this day - 26 children of both neophyte and gentile parents.[3]

Later in the month, Fr. Altimira made the following entry in the leather bound book of

BAUTISIMOS
LIBRO OF SONOMA
No. 1

No. 46   Dia 17 April 1824
A un hombre llamdo de
Gent Quelloy, Le puse pr.
nombre Franco Solano.

Franco Solano
     Adto

(A man called in his pagan state Quelloy, I give him the name Francisco Solano. Baptismal register of Mission San Francisco Solano.)

This year of 1824 was a busy one at San Francisco Solano. There were permanent buildings to plan for and erect, thousands of adobe bricks to be made, tiles to be formed and fired for the floors and roofs, timbers and planks to be hewn from the logs, and iron work to be made. Then crops had to be sown and harvested and the hundreds of workers housed and fed daily. Experience gained at the older mission enabled the padre and his helpers to accomplish a great deal during the year.

At the year's end, Fr. Altimira was able to report that progress of his mission included a large adobe building now housing the padre and some stores. It was 10 *varas* wide and 40 *varas* long, 7 *varas* high, with a full length corridor - all roofed with tiles. It was divided into four rooms and a large *sala*. The rafters of unhewn poles supported hewn planks that were covered with bundles of brush on which the red roof tiles were bedded. The corridors were

Informe Anual J.J. del Estado de esta nueva Fundación de S. Fran.co Solano ..... f.

..... "0006"

en 31 Dbre. de 1824.

..... "0002"

Se han bautizado este año ..... "000 2/y/2." n.o Rancho de S.ta Eu

Baut.mo
Adultos ..... "0036" }
Parbulos hijos de Gentiles y Catecumenos ..... "0024" } 0095" y f."..0710"...
Dr. de Neofitos congregados ..... "0035" }
Dr. de gente de razon ..... "0000"
El año antecedente ..... "0000" 0000"

Matri-monios
Se han celebrado matrimonios de Ind.s ..... "0017" } 0018"
Dr. de gente de razon ..... "0001"
El año antecedente de Ind.s ..... "0000" 0000"
Dr. de gente de razon ..... "0000"

Difuntos
Han muerto Indos. Adultos ..... "0023" } 0041"
Dr. Parbulos ..... "0017"
Dr. de gente de razon ..... "0001"
Los años anteriores de Ind.s ..... "0000" 0000"
De Gente de razon ..... "0000"

Existentes
Los Indios q.e actualmente existen empadronados,
y en toda instruccion cristiana y civil son Adultos
de 9 años para arriba ..... "0305" } 0384"
..... "0079"
Parbulos hombres ..... "0234" } 0308"
Adultas mugeres ..... "0074"
Parbulos id. .....

Yglesia y
Sacristia.
No se hallan ni medianam.te surtidas. Aunq.e yo he andado con alguna diligencia, mercando à los Ru[s]os de la Bodega, algunas ropas, candeleros, cuadros, espejos, floreros &.a ò pagar cuando pueda la Fund.r con semillas, de suerte q.e cuando se solemniza alguna fiesta causa el adorno de la S.ta Capilla, mucha devocion y respeto; y ojala hubiese alguna campana.

Ganado
Mayor.
Entre grande y chico (inclusas 7.o Juntas de bueyes) hay cab.l ..... "1100"
Caballos. ..... "4000"
Dr. Lanar. Entre grande y chico hay cab.l ..... "0130"
Caballada. Entre mansos y quebrantad.s hay cab.l ..... "0300"
Yeguas. Hay seis manadas y cab.l .....
Mulada. Hay mulas mansas con una nueva bronca ..... "0016"

Se han sembrado este año f. | Se han cosechado ..... f.
Trigo ..... "0480" de Trigo | ..... "0600"
Maiz ..... "0002" de maiz | ..... "0200"

... se debe informar en orden a lo mandado.
N.va Fund.n de S. Fran.co Solano. 31 Dbre. de 1824.

Fr. Jose Altimira

Fr. Altimira's Informe - 1824, report of the year's progress at Mission San Francisco Solano, signed December 31, 1824. Courtesy Santa Barbara Mission Archives.

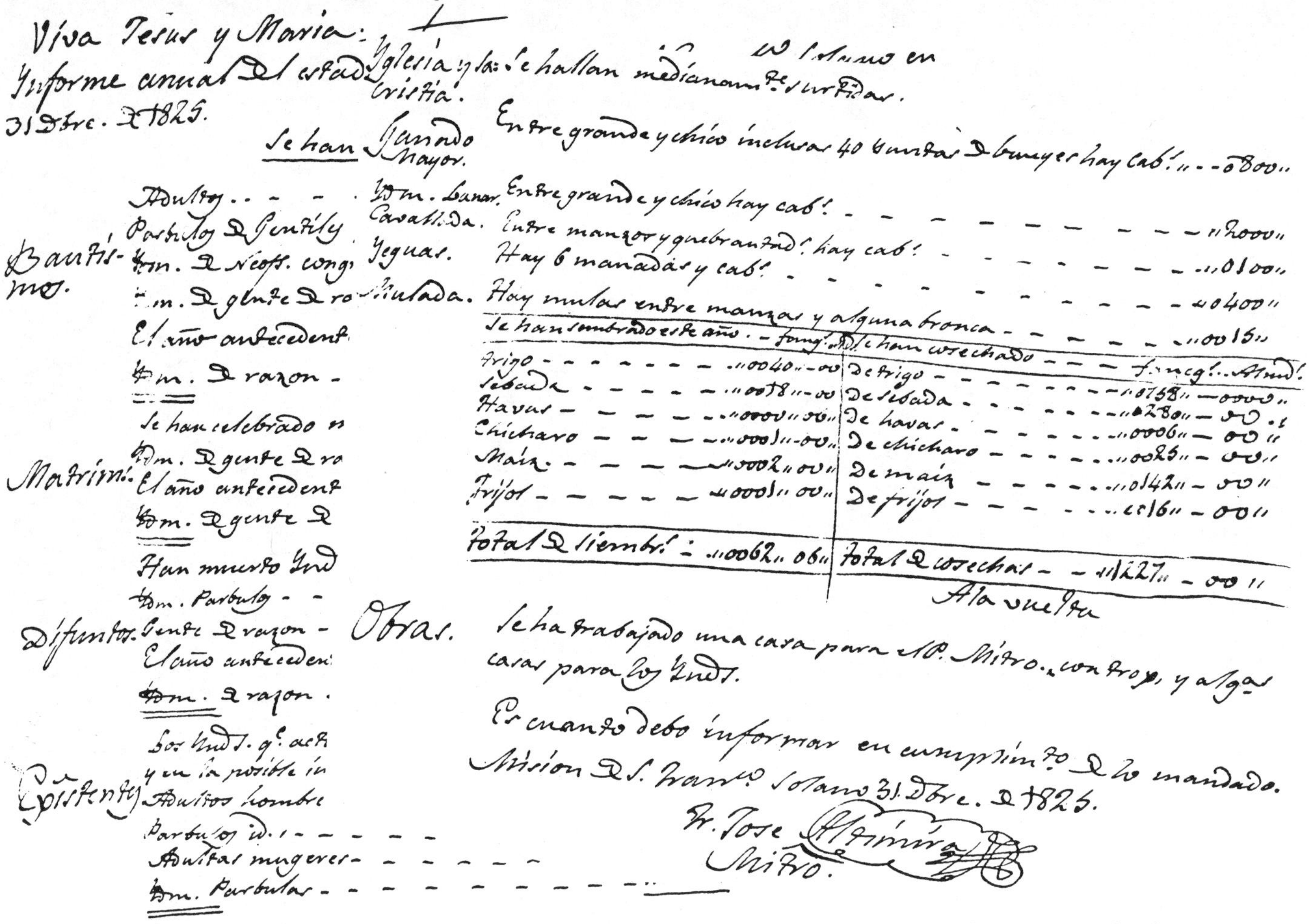
Viva Jesus y Maria:
Informe anual del estado
31 Dbre. de 1825.
Yglesia y sacristia. Se hallan medianam.te surtidas.
Se han Bautismos. Adultos. Parbulos de Gentiles. Idem de Neofs.
Ganado Mayor. Entre grande y chico inclusas 40 yuntas de bueyes hay cab.s ... 0800
Idm. Lanar. Entre grande y chico hay cab.s ... 4000
Caballada. Entre manzos y quebrantado hay cab.s ... 0100
Yeguas. Hay 6 manadas y cab.s ... 0300
Mulada. Hay mulas entre manzas y alguna bronca ... 0016

Se han sembrado este año	fanegas	Se han cosechado	fanegas
Frigo	0040 - 00	De trigo	0158 - 0000
Sebada	0018 - 00	De sebada	0280 - 00
Havas	0000 - 06	De havas	0006 - 00
Chicharo	0001 - 00	De chicharo	0025 - 00
Maiz	0002 - 00	De maiz	0142 - 00
Frijol	0001 - 00	De frijol	0016 - 00
Total de siembras	0062 - 06	Total de cosechas	1227 - 00

A la vuelta
Matrim. Idm. de gente de ro. El año antecedent.
Difuntos. Han muerto Ynd. Idm. Parbulos. Gente de razon. El año antecedent.
Existentes. Los Ynds. q.e act. y en lo posible in. Adultos hombres. Parbulos id. Adultas mugeres. Idm. Parbulas.
Obras. Se ha trabajado una casa para el P. Mitro. con otros, y algunas casas para los Ynds.
Es cuanto debo informar en cumplim.to de lo mandado.
Mision de S. Fran.co Solano 31 Dbre. de 1825.
Fr. Jose Altimira
Mitro.

Informe - 1825, *indicating baptisms, marriages, deaths, a census and the harvest results for that year. Note near end of report it says "This little scraping report in compliance with the mandate." Courtesy Santa Barbara Mission Archives.*

roofed with rough rafters supporting round willow rods bound with rawhide, then covered with red tile.

A forge shop 10 *varas* by 7 *varas*, and a weaving building 20 *varas* by 8 *varas*, both without roofs, were built. The garden, 150 *varas* square north and east of the church - containing over 160 fruit trees, was set out and fenced with willows. A corn field close to the church was walled in also. A vineyard had been started with over 1,000 growing vines.

Cattle ranches were established in the nearby Sonoma Valley and, in the Valley of the Suisuns, a large number of cattle were pastured on the rancho named Santa Eulalia where an adobe house and horse corral had been built to care for the padre's visits. A neophyte *alcalde* (mayor) with his family, was in charge of this large rancho, 12 leagues to the east.[2]

The mission now had many cattle, horses, and sheep on its lands. These had increased from the allotment originally received from Mission San Francisco de Asís of 20 yoke oxen, 25 bulls, 50 cows, 60 horses, and 300 sheep, as well as stock from other missions. Field crops began to produce good harvests from the virgin soil of the valley and the storerooms were beginning to fill with food for the coming winter.

Neophytes were coming to the mission in increasing numbers. These included 322 from San Francisco de Asís, 153 from San Jose, and 92 from San Rafael Arcangel. Fr. Altimira's annual report of December 1824 advised that: 36 adults, 24 children, and 35 neophytes were baptized - a total of 95 persons. Marriages were performed for 17 Indian couples and one Gente de Razón (white) couple - a total of 18. Burials were conducted for 23 adult Indians and 17 of their children, as well as one Gente de Razón - a total of 41. There were 305 Indian men and 79 boys as well as 234 Indian women and 74 girls at the mission - a grand total of 692 persons.

At the ranchos he lists 1,100 cattle, 4,000 sheep, 130 horses, 300 mares and 16 mules. Over 200 head had been killed to supply the mission, the *escolta* and herdsmen. Crops were producing for the year as follows:

Wheat	500 *fanegas*, for 130 planted
Corn	200 *fanegas*, for 2 planted
Frioles	6 *fanegas*, for ¼ planted
Garbanzos (chick-peas)	2 *fanegas*, for ¼ planted
Lentils	2½ *fanegas*, for ¼ planted[3]

The progress of Mission San Francisco Solano

carried on into the next year, 1825. William Antonio Richardson, a friend of Fr. Altimira while at San Francisco de Asís, helped in teaching the neophytes carpentry and building skills. He brought up a new bell for the mission in his launch a few days after his marriage there to Maria Antonia, the daughter of the Presidio *Comandante*, Ignacio Martínez. It was hung on a heavy beam in front of the mission church.[4] William Richardson assisted in laying out the buildings and the planned quadrangle and, being an experienced ship's carpenter, was able to plan substantial structures for the mission.

The rains of the previous winter had damaged the walls of two buildings, the forge and weaving shops which had not been roofed. These were rebuilt and roofed with tiles. Some adobe houses for a few Indians were built opposite the padres' house in the Indian village, as well as a new guardhouse and *calabozo* in the same area. The Indian neophytes lived in huts which they built of willows and rushes, partly in the ground, and thatched against the weather. These were grouped in the Indian village area south of the mission buildings.

During the summer, Fr. Altimira left the mission and visited as far south as San Buenaventura, where he officiated at Burial No. 85 on June 3rd and a Baptism No. 1043 on August 21st of 1825.[5]

During the year, new fields were cultivated and planted to grains and vegetables and the cattle ranchos extended farther out into the adjacent valley and foothill grazing lands.

Fr. Altimira in his short *Informe* at the end of the year 1825 reported:

"We have built a house for the Minister, with granary and thatched houses for the guards."

Baptized	100
Married	24
Buried	41
Indian population	338 male
	296 female
Cattle	800
Sheep	2000
Horses	100
Mares	400
Mules	15
Field Returns -	
Wheat	758 *fanagas*
Barley	280 *fanagas*
Beans	6 *fanagas*
Peas	25 *fanagas*
Corn	142 *fanagas*
Frioles	16 *fanagas*
Total	1227 *fanagas*[6]

The spring of 1826 found the new Mission San Francisco Solano in the midst of activity. There was a large quantity of seed from the previous harvest and extensive fields to be planted with grains, beans, and other field crops. The cattle were multiplying on the grazing lands and had to be rounded up and branded.

At the mission, new buildings were laid out and an adobe wall enclosing the quadrangle built and topped with tiles. The sowing field was cleared of rocks and they were used to enclose it with a rock wall to keep the cattle and wild deer from destroying the growing crop. Many new neophytes were coming to the mission from the gentile *rancherías* attracted by the abundance of food offered and the protection from hostile outlying tribes.

The weaving rooms were now completed and the young females kept busy making the blankets and rough cloth for their clothes. The *monjas*, or unmarried girls, had their own temporary *monjerio* or residence. The smithy was making the tools and implements for the building and ranching, while the *pozolera* (kitchen) in the quadrangle was busy preparing the pinole and other foods for the growing population. The brickyard was a busy place as thousands of adobe bricks were needed for the proposed buildings and the walls being built. The tile kilns were turning out hundreds of red roof tile, and now many one inch thick floor tiles were being made to floor the permanent buildings and corridors.

The lack of good housing for the many Indian neophytes and the newcomers from the nearby *rancherías* was proving a problem at the new mission. Many Indians traveled back and forth to their *rancherías* and, when work became too tiresome, left the mission. They were allowed to go and come, and, when crops were harvested, were glad to help as they received part of the harvest to take home. Fr. Altimira was crowding the Indian help and was not too successful in handling them. Complaints from the Indians had reached the Father Commissary Prefect during the earlier years and he passed the information on to the governor.[7]

The harvest of 1826 was a large one and the mission seemed in a good position for the Winter of 1826-27 with the storehouses full and the livestock ample and multiplying.

With the harvest in and lots of food in sight, some of the Indians became restless and hostile. The hostility finally erupted in the early Fall of 1827 with some of the troublemakers and other gentiles raiding the supplies and setting fire to some of the buildings. As there were still a number of *palizada* or pole buildings with tule thatched roofs, it was an easy matter for fires to

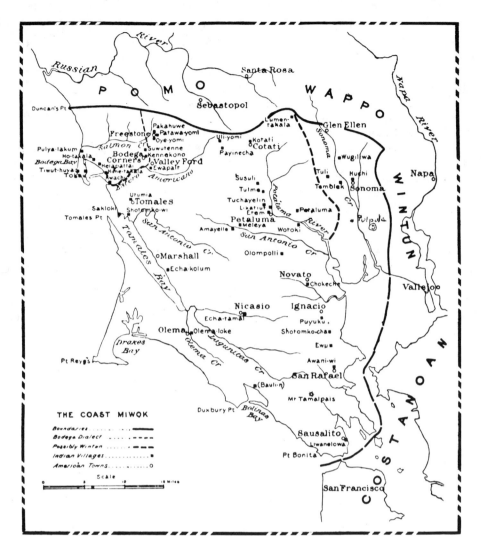

THE COAST MIWOK

Boundaries ....
Bodega Dialect ..... — .—
Possibly Wintun ...... — .— —
Indian Villages .... ■
American Towns .... o
Scale

Coast Miwok territory and Indian settlements. Sonoma Valley up to about Glen Ellen has been attributed to the southwestern Wintun as well as the Coast Miwok. Conflicting evidence makes a positive decision impossible. Tchokoyem or Chocuyen has been used as a designation for the Coast Miwok in Sonoma Valley or in general. Its origin is unknown. Courtesy University of California.

spread and consume them. The Indian village, mostly conical wicker huts with thatched walls and roofs, was easily destroyed.

Though this had happened at quite a number of the other missions during their early years, Fr. Altimira was very discouraged. He left the mission and moved at once to San Rafael Arcangel, then on to Mission San Francisco de Asís.

However, the damage was not too extensive to the permanent structures or the ranchos and growing crops as the harvest of the year testifies. No Indians were punished or expeditions made in retaliation.[8],[9]

Fr. Altimira requested that he be transferred to Mission Santa Barbara but ended up at Mission San Buenaventura. There had been a recent decree passed by the Mexican National Government that required the deportation of all persons who would not sign the oath of allegiance to the new National Government. Fr. Altimira was a strong adherent to the Spanish regime as was proven later by his secret departure from his station at Mission San Buenaventura for Spain in January 1828. This was done without the knowledge or permission of his superiors.

PART II

THE MISSION DOMAIN
A PROSPEROUS INDIAN MISSION

V

Padre Buenaventura Fortuny
The Builder

In September of 1826, soon after Fr. Altimira left, Padre Buenaventura Fortuny was assigned to Mission San Francisco Solano. He had been at Mission San Jose for the past 20 years with Fr. Narciso Durán. He was a quiet, simple in his tastes, unobtrusive man, strict in his religious life. He had been especially successful in handling the mission Indians and they had been well taken care of at his mission. Mission San Jose had become one of the best operated and richest missions in Northern California under his and Fr. Durán's guidance and excellent administration. Padre Fortuny was 52 years old at the time, having been born in 1774 at Moster, Archdiocese of Tarragona, Catalonia, Spain. As a student, he had been tall, dark haired, with hazel or dark brown eyes, a scant beard and pockmarked face.[1]

He joined the Franciscan Order in 1792 and, in 1803, embarked for Mexico with Fr. Narciso Durán. There, he entered San Fernando College until February 1806 when both he and Fr. Durán were sent to California. Both were assigned to Mission San Jose where they remained together for 20 years, Padre Fortuny as the Superior.

The large Mission San Jose adobe church building had been started and Padre Fortuny finished it, as well as building a two-story padre house, dam and water works, water powered flour mill, large gardens, tannery, soap factory and long adobe buildings of the Indian village. The mission ranchos were very extensive and their herds of animals were among the largest of the missions. Mission San Jose was considered the largest of the California settlements next to Mission San Luis Rey and Padre Fortuny had well earned the major credit for its position along with his co-worker, Fr. Durán.

Fr. Presidente Mariano Payeras stated, "His merit is as laudable as his simplicity and zeal. His aptitude for being a good missionary renders him suitable for labor among both faithful and infidels."[1]

Arriving at Mission San Francisco Solano in 1826, Padre Fortuny found the mission in bad shape. The neophytes were disorganized as a result of the earlier trouble, fires and the departure of Fr. Altimira. But, with a small number of loyal neophytes and the *escolta* (squad) of soldiers, he soon had created order out of chaos. Living quarters were cleared and refurnished, houses for the Indians were soon built, the soldiers' houses were repaired and soon the mission was functioning again under his experienced supervision.

At the end of the year, the grain fields were ready for the new crops and the orchard and vineyard were cleaned up for the winter. The cattle on the outlying ranchos were again in the charge of their *vaqueros* (cowhands). The Indians from the surrounding *rancherías*, when they saw the mission was operating and food was again abundant, soon returned and a large work force was available. The buildings that had been built of adobe and tile survived the fire, and now new bricks and tiles were being made for the new buildings to be constructed next year. A circle of rock walls was built around the cultivated area to protect the plantings and a wall of adobe now enclosed the *campo santo* or cemetery. Thirty-four large trees were cleared from around the mission area as well.

The church received the following gifts from Mission San Jose, Fr. Fortuny's former station:

2 chasubles - with white ribbon stoles, maniples and corporal cloths

2 albs

2 *cingulos*

6 purifiers

6 *amices*

1 Misal with Stos-middle border of the Order of N.P.S. Fr.

1 *platito de pelora* (pewter) with altar wine glasses of crystal

1 pan, for cleaning hands.

The padre and two neophytes made a dust guard for the mission articles.[2]

By year's end, Padre Fortuny was able to report for 1826:

  641 neophytes at the mission, with
  107 baptized during the year, and
  61 deaths and burials in the *campo santo*

The fields produced:

  2627 *fanegas* of grains
  582 cattle
  500 horses and mares
  1439 sheep, and
  11 mules were now in the pastures[2]

The many herds of large elk that roamed the nearby valleys were used for meat and *manteca* (butterfat) as well as tallow and hides, in these earlier years, to allow the domestic cattle to increase and also to clear the pasturage of wild animals.

The main project at the mission quadrangle for the new year of 1827 was to lay the foundation and start building the permanent adobe church at the east end of the padres' house.

This church was 55 *varas* long and 12¼ *varas* wide. It was to fill nearly the entire east side of the quadrangle. Its 1½ *vara* thick walls on heavy rock foundations were to rise 11 *varas* and support a wide tile roof. To the east of the new adobe church was established the *campo santo*, or new cemetery.

Enlargement of the curates' or padres' house was begun this year, making more useful quarters for the padres - living rooms as well as bedrooms for both padres and guests. It extended the building to the east, partly closing the front or south side of the quadrangle. The new and rebuilt sections would total 12 *varas* wide by 50 *varas* long inside.[3] The padres' house would be divided by the center wall and cross partitions into a *sala* (main room), dining room, and priest and guest rooms. There were also storerooms for the more valuable stores. A heavy plank ceiling would cover all the rooms.

Along the front and rear extended the corridors which were 3 *varas* wide, giving shelter and access to the various sections. When completed, there were to be 27 rooms in all - some in the extensive attic.[4] Over all, a red tile roof that extended over the corridors would be placed the next year. The rooms would have tile floors and soon the corridors would also be tiled.

The shops in the rear of the original church were operating and the tallow vats out in the back were set up with their large iron cauldrons. The weaving rooms, though still small, were busy as were the rooms where the Indian women ground the corn and grain on their *metates* (grinding stones).

Out on the ranchos the cattle and sheep were increasing in numbers as well as supplying the mission with daily food. Ranchos were established east of the mission at Huichica, at Agua Caliente the ancient Indian hot springs to the north, and beyond at Los Guilucos where the Valley of the Sonomans ended. To the east, in the Valley of the Napas, the mission horses grazed and cattle were pastured on the lands of Rancho St. Eulalia on the plains of the Suisuns. Sheep were herded in the upper hills and farther west. The general crops were planted but Padre Fortuny did not have much time or help for extensive field work or row crops this year in the extensive irrigated fields south of the mission.

In late summer, the mission was visited by Auguste Duhaut-Cilly, captain of the French ship *Le Heros*. He was on a trading trip to the Pacific Coast, visiting and trading with the pueblos and missions in California. His report of conditions at Mission San Francisco Solano, during this period, is quite complete as the following will indicate:

Trip to San Francisco Solano - August 4, 1827

While the transfer of the goods from Santa Clara and San Jose was continued, I undertook an expedition to San Francisco Solano, the last one established of the five bordering the bay. I was informed that a certain amount of deer tallow was to be found there, and I did not like to leave it for others to buy. The 4th, at four in the morning, I set out in the ship's long boat, well armed, having with me eight sailors, the second lieutenant, Dr. Botta, and Mr. Richardson, who took upon himself to be our pilot. We profited by what remained of the ebb tide and by a light breeze from the northwest to cross the bay, going by Alcatraz Island (Pelican Island). We recognized this name had been given to it with good reason, for it was covered with a numberless quantity of these birds: a rifle shot we fired across these feathered legions made them rise in a dense cloud with a noise like that of a hurricane.

We then passed between the right bank of the bay and Los Angeles Island (Island of the Angels) (Angel Island) where the flood began to favor us. The coast we were passing is formed of mountains of moderate height, covered with grass, at that time somewhat parched; in the ravines we saw clumps of oaks. From time to time we descried large deer herds. They were wandering in bands over these sloping pasture grounds, and we saw them run, browse, rush over these sloping pasture hills, so steep sometimes, that we could hardly imagine how they were able to hold themselves there without falling.

There are also many bears in these wooded places; but as these animals seldom appear except at night, we saw none. But a man named Cipriano, who was with us in the long boat, related to me that, passing some months before in this channel, one of these ferocious beasts, which was swimming to Los Angeles Island, approached the boat, intending to climb into it, when some soldiers who were in it,

Fr. Fortuny's Informe - 1826. "Fabricas. We have built a circle of rock [rock wall] sufficient for cultivation, we have enclosed with a wall of adobe the cemetery, we have removed a circle of 34 trees." Courtesy Santa Barbara Mission Archives.

with their arms, fired four balls at it at close range, just as the bear was getting its claws upon the boat, and killed it stone dead.

We had made about five leagues when we found ourselves in front of Mission San Rafael, placed at the farther end of a bay, on the north side of the harbor. This mission is very poor and has nothing for barter: we did not stop there. The east side of this little gulf makes, with a peninsula from the opposite coast, a strait a league wide, and contracted by four small islands, of which the principal two bear the names of San Pedro and San Pablo: the name San Pedro is also given to a rancho occupying the isthmus joining the peninsula to the mainland.

Coming out from this strait we saw opening before us a new sea, whose bounds we could hardly discern, and soon our attention was called to another passage serving at once as a mouth to the large river called the Sacramento coming from the north, and to another, not so considerable, which flows from the southeast.

With the assistance of oars and of the current we steered north-northwest, toward a group of mountains at the foot of which is built Mission San Francisco Solano. I reckoned we had made thirteen leagues from Yerba Buena when we reached the opening of a small channel meandering in the mid-

dle of a marsh covered with reeds, and into which we entered. This stream makes a thousand turns as it advances into the interior; and although from its mouth to the spot where we landed there are not more than three leagues in a straight line, we made fully double that many in following its windings.

This passage, however, could not be shortened by making it by land; for, up to the landing place, there is no solid ground: the banks of the channel are indicated only by rushes or reeds growing in the water, or at most in a kind of mud. Having arrived at solid ground, there still remained a league to make before reaching the mission; but Padre Ventura Fortuni (this was the name of the president), apprised of our landing, having sent us some horses, we were not long in repairing thither.

From my reckoning we had made about seventeen leagues, in a direction very close to north, since leaving the ship, a calculation agreeing well with the difference in latitude between the two points, Yerba Buena being on parallel 37° 48', and San Francisco Solano on 38° 39'.

This establishment is the northernmost of those the Spanish possess on this coast. It was founded the 25th of August, 1823, by Padre Altimira, who placed it in the middle of a plain of great extent, bounded on the north by mountains and hills, on the south by the bay, and everywhere watered and crossed by streams of fresh water. There are few happier sites, and this mission might become a very important one in a little time; but it was yet of small account at the period of my visit: therefore poor Padre Ventura Fortuni, in spite of his desire to treat us well, could offer us only cakes of Indian meal and dried beef. This want did not incline us to prolong our stay with him, and having hurried to buy all the tallow to be found at this mission, I fixed our departure for the next day.

I have said before that this tallow was deer tallow; and as this name may appear extraordinary, it is right that I explain the manner in which it is procured. The hills of this part of California, and the plains they leave between them, support an immense quantity of deer of prodigious strength and size. The animals find such plentiful pasture ground here, that, in the month of July, they become so fat that their agility is much lessened therefrom; this is the time the Californians choose to take them.

Mounted upon the swiftest horses, armed with a hunting knife and with the fatal rope, they betake themselves to the places where the deer are numerous, and pursue them to the utmost. Although these swift guests of the plains have lost part of their speed, enough still remains to them that they do not fear an ordinary horseman; but these men, born, so to say, on their horses, seldom fail to reach them and to throw the lasso at them with inconceivable skill. As soon as the deer is snared, it is overthrown and it is frequently pierced with its own weapons, rolling upon the sharp points of its antlers. This accident is not a rare one; but if it does not occur, the rider gets down from his horse, and, aided by his companions, he severs the hamstring, leaving it in this condition in order to follow the others. They do not always use the rope; when they succeed in nearing one within arm's length, it is the hunting knife they employ to cut the tendons of the leg.

This hunting is not done without a sort of tactics: one must know how to withdraw the animal from the woods and mountains, and to act so as to hunt it with the wind, in order that the deer, which runs away with open mouth to breathe and to be cooled, may want air sooner and be more quickly hunted down. But if this exercise demand much skill, it offers no less danger. Sometimes the rider, carried away by his eagerness, cannot avoid being thrown down with his horse into the clefts and fissures of the ground; sometimes darted ahead with too much speed, he cannot turn aside his steed soon enough, causing him to strike cruelly against the branches or trunks of the trees often met on his way. Even when the deer is snared and thrown down, great precautions are necessary in approaching and killing it: one has equally to fear the points with which its forehead bristles, and the toes of the hoofs arming its feet. I saw a horse which appeared to have received a thrust from a sword upon the thigh, but which had been wounded only by the cutting foot of a deer.

The flesh of these dead animals, from which the fat had been removed, remaining abandoned on the hunting ground, bears, attracted by this prey, come from all sides to feed upon it; and the hunters must often contend for the ground with these dangerous animals, which occasionally desert the battlefield only in losing their life.

I was pointed out a child of sixteen who had captured twenty-three deer in one day. Assuming that each one had yielded three *arrobas* (1) of tallow, this young man had earned, in his day's work, one hundred and thirty-eight piastres (about seven hundred francs). I bought from the soldiers of the guard at this mission for four thousand francs, a supply of this product, the result of their hunting.

(1) (An *arroba* is equal to twenty-five pounds.)

Before leaving, I accompanied the padre into his garden which I found in the most deplorable condition: thick grass and marshes had invaded a portion of it, and the rest was as badly planted as it was badly cared for. He showed me the place where, a few days before, some wild Indians of the neighborhood had killed two men of the mission, shooting them with their arrows while asleep. This murder was attributed to the hatred that *los gentiles* bear toward all the Christian Indians; but this time it appeared to be the result of revenge and reprisals.

The Spanish government of California has always followed the atrocious system of ordering, from time to time, excursions to the settlements of the interior, either for retaking the Indians escaped from the missions, or driving away *los gentiles* by exciting terror among them; expeditions which, while costing the life of some soldiers and many natives, have served but to nourish hatred. The last and most ridiculous one of these little campaigns was made in 1826, under the command of Alférez (second lieutenant)-ensign-Sánchez. This is the cause of it.

After the harvest, the padre at San Francisco Solano had given permission to eighty of his Christian Indians to visit their old native settlements; and they were on the way in a large boat, going up the Sacramento River, when the savages, attacking them unawares in a confined spot where they could neither flee nor defend themselves, killed more than forty of them. As a result of this, an incursion was ordered and entrusted to the passionate ardor of Sánchez, who advanced into the country at the head of twenty or thirty mounted soldiers. At their approach, all the Indians able to defend themselves lay in ambush in the woods, when they shot their arrows at the troop, while it was impossible for the horsemen to reach them or even to see them; but they, enraged, revenged themselves upon the women and children who had not been able to flee; they massacred thirty of them, and returned, in shameful triumph, with two young girls and a child whom they brought prisoners, as a token of their victory.

Were one to ask these imitators and descendants of the Spanish if there be no other way of gaining peace with these people; imbued with the ideas of their ancestors, they give the Indians so inhuman a character that, to hear them, it is impossible to treat them otherwise. "They live," they say, "in separate villages; and if peace be made with one of these hamlets, it is a motive for attack by the neighboring villages, who regard its inhabitants as traitors, and who join together to destroy it." But if one considers that the missions are peopled only by these same men, and that the padres, using in turn mildness and severity, have been able to acquire over them the immense influence which keeps up these establishments, one cannot help thinking that the commandants at the presidios have taken the reverse of good policy as well as of humanity.

I noticed one thing which would seem to prove that the resentment against so lamentable a system has not gone so far as to render the natives unruly. At the time of the harvest, the missionaries at San Rafael and San Francisco Solano obtain as many gentiles as they want for helping them gather the grain. They come to these missions with their wives and children, construct their temporary huts, and work in the harvesting for a small quantity of corn or maize which the padres give them. We found two to three hundred of them who had been at San Francisco Solano for several weeks.

Nothing is more miserable than the people at the little camp they had pitched in front of the padre's dwelling. The men are nearly naked, and the women have only a cloak made of narrow strips of rabbit skin twisted into strings and sewed together. This garment is very warm; but being thick it serves as a retreat for an immense number of those parasitic insects so disgusting to us; . . . . .

I could carry away in the long boat only part of the tallow I had purchased; and notwithstanding that, it was heavily enough loaded for the long trip we had to make. We set out at two in the afternoon and we rejoined our ship at two in the morning.[5]

Disturbing news to the older padres of the missions, who had come from Spain and felt that it was still their homeland, was the report that the new Mexican government had decreed that all Spaniards under 60 years of age, unless married to Mexican citizens and had taken the oath of allegiance to the new government, would have to leave the country. But most of the older padres felt it was prudent to wait and see what would happen - especially as there were no padres coming to California to care for the churches and missions.

The annual reports for the year 1827 showed the progress that was being made at the mission. There were 90 baptisms and 41 marriages, while 64 burials were added to the *campo santo*. The neophyte population had increased to 667 at the mission. Cattle on the ranchos now numbered 1,200, with 3,500 sheep grazing on the hills. Horses, mares and mules totaled 550 head, including 50 head of oxen, and the padre now had 8 pigs. Grains were harvested: 1,150 *fanegas* wheat, 200 *fanegas* barley, 48 *fanegas* beans, 75 *fanegas* peas, 250 *fanegas* corn, 9 *fanegas frioles* and 5 *fanegas garbanzos* -- 1,739 *fanegas* in all.

The church was enriched with the following items also: 1 chalice, 1 large cup, 3 albs, 1 altar cloth, 2 vestments for deacons, and 3 chasubles of white velvet - gifts from the Mission of San Jose. Mission San Rafael sent a *crismera*, or consecrated oil vessel, with *sto casito* and lid

(storage case). A bridge and two dust guards and a rain gauge had been made at the mission.[6]

The buildings and adobe walls now enclosed an area 51 *varas* square with roofed corridors along the sides of the buildings. Access was eventually restricted to one entrance on the front so that the padre and major-domo could keep track of their neophytes. Also, in case of an Indian attack, the mission would be a closed fortress.

The year 1828 was also one of building at the mission and the large number of neophytes and artisans were busy on the new buildings. Roofing with new tiles was the important work for the year. The new padres' dwelling house of 50 *varas* building front with double roof was covered with 12 *varas* width of tiles. Also, 30 *varas* of the same width of sod were changed to tiles.[7]

The large adobe church walls were going slowly up as the hundreds of bricks were made and seasoned. The timbers were being brought in from the mountains and hewn for the door, window frames, roof beams and rafters.

A new forge building, 12 by 30 *varas*, was replacing the old original one in back of the wooden church, as well as new shops, 12 by 50 *varas*, in the rear. The granaries were enlarged to care for the increased harvest and storage for soap, tallow, and hides was needed.

Opposite the front of the church and large padres' house, the major-domo and soldiers had their houses with the ever ready guardhouse nearby. Beyond to the south, the neophytes built their conical grass and tule huts on the level land. Here, a small stream supplied the necessary water for their few needs.

News arrived early in the year from Mission Santa Barbara that Fr. José Altimira, the zealous founder of Mission San Francisco Solano, had secretly left for his homeland Spain on the American brig *Harbinger*, January 23, 1828. He was accompanied by Fr. Antonio Ripoll of Mission Santa Barbara, another young Spanish padre. The Mexican government decree of December 29, 1827, expelling all young Spaniards from the country caused them to act, anticipating that soon such action would be taken. Fr. Altimira was later heard from in Teneriffe, Spain.

Padre Fortuny still remained the only padre at Sonoma as there were few new padres coming from the college in Mexico and, of course, none from Spain. So they were being spread out along the mission chain and the older members pressured to remain beyond their usual terms of service. However, he had good control of his mission and was able to accomplish a great deal of work during the year.

The results of his year's work in 1828 were: 127 baptisms and 35 marriages with 89 burials among his neophytes, who now numbered 667 persons.

Despite the increased daily food requirements of his establishment, the ranchos now pastured 1,400 cattle, 4,000 sheep, 531 horses, mares and mules, including 60 oxen - or a total of 5,931 head. The year was a poor one for field crops, however, as only 770 *fanegas* of all grains were harvested.[7]

Cattle brand of Mission San Francisco Solano de Sonoma.

Viva Jesus

Informe anual de esta M.ⁿ de S. Francisco Solano en 31 de Dic. de 1830.

Bautismos ___ Se han bautizado este año Adultos 6. Parvulos 19. De estos 3 son hijos de Gentiles. De Neg. recien baut.ˢ o. De gente de Razon o. De Neof.ˢ antes congregados 16. Son por todos 25. Los años an. 624. Desde la fund.ⁿ 642.

Matrimonias ___ Se han celebrado 20. Matrimonios de Yndios. Ninguno de Razon. Los años ant. 174. desde la fund.ⁿ 194.

Difuntos ____ Se han muerto Yndios 24. Adultos, y 13. parvulos. De Razon o. Son por todos 37. Los años ant. 340. Desde la fund.ⁿ 377.

Existentes ___ Los Yndios que actuam.te existen empadronados, y en la posible instruccion Cristiana, y Civil son Adultos 318. De 9 años abajo 75. total de homb.ˢ 393. Adulta. 29. De 9 años abajo 71. total de mugeres 367. total de existentes 760.

Ganado May.r Hay entre chico y grande 2000. cabezas, inclusas 40. yuntas aperadas, y 20 sin aperar.

Ganado menor Hay entre chico y grande 4000. cabezas. De Cerda 60. cabezas.

Cavallada Hay 6 manadas de Yeguas que componen el n.º de 600. cabezas entre chico y grande. Cavallos mansos, y quebrantados 125. Bestias mulares 4.

Siembras ___ Se han sembrado para este año. De trigo 37 ½ f. De Cevada 19. De Hava 2 ½ f. De chicharo 2. f. De Maiz 4 f. De Frijol 3 f. De Garvanso 6 almudes.

Cosechas ___ Se han cogido de trigo 1190 f. De Cevada 140. f. De Havas 12 f. de chich.º 3 f. De Maiz 300 f. De Frijol 24. De Ganso 6 almudes.

M.ⁿ de S. Fran.co Solano 31 de Dic. de 1830

Fr. Buenav. Fortuny

Informe - 1830, penned by De la Rosa for Fr. Fortuny. Courtesy Santa Barbara Mission Archives.

VI

The Prosperous Years
El Camino Real

By this time, life at Mission San Francisco Solano had settled down to a daily routine. At dawn the peals of the large bell on the beam in front of the padres' house rang out over the settlement.

The first duty was attending mass for all but the young children. Here, in the tall wooden church, the neophytes stood while the padre celebrated Holy Mass, the prayers for the day, and the *Doctrina* (catechism) recited aloud with the Indians. Concluding, the *Alabado* (in praise of the Sacrament) was sung. Sometimes simple lessons in Spanish were given before dismissal. Often, parts of the service were spoken in the Indian's own language.

Then, all received their breakfast of *atole*, a gruel of roasted corn or grain, at the *pozolera* or kitchen where the big iron kettles were kept boiling. The girls and young men took their meals at their own quarters while the families carried their share home in bark or earthen vessels. After breakfast, the young girls and single women went to work in the spinning and weaving shops under their matron. The men and larger boys left with their leaders for their work in the fields, shops, and on the new buildings.

At noon the large bell pealed out the Angelus, the welcome three peals -- three times and then nine, and all returned for dinner. This was served from the big kettles of the *pozolera* also, but was usually *pozole*, a gruel or broth with meat, beans, peas, lentils, or *garbanzos* added -- according to the season and state of the harvest stores. A siesta period followed the noon meal until about two o'clock when all went back to their tasks for the balance of the afternoon. The welcome peals of the bell about five o'clock ended the day's work.

All attended the church and evening service for the recitation of the Doctrina and religious devotions. After instructions in Spanish or Indian by the padre, the service was concluded with the singing of the *Alabado*. The neophyte choir was trained in the singing and performance on the musical instruments. Six o'clock usually found a supper of *atole* ready for the entire settlement. After which, they could indulge in various amusements, in which they enjoyed much latitude.[1]

A small bell hanging by the major-domo's house on the south side of the mission plaza was used for calling the neophytes together for meals, work duties and attendance at Church. Eight o'clock curfew was signalled with the ringing of the "poor souls" bell.

On Sundays and Holy Days (*dias de fiesta*), there was no general work. After divine service in the morning and devotional exercises in the afternoon, consisting of the Rosary, the Litany of the Blessed Virgin, and other short prayers in Spanish, the neophytes were free for the day. Games, races, and other amusements dear to an Indian's heart were in order - helped along by the padre. July 14th, Day of Patron Saint Francis Solano apostle of Peru, was an important annual celebration.

Work had progressed during this year of 1829, with the church walls going up higher and the other permanent buildings of adobe receiving their heavy roof beams and rafters and being covered with red tile from the busy kilns.

PATER NOSTER
MISSION SAN FRANCISCO SOLANO

Allá-igamé mutryocusé mi zahuá om mi yahuatail cha usqui etra shou mur tzecali ziam paconjinta mul zhaiíge. Nasoyate chelegua mul znatzoitze tzecali zicmatan zchiitiilaa chalehua mesqui pihuatzite yteima omahuá. Emqui Jesus.

(The Guilitoy language.)[8]

Out in the planting fields the neophytes were now well trained in preparing the soil and planting the crops. A crude plow made from a tree limb and fork was shod with an iron point. A yoke of oxen pulled the plow, the yoke at the end of the long beam being fastened to their horns with rawhide. After seed was sown, brush dragged over the furrows covered the seed. Corn was planted by hand in furrows and covered with soil, using the feet to compact it.

When harvest time came, hand cutting was resorted to and the sheaves were hauled in the *carretas* or carried to the threshing floor. This was a level area paved with flat stone, six or ten *varas* in diameter with a wall of stone around it. The grain was scattered over the floor, and horses, often the wild mares were driven over the grain round and round the enclosure. When they had the grain well trampled, the neophytes tossed it in the air so the wind would blow off the chaff and dirt, leaving the grain ready for storage. It was measured by *fanegas* (1.6 bushel). Corn was also harvested and stored, sometimes on the ear and sometimes shelled. The dried beans, peas, lentils and *garbanzos* were dried and flailed out of their pods and stored in the ample storerooms.

Some distance from the quadrangle was the *mantanza* or slaughter field where selected cattle were driven every few days and slaughtered. The meat was brought to the kitchens and the heavy fat to the tallow vats for rendering, as was the *manteca*, or butterfat, for the kitchen use. The hides were staked out on the ground to dry and then stored for trading purposes, unless they were made into rawhide strips for lashing the roof rafters and coverage of the new buildings. They were also used for chairs, and, covering a frame, made the beds in use at the mission. Some hides would soon be used in a proposed tannery where various leathers would be produced for shoes, saddles and harness. The soap vats were also set up and used the tallow and lye from the ash heaps to make the heavy bars of soap used in the kitchen and laundry. Roofs were tiled for 50 *varas* in length. They were double or hip roofs, 12 *varas* wide, including the new corridors.[2]

Many neophytes were vaccinated by Mr. William Richardson of Yerba Buena as some epidemics were reported in the territory to the south.

The year of 1829 was about over when Padre Fortuny reported the following: baptized were 119 persons, and 36 marriages were performed, while 51 burials were added to the *campo santo*.

The field crops had a poor year again and the harvest totaled only 523 *fanegas*. On the range land, however, increases continued with 1,500 cattle, 5,000 sheep, 529 horses, mares and mules, including the 60 oxen. Pigs numbered 5 this year - a total of over 7,000 animals.[2]

The mission bell that hung on the heavy beam in front of the padres' house was moved along the beam so that the new bell, recently cast in Mexico especially for Mission San Francisco Solano, could be hung. It was a large heavy bell with decorated rim and crown on top through which the rawhide lashings fastened it to the large beam. The clapper, with its leather cord, made a strong pleasant tone that complemented the earlier bell by its side. On one side was the symbol of the cross made in stars. Around the bell were the words -

MYCON DE
SAN FRANCISCO SOLANO
1829
(Mary, Immaculately Conceived.
Belonging to San Francisco Solano
1829)

After the new bell was in place, Padre Fortuny assembled his flock and the new addition to their mission's daily life was blessed. It soon rang out its cheerful peals over the quiet valley along with those of its older companion bell.

Work on the buildings continued throughout the year. The large adobe church, on the east side of the plaza, was receiving its heavy bricks as soon as they were sufficiently cured and was near the desired height of 11 *varas*. The massive roof beams and rafters were being brought in from the nearby mountains and hewn down to size. All the earlier *palizada* or wooden buildings, except the first church, had or were being replaced with adobe walled structures with the tiles replacing the temporary tule roofs.

The mission launch was busy bringing the needed supplies from the other missions on the Bay and from ships anchored at Yerba Buena. These consisted of cloth, foodstuffs, church supplies, iron, and what implements were obtainable. The embarcadero on *Arroyo* Sonoma, a long league to the south, was the landing place and the mission pack trains brought the shipments to and from the mission. Payment was usually in hides, tallow or grains.

The ranchos were also served by the pack trains of horses or mules. Each animal, fitted with *basta*, a pack saddle, and *alforjas*, pack bags, could carry 75 to 150 pounds and afforded an excellent means of transportation. The *carretas*, drawn by oxen, were often used for heavy loads but were slow and needed a better road. Timbers, before being hewn, were often dragged long distances by yokes of oxen.

El Camino Real, the King's Highway, with its northern terminal at Mission San Francisco Solano was often used to travel to and from Mission San Rafael Arcangel and from there,

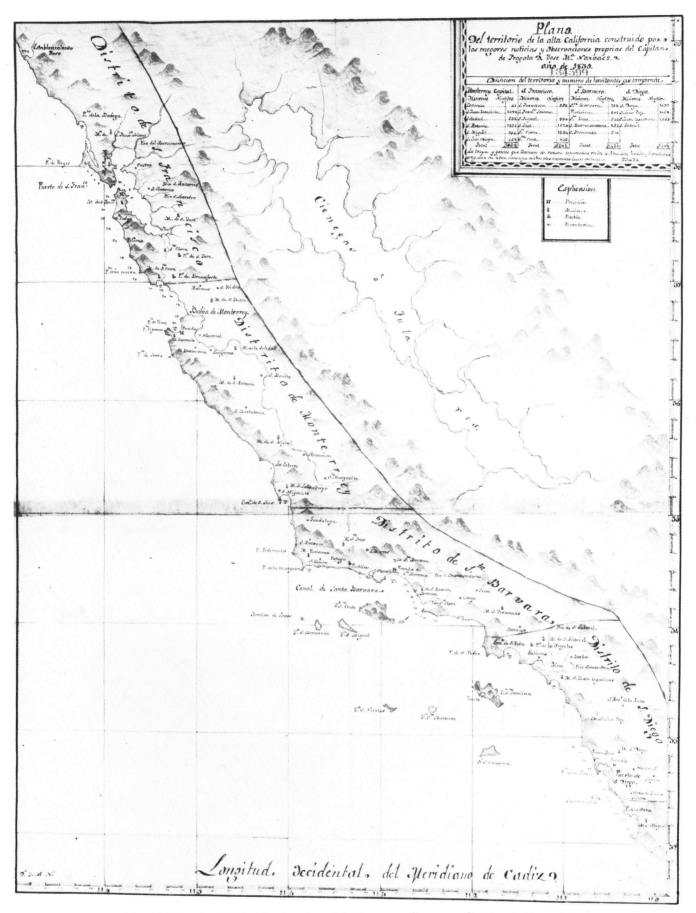

Alta California - 1830. Map by Jose M. Narvaez. Courtesy California State Library.

by boat to Mission San Francisco de Asís or the Presidio de San Francisco. It supplemented the direct water route from the mission embarcadero on *Arroyo* Sonoma.

From Mission San Francisco Solano plaza, El Camino Real led past the Indian village and south along higher ground and then southwest to a *vado* or ford across *Arroyo* Sonoma, one half league southwest of the mission plaza.[3]

The Plain of Sonoma was crossed to the southwest and through the low hills to the Tolay *Portezuela*, and Laguna Tolay with its Indian *ranchería* beyond. From here, El Camino turned north along the base of the hills to another *arroyo* that led on to the old camp site of Fr. Altimira on *Arroyo* Lema.

From Lema, the exploration route was followed west across the *Plano de* Petaluma to Chocuay, *la Punta de los Esteros*, and then south along the west side of Rio de Petaluma to Olompali. Here, the camino to the Ruso settlement led west up the *arroyo* to *Puerto* (Port) Bodega.

El Camino Real continued south from Olompali on the well-worn exploration route through *Portezuela* (gap or pass) Novato and, crossing Rancho San Jose to the San Rafael *portezuela*, continued around the hill to Mission San Rafael Arcangel. From the nearby San Rafael embarcadero, boats were used to and from Presidio de San Francisco and Mission San Francisco de Asís on their well established positions on El Camino Real.

Mission San Francisco de Solano drew its neophytes from the area covered by El Camino Real north of Novato and all of Sonoma, Mendocino, Lake, Napa and Solano counties.

Gentile *rancherías* in the *Frontera del Norte Este* which were the original homes of the mission neophytes were as follows (the location of some are indefinite:)[4]

NAMES	PROBABLE LOCATION
Aloquiomi	
Atenomac	
Canoma (Cainama or Camameros)	Santa Rosa
Canijolmano (Calajomanas)	Bale Rancho, Napa County
Caymus (Kaimus)	Yountville, Napa County
Chemoco (Chemocoytos)	Upper Suisun area
Chichoyomi (Chicoimi Stream)	East of Petaluma
Chocuyem	Sonoma Mission site area
Churvato	Cache Creek
Coyayomi (Joyayomi)	
Huiluc	
Huymen	
Lacatiut	San Rafael, Marin County
Loaquiomi (Locollomi)	Napa County
Linayto (Libayto)	North Suisun Valley
Locnoma	1 mile east Middletown - "Goosetown"
Mayacma (Mayakma)	Calistoga area, Napa County
Muticolmo	
Malaca	Above old Suisun area
Napato	Napa area
Oleomi (Oleyome)	Northeast of Middletown, Lake County
Putto or Putato (Pultoy)	Punta Creek, Lake County
Polnomanoc	
Paque	
Petaluma	Lake Tolay, Sonoma County
Pulpul	Lower west Sonoma Valley

Suisun	Old Suisun Creek, west side
Satayomi (Sotoyomi)	North of Santa Rosa
Soneto	
Tolen (Tolenos)	North side Suisun Valley
Tlayacma	
Tamal	Mt. Tamalpais, Marin County
Topayto	Monticello Valley
Ululato	North side Suisun Valley
Utinomanoc	
Yulyul	South of Suisun
Zaclom	

Reports for the year 1830 sent in by Padre Fortuny to Fr. Commissary Prefect showed that baptisms were only 25 and marriages performed 20 - with 37 burials. Altogether, 760 neophytes belonged to the mission.

The cattle numbered 2,000 now, with 4,000 sheep, 729 horses, mares and mules also in pasture and the pigpen now had 60 pigs in residence. The field crops were abundant with 1,190 *fanegas* of wheat, 140 *fanegas* of barley, 12 of beans, 3 of peas, 300 *fanegas* of corn, 24 of *frioles* and half a *fanega* of *garbanzos* - so the storerooms and granaries were bulging again with 1,670 *fanegas* total.[5]

Mission San Francisco Solano in its sixth year under the guiding hand of Padre Fortuny was well on its way to becoming a strong and populous unit of the long chain of California Missions and was expanding its influence farther to the north and northeast each year. The gentiles from the far *rancherías* were joining the neophytes at the mission and the old and young were being baptized and instructed in the ways of the church. At the same time, they were being taught the many skills and trades necessary for the building up and maintenance of the mission and the fields and ranchos of grazing land.

The new church was nearly complete and the additional small utility buildings, closing the quadrangle, well on their way. These were not progressing as fast as the padre desired but the work of preparing the daily tasks and meals, and planting, tending and harvesting the crops was most important for the year.

On October 24, 1831, a fire consumed some of the straw and tule huts in the neophytes' area to the south of the padres' house. Before it was controlled, a man and four women had perished. The huts were soon rebuilt after the area was cleared. More adobe houses with tiled roofs were needed in the Indian village and plans were made to rebuild this section as had been done at all the other missions.[6]

The big event of the year was the rodeo which was held at the various ranchos. Here, the cattle were driven in from the grazing lands and kept together while they were singled out and counted, brands sorted out, young unbranded cattle and horses were lassoed and operated on, if desired, and branded with the mission brand "F".

The herds were becoming large enough now so that older animals were driven to the slaughter areas where they were thrown and killed. Then their hides were taken off and staked out to dry. The fat was taken to the tallow vats and rendered into tallow. A hide was hung by the four corners, or in a hole, and filled with tallow which was allowed to harden - each holding about one *arroba* (25 pounds). Certain richer fats, or *manteca*, were rendered out for use in the kitchen. The hides, dry and stiff, and the bags of tallow were now ready for sale or barter with the sailing ship traders who visited the San Francisco Bay and Sausalito anchorage. The pack trains carried the hides and heavy *arrobas* of tallow down to the embarcadero on the *Arroyo* Sonoma where the ship's launches or boat of the mission carried the products to the waiting vessels. Articles and supplies badly needed by the mission were brought back on the return trips.

By the end of the year 1831, Padre Fortuny could submit with pride his annual report of progress, both spiritual and material.

Baptisms	232
Marriages	35
Burials	53
Total population	939 neophytes

The horned cattle on the ranchos totaled 2,500, sheep 5,000, horses, mares and mules 729, including the same 60 oxen. The pigsty held 50 pigs. The granaries and storerooms were full with the total 1,640 *fanegas* consisting of 1,171 *fanegas* wheat, 211 barley, 5 beans, 19 peas, 200 corn, 24 *frioles*, and 2 *garbanzos*.[7]

Mission San Jose de Guadalupe, founded June 11, 1797, by Father Lasuen. The fourteenth mission in order of founding, it was at one time second in the number of neophytes under its control. Courtesy Pictorial History of California, *University of California.*

Indians in ceremonial gathering at adobe church - 1832. From a painting by Oriana Day, 1882-83. Courtesy Bancroft Library.

SAN FRANCISCO SOLANO, 1832.

Adobe church at San Francisco Solano, 1832. From a drawing by Edgar Vischer under instruction of M.G. Vallejo, 1874. Courtesy Bancroft Library.

VII

The Great Adobe Church

The years of 1832-33 were years of much rejoicing in the Valley of the Sonomans for the great new white adobe church, with its red tile roof, was completed. It stood high and clear beside the padres' house and the older wooden church - against the background of the green hills on the eastern side of the valley.

It was 12¼ *varas* wide and its walls were 1½ *varas* thick and 11 *varas* high, extending back 55 *varas* and filling most of the east side of the quadrangle or patio.[1] The facade was plain and the large doorway was bordered with a square timberlike trim. Above, a square window with like trim lighted the choir loft. Up near the peak of the roof was a smaller round window. Along the sides, high windows let in the light over the interior. The wide overhanging roof was covered with the red tile of which hundreds had been made in the busy kilns.[2]

The church building extended a short distance out from the front corridor, similar to the majority of other mission churches.[2] The vestibule was in the front with the choir loft above and the long nave was clear to the sanctuary where the elaborate altar was now installed. With the Stations of the Cross in their places along the walls, the new church was a great tribute to Padre Fortuny and his fine administration of the mission.

Alongside the new church on the east side was the new *campo santo* - 11 *varas* wide, enclosed with its adobe wall and an arched gateway in the front wall. This cemetery had replaced the original one on the west side of the first wooden church.[2] At the rear of the church was an ample sacristy, 5 *varas* long, with a doorway into the sanctuary as well as an entrance from the patio.[3]

The old original church of wood was retained for the present as buildings were needed for many things, especially for storage of grains and other supplies.[4]

The padres' house extended the full length between the old and the new churches except for a small passageway with gate beside the older church. The east end had been extended to the wall of the adobe church, adding more needed rooms to the large building.

On the west, the old church filled in half of that side, with the smith, carpenter, and old weaving shops and an adobe wall closing up the patio.

Along the buildings facing the patio were the covered corridors. The wide 3 *vara* corridor along the rear of the padres' house was floored with the large red tiles, as was the corridor alongside the old wooden church on the west side.[5] The patio or quadrangle, 51 *varas* square, was the center of the mission's activity where the work could be done under the direction of the padre, his major-domo, and the artisans with their various crews.

In front of the church and padres' house was the open mission plaza where the neophytes assembled and many of their games were held. Fronting on and beyond this plaza were the quarters for the major-domo, the *escolta*, the *cuartel* or guardhouse, and some houses for retired soldiers and their families. Beyond, on the wide plain, was the village of the neophytes - a few adobe huts but many rows of their conical willow and tule huts. When possible, the native huts were being replaced with tiled adobe houses similar to those at Mission San Jose de Guadalupe, Padre Fortuny's former mission.

Outside, and to the west and northwest of the quadrangle, were the adobe brick yards, the tile makers' buildings, and kilns, the tannery and soap vats. Small streams from the springs at the base of the nearby hills were brought down in ditches to these work areas. On one of the streams was the *molino* or grist mill being built with its water wheel and mill stones, quarried from the nearby hills.

Nearby, 346 *varas* to the east, was the mission vineyard now producing ample grapes for

Informe - 1832. "*Fabricas. The new church of 55* varas *long and 12¼* varas *wide has its roof covered.*" *Signed by Fr. Fortuny, December 31, 1832. Courtesy Santa Barbara Mission Archives.*

the table and the wine barrels. It was 250 *varas* by 300 *varas* with a stone and adobe tiled wall surrounding it. A small adobe hut was built for the caretaker. The water from a good spring was used for irrigation, coming along the hill in a *zanja* or ditch. At the mission the grapes were pressed and the wine now filled the small cellar.

The mission orchard with its many fruit trees was now in full bearing - back of and to the north and east of the quadrangle buildings. Some badly needed adobe granaries were being built outside the quadrangle to the north.

The mission quadrangle had its own water ditch or *zanja*, bringing water to a patio fountain for domestic use. A natural stream from a large spring ran south beyond the far wall of the new adobe church and continued on past the soldiers' houses and *cuartel* and through the Indian village.

Ranchos were being operated at the Valleys of the Libantikiyoma (Santa Rosa), the Petalumas, Napas, and at St. Eulalia (Suisun), Huichica just southeast of Sonoma, and Los Guilucos to the north, while herds and flocks were also pastured in the nearby valley itself.

Padre Fortuny claimed for the mission's use a vast area, 7½ leagues north from the Estero de San Pablo and 11 leagues wide from east to west, over 80 square leagues, which included four large fertile valleys and their rolling hill pasture land - a small empire in itself. This area was being developed as the neophytes from the many *rancherías* joined the population at the mission or were under its influence.

Fr. Amoros of Mission San Rafael died in 1832 and Padre Fortuny cared for the burial of his neighbor padre in Mission San Rafael Arcangel.

The year 1832 was the most prosperous of mission San Francisco Solano and the reports of Padre Fortuny showed the following results:

127 baptisms	1008 to date
34 marriages	263 to date
70 deaths	500 to date
Neophytes	996 at present
Cattle	3500
Sheep & goats	6000
Swine	50
Horses & mares	900
Mules	13
Wheat	800 *fanegas*
Barley	1025 *fanegas*
Beans	3 *fanegas*
Peas	52 *fanegas*
Corn	300 *fanegas*
Frioles	32 *fanegas*
Garbanzos	2 *fanegas*
Total	2214 *fanegas*[6]

It appears that for the last three annual informes Padre Fortuny had a secretary or helper to write them as these three are clearly written in near printing script and signed by Padre Fortuny in his regular hand.

At the end of this 1832 informe, the modest padre made just one very important statement: "*Fabricas - Se ha techado la nueva Yglesia de 55 vs largo, y 12 y cuarto de ancho.*" The new church of 55 *varas* long and 12¼ *varas* wide has its roof covered (been roofed). NOTE - This is the new adobe church at the east end of the padres' house.

VIII

The Builder Padre Leaves

The mission now was equal to many of the older missions in the other parts of Alta California, both in permanent buildings, neophytes, cattle, and ranchos. It had a potential for becoming larger and more important as the plans for expansion could be carried out. Padre Fortuny had accomplished this without the help of an assistant padre throughout the six and a half years of his residence.

Feeling that he had brought the mission up to a going operation, Padre Fortuny wished a transfer to a less strenuous post at one of the older missions. A young padre should carry on here at Sonoma. He wrote as follows:

Viva Jesus

San Solano 2nd of January
Year of 31.

R.P. Fr. José Sanchéz,
My Father President: Health and grace in the Lord.
May the year I have had a good beginning and as well a good ending. Amen.
Here are the reports, modest in both temporal and spiritual matters; in the same manner in which St. Paul speaks, first of which is corporal, then that which is spiritual. Consequently where the first are lacking, the second fail. There is a great harvest in these hills but for lack of clothing we have not been able to harvest it.

The quadrangle of Mission San Francisco Solano de Sonoma, circa 1836.

Because 5 or 6 padres are arriving see if some person can come here, tho I consider that there will be many candidates because there will be some who desire to leave, and I, one of them, because now I lack those strengths of the mind and the body. Therefore I have made it known on the other side. (i.e. Mexico)

There is much which to be done in one occupation and in this remote district, and I am not able to do it. Presently for in order to go to confession I have to travel by water and although we possess a launch the estuary is not always usable for service. Since the 15th of September, when I was with P. Marceso, I have not had a visit with another padre, and then I did not have a greater want because I had someone to look after the house, and the sick, and at present I do not have such a one. Indeed there is an Englishman here who is deaf, called Santiago, but the Indians do not pay much attention, according to what he tells me.

I do not have anything else to communicate.

Get along well with Ignacio, whom I salute, and I kiss your hand.

Fr. Ventura Fortuny

P.S. The said Englishman states that he had been at Mission San Gabriel, in the capacity of a servant.

Farewell[1]

At his request, he received a transfer to Mission San Diego where he would serve with another padre at the oldest mission of Alta California.

It was a sad day when Padre Fortuny announced that he was leaving, for he had become as a real father to the many neophytes and their children. He had cared for them and taught them through the years. He had built them a fine mission and had kept peace and happiness throughout the widespread lands of his domain. Mission San Francisco Solano was a monument to his ability as a builder and its prosperity to his excellent management.

Padre Buenaventura Fortuny baptized for the last time on March 15, 1833, and turned the mission over to Fr. José de Jesús María Gutiérrez, who had newly arrived from Mexico and had officiated at a baptism on the 1st of March. Padre Fortuny left the mission at Sonoma and traveled south to his new post at Mission San Diego de Alcala. On the way, he baptized persons at Mission San Buenaventura on the 18th of April.[2]

Fr. Gutiérrez was born in Mexico and was a Franciscan from the College of Nuestra Señora de Guadalupe de Zacatecas. He was new to the *frontera*, having arrived in Monterey January 15, 1833, and had a difficult time handling the neophytes and the gentiles of the surrounding tribes.

Yet the mission prospered under his control with good harvests and ample increases in the herds of cattle and horses and flocks of sheep. In the fall of 1833, a pestilence of an unknown

The only existing letter from Mission San Francisco Solano - a request for relief from Fr. Fortuny to Fr. José Sanchéz, 1831. Courtesy Santa Barbara Mission Archives.

40

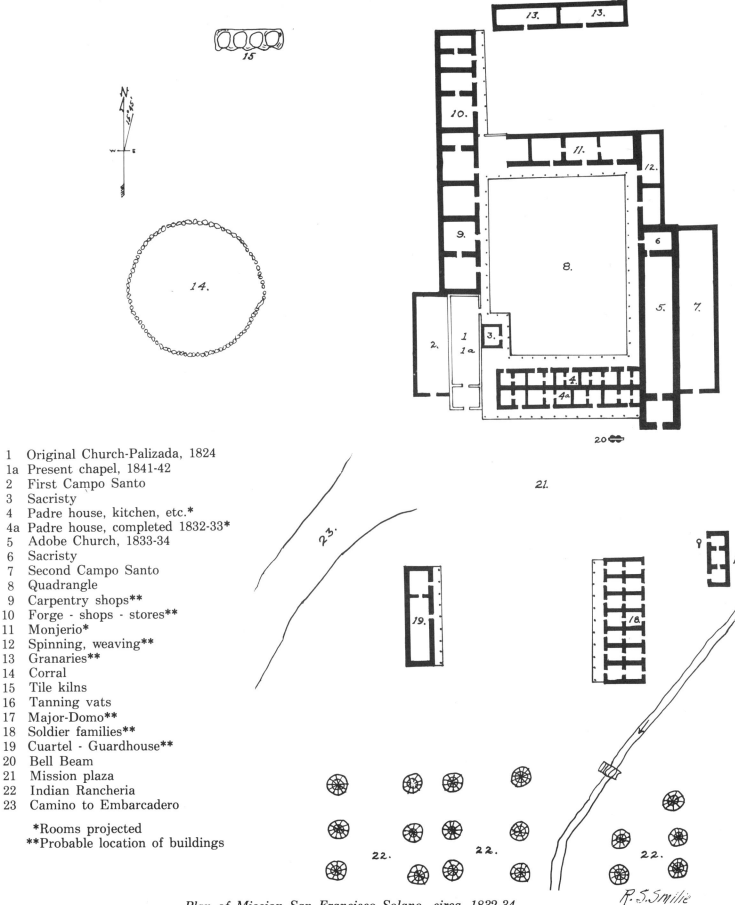

1 Original Church-Palizada, 1824
1a Present chapel, 1841-42
2 First Campo Santo
3 Sacristy
4 Padre house, kitchen, etc.*
4a Padre house, completed 1832-33*
5 Adobe Church, 1833-34
6 Sacristy
7 Second Campo Santo
8 Quadrangle
9 Carpentry shops**
10 Forge - shops - stores**
11 Monjerio*
12 Spinning, weaving**
13 Granaries**
14 Corral
15 Tile kilns
16 Tanning vats
17 Major-Domo**
18 Soldier families**
19 Cuartel - Guardhouse**
20 Bell Beam
21 Mission plaza
22 Indian Rancheria
23 Camino to Embarcadero

   *Rooms projected
  **Probable location of buildings

Plan of Mission San Francisco Solano, circa 1832-34.

type among the neophytes caused the death of more than 60 before it ran its course by the end of November.[3]

Fr. Gutiérrez' methods came under criticism during his year at Mission San Francisco Solano. One was a letter sent to Governor Figueroa by Mariano Vallejo after his 1833 trip to Fort Ross.[4] Fr. Gutiérrez answered them, citing the situation here on the *frontera* and his troubles with the going and coming of the neophytes.

'I must say,' Fr. José Gutiérrez replies from San Francisco Solano to the governor's dispatch of May 13th, 1833, 'that in keeping with my character my way of proceeding with the neophytes is rather too indulgent. I now see that it has brought down upon this mission some disorders which formerly had not occurred. The Indians stay away from holy Mass. They do not come to be instructed in their Christian duties. They do not attend to their work though there is so much to be done. They run away to the mountains and stay there fifteen, nineteen, and more days without letting me know. If we do away with flogging, with what punishment does Your Honor wish these transgressions to be chastised ? Will it suffice to punish them with a mere reprimand? It is plain to me that they despise this, and so it is useless, for afterwards they ridicule the Father and return to their evil habits. These results, I am sure, were not reported to Your Honor by the one who elicited your official note to which I am now replying. It is true that I do order some flogging, but very seldom and with moderation, after I have overlooked many things in the one who deserves the punishment.

'It is not the same thing to contend with uncivilized as with civilized people. Law directs the latter; reason enlightens them; shame curbs them; and not unfrequently the point of honor stimulates them. It is not thus, however, with those who recognize no law, whom reason does not influence, whom neither the point of honor nor shame, nor anything else holds in check, except fear. This it is which flogging effects. To this the Indians have been accustomed from the founding of the missions. As they are deficient in understanding, they comprehend as good only that which in them is not chastised, and as evil that which is prohibited under pain of castigation.[48] Nevertheless, Your Honor on this account must not think that I desire to fill the position of flogger; that is perhaps the last in which I would take delight; but I want to make it evident to you that it does this mission in my charge no good to deprive it of said penalty, unless another is substituted. By all means, let it be moderated; and this, as far as I am aware, I have already done.

'The decree of August 17th, 1833, and the government order of August 12th, 1822, which Your Honor quotes, hold good and speak only in connection with civilized people in the towns of our Mexican Republic who possess abundant intelligence for correcting and improving themselves; but they do not concern these neophytes, who lacking the mental light in which the former abound are but just beginning to emerge from their political and religious infancy in which, as is evident, they still are.

'From all that has been said Your Honor will understand my method and my sentiments on the subject, and you will at the same time be convinced that my manner of proceeding is regulated by the compassion which animates me for these poor people upon whom I look as upon my little children, and likewise as upon Mexicans like myself.

'In conclusion, if Your Honor, after due consideration, should deem it advisable to abolish absolutely the whipping which has been applied as paternal correction, I am ready to obey Your Honor, but I should appreciate it the better if it came with the knowledge and command of the Rev. Comisario Prefecto.'[49]

What steps Figueroa took in return, is not on record.

[48]"*Como escasos de luces, solo aprehenden por bueno lo que no se les castiga; y por malo lo que se les prohibe mediate del dicho castigo.*" This was the experience of the missionaries from the beginning, and accord to this fact they had to choose their methods.
[49]Cal. Arch., Dep. St. Pap., Ben. ii, 142-144.[5]

IX

The Russian Menace
Colonization of Frontera Del Norte

As 1833 opened, events had begun to happen in the *Contra Costa del Norte* that indirectly concerned Mission San Francisco Solano. The government in Mexico City was becoming alarmed at the interest foreign countries were showing in the Pacific Coast, especially their choice Alta California and its fine harbors. Governor Figueroa received instructions to colonize Alta California up to the 42° parallel, the border of Oregon territory, and to pay particular attention to the northern areas.[1] The French visitors had been reporting favorably on the territory and its lack of military strength. The many English as well as Yankee ships sailing the Pacific and calling at California ports added to the anxiety of the Mexican authorities.

The Russians now had a foothold on the northern California coast and were enlarging their settlement north and south of their busy headquarters at *Rossiya* (Fort Ross) at Lat. 39°30' - established in 1812. They had a strongly fortified headquarters and, at Bodega Bay, a busy shipping center. However, they had not penetrated more than three leagues inland at that time.

In 1806 Count Nikolai Rezanov had made a "trading" voyage to California from the Russian base at Sitka in Alaska - on the *Juno*. Three years later Ivan Aleksandrovich Kuskov, on the *Kodiak*, entered Bodega Bay and called it Port *Rumiantsoff*. Here, he established temporary buildings and made friends with the neighboring Indian tribes. He remained until August before returning to Sitka. He advised the Czar of the trip and received his approval for a settlement.

In 1811 Kuskov again arrived on the

View of Fort Ross in 1828. Woodcut. Courtesy of Society of California Pioneers.

schooner *Chirkof*. He explored the coast and decided on a site 6 leagues north for the main settlement. It had a good anchorage, though not protected from southwest storms; but had good water, soil, wood and timber. Indians called it *Madshui-nui* - and the table land was ideal for the fort and settlement.[1]

By September, the original buildings were up and the 95 Russians and 80 Aleut Indian hunters celebrated their new home - Ross. Twelve cannon were mounted and were increased to 40 later on. The buildings, although of wood, were of heavy redwood hewn plank and timbers - with a heavy palisade wall enclosing the main area. They paid the Indians for the land in merchandise and made a treaty with them, using the leading tribe to govern and handle the other nearby tribes and protecting them against the inland enemy tribes.

There were two objectives in establishing the settlement. One was as a base for the extensive otter and seal fur hunting along coast waters, which the Aleut Indians in their skin *bidarkas* (canoes) cared for. The other was to raise food stuffs for their Alaskan headquarters, especially grains and cured meats. They had extensive grain fields and orchards at Ross and, inland from Port Bodego on the Arroyo Salmon, a large area produced grains; also, the ranchos along the coast added to the harvest. At Port Bodega was the marine base and warehouses and, here, the ships were protected in a secure harbor. A sled road along the coast ran from the port north to the headquarters at *Fuerte del Ruso* - as the Californians named it.

Sonoma was the farthest north Spanish settlement at 38° 17' 19" north latitude and 122° 18' 26" longitude to date. It was now a well established mission but not a military post, the Presidio at San Francisco being the only military post north of the capital at Monterey. Lieutenant Mariano Guadalupe Vallejo had assumed command there in September 1831. He was a young man of Spanish parents who had married Francisca Benicia Carrillo of the San Diego Carrillo family March 6th, in San Diego, the previous year and they were now living at the San Francisco Presidio officers' quarters.

On April 11, 1833, the governor announced his intention of founding a presidio north of San Francisco Bay. On the 19th of April, he ordered Lieutenant Vallejo to conduct an exploratory expedition to the Contra Costa del Norte, select a site for the future presidio and settlement and then offer land for the settlers to populate the area.[2]

Earlier in 1831, a large land grant was granted in the Valley of the Cainameros, halfway between the Russian settlement at Port Bodega and Mission San Francisco Solano. The area was called Santa Rosa, a name given by Padre Juan Amoros of Mission San Rafael Arcangel to an Indian maiden that he baptized alongside the stream the Indians called Chocoalomi (Santa Rosa Creek) on the day of the Feast of Santa Rosa of Lima. Governor Echeandía granted it to one Rafael Gómez as a buffer against the Russian expansion. However, Don Gómez did not proceed with settlement of the rancho and Gómez' claim was abandoned.

Lieutenant Vallejo was also to assemble the members of the Presidio Company who were working for private individuals. They were to be provisioned and sent to Mission San Rafael Arcangel and Mission San Francisco Solano where the padres would employ them until they were needed for regular military duty, thus increasing the military strength of the *Frontera del Norte*.[3]

The next week, Lieutenant Vallejo with a party of mounted troops left the Presidio of San Francisco and, by way of Mission San Rafael Arcangel, traveled up the Valley of the Petalumas and on to the valley above before turning west towards the coast and the Russian Port of Bodega. The season was a wet one and the valleys were flooding. However, from some high hills Vallejo was able to look over the country far to the north and to the hills on the east.

This was Vallejo's first trip to the *Frontera del Norte* area.[4] While in the upper Valley of the Cainameros (Santa Rosa area), he had a chance to meet their Chief Daniel and they signed a treaty of peace which was kept faithfully for many years.

Arriving at the coast, his party followed the Russian sled road north to the river crossing near the mouth of the *Rio Slavianka*; then on up the coast to the fortified headland of Ross or, as the Spanish called it, *Fuerte del Ruso*.

Lieutenant Vallejo carried letters from the governor to the commander of the fort, Pedro Kostromitinoff, who received him cordially. One excuse for the visit was to ask the Russians, especially their Governor Baron Wrangel (who was expected soon) to help obtain recognition of the new Mexican Government by the Russian monarchy. The visit lasted three days, after which Vallejo and his party left, returning down the coast to Port Bodega where he looked over the port activities. The return trip was direct to Mission San Rafael Arcangel and by launch to the Presidio San Francisco, arriving May 5th.

Lieutenant Vallejo made a detailed report, May 6th, of what he saw at the Russian colony and also of the desirability of the planting of a Mexican fort in the Valley of Santa Rosa, to the north, to contain any further expansion of the Russian colony to the interior.[4]

In August, Lieutenant Vallejo issued a circular to all corporals of the guard at the Presidio, Mission San Rafael Arcangel, and Mission San Francisco Solano. He ordered them to permit no one to travel to or from *Fuerte del Ruso* into the interior without valid passports issued by the Commandant General or, at least, by the authorities at San Francisco. To disregard his orders meant military punishment for the offenders.

Down at the Presidio of San Francisco, Vallejo, following his orders from the governor, began to assemble the families to settle the new country to the north. Ten families, totaling 50 persons, agreed to go and take up the free land. October 1833 found the party at the land of the Petalumas where they laid out their claims to small ranchos. On arrival, the settlement party found that the area had been claimed by Mission San Francisco Solano as one of their ranchos and that the mission men were busy erecting small houses for their herders and a large drove of horses was pastured on the land.

Most of the families returned to the Presidio of San Francisco, not wishing to confront the mission claims or the hostile tribes of Indians to the west and north. Three families stayed and planted grain to establish their ownership and Vallejo had six *fanegas* of wheat sown for his own account. The mission rancho unit remained in occupancy also, disputing any claims of the settlers.

The settlers who were left were then moved north eight leagues to an area called Santa Rosa where a large stream, Arroyo Tahuiyumi, came in from the eastern hills. A second settlement was started. Here again, the settlers found that they were on a rancho claimed by the Mission San Francisco Solano as there was a herd of swine with two swineherds in possession. However, they settled here for a short while, laying out their claims as before. This was a location selected for a military post to be established for the protection of the settlers as well as a buffer to the expansion of the Russian settlements at Fort Ross on the coast.

The padre later consented to the settlers remaining on this site though only on a temporary basis and Vallejo so advised the governor. However, as winter approached, the settlers became apprehensive of the isolated situation and the nearness of the hostile Indians. By the end of the year they abandoned their settlement and returned to the Presidio of San Francisco, leaving the land in the possession of the mission padres at Sonoma and the local Indian tribe.[6]

Downstream near the junction with the large

Rio Ruso, or Taniyomi, Don Juan B. R. Cooper, who had married Lieutenant Vallejo's sister Encarnacion, received a large 14 square league grant of land called Rancho Molino, where he planned to build a water powered sawmill.

At the closing of the year 1833, Fr. Gutiérrez at Mission San Francisco Solano reported on his *Informe* that the cattle had increased to 4,849, the sheep to 7,114, the horses and mares to 1,048, and mules 18. At the church, baptisms totaled 22 while there were 15 marriages. Burials in the *campo santo* were 118. The Indian population was down to 750 neophytes. The field crops were bountiful for the year:

	Planted	Harvested
Wheat		
Barley	86 *fanegas*	931 *fanegas*
Beans	46 *fanegas*	500 *fanegas*
Peas	2 *fanegas*	9 *fanegas*
Corn	2 *fanegas*	24 *fanegas*
Frioles	3 *fanegas*	90 *fanegas*
Garbanzos	7 *fanegas*	15 *fanegas*
	1 *almud*	20 *almuds*
	A total of 1569 *fanegas*	

He also reported: "*Fabricas* - We have prepared foundations in the same manner as round about the house and new church of 200 *varas* and made 20,000 adobes." This was probably for the new *monjeria* (young woman's dormitory, etc.) and "Note - The census of the people has been made out anew and since I do not have an account of the true state of affairs, I was forced to include people who already have died and as a consequence there will be expressed a considerable difference in the number of existing Indians."[7]

Informe - 1833, *Fr. Jose Gutierrez, Mission San Francisco Solano. Courtesy Bancroft Library.*

X

Father Quijas—Lieutenant Vallejo
Secularization

In February of the spring of 1834, after serving at Mission San Francisco Solano for a year, Fr. Gutiérrez was sent to Mission San Francisco de Asís, or Dolores, and Fr. José Lorenzo de la Conceptión Quijas from that mission came to Mission San Francisco Solano in his place.

Fr. Quijas was a large, fine looking man over six feet tall, of more than ordinary abilities and education - and a fine horseman. He was a native of South America, probably Ecuador; had been a muleteer and trader before becoming a friar. He was kindhearted and popular both with the noephytes and the other padres and *gente de razón* of the California colony - and a genial host to visiting travelers at the mission. However, he stood up for his rights and for those under his charge.[1]

The mission, as well as all the missions from Mission San Carlos Borromeo at Carmel north, was now governed by the College of Nuestra Señora de Guadalupe de Zacatecas. The new Commisary Prefect from this college was Fr. Francisco Garcia Diego - with residence at Mission Santa Clara.[2]

Fr. Quijas took charge of Mission San Francisco Solano and, once again, it was in capable and strong hands. He carried on the plans that Padre Fortuny had laid out and the settlement prospered under his guidance. There were now 20 buildings of adobe, large and small, at the mission, built and under construction. This included the new *monjerio* started by Fr. Guiterréz across the north side of the quadrangle. The adobes were on hand and soon it was ready for the use of the single women and girls of the mission.

This building was 34 *varas* long, 10 *varas* wide with adobe walls a *vara* thick. An ample corridor ran the full length of the patio side, and it, as well as the main building, was covered with red tile. Floor tile was ready for the floor of the rooms. The west end was extended 8 *varas* but never closed at the far end short of the northwest corner of the quadrangle and complete closure. A small storage building connected the east end with the sacristy of the adobe church.

There were, however, one or two clouds on the horizon that were far beyond local control. One was the Mexican government's orders for secularization of the missions and the other was to extend the Mexican domain over the *Frontera del Norte*, not with missions as in the past but with groups of new settlers and, eventually, new pueblos and military posts.

Secularization of the missions dates back to the Spanish days when the original rule was that after a mission had operated for 10 years among the gentiles and they were converted and trained, a town should be developed for them and the missionaries moved on into new fields. In 1813 the Spanish Cortes passed a law declaring for immediate secularization of all missions 10 years and older. In Alta California it had not been enforced, nor after the Mexican independence, though published there in 1821.

In 1826, Governor José María Echeandía ordered that married Indians of missions south of Monterey, on proving that they had been Christians for 15 years and could support themselves, could leave the missions, but few Indians took advantage of this order.

Again in 1830 Governor Echeandía, under pressure from Mexico, issued a provincial law approved by the national government that the missions were to be gradually secularized. This was the result of envy on the part of soldiers and other Spanish and Mexican settlers of the wealth and prosperity of the mission establishments; also there was the desire by many to obtain possession of the vast ranchos and land holdings of the missions for their own use. And the Indians were often restive and many desired freedom and their part of the mission wealth, an idea of freedom announced by the governor. Agents for each mission were to be appointed by the governor to take charge of the properties.[3]

When word of the impending action reached the missions, it caused a great deal of trouble among the padres, the soldiers, and the neophytes. Some missions turned many of their cattle into saleable hides and tallow as soon as possible. Future planning stopped and building delayed. Many neophytes left the missions so labor was scarce and crops suffered.

In January 1833, Governor José Figueroa, newly arrived from Mexico, after a trip over the mission chain, felt that the neophytes were not ready to assume responsibility and care for themselves as Christians and that secularization would have to come gradually. In this he agreed with Fr. Presidente Durán and Fr. Commissary Prefect Garcia.[4] He was opposed to the granting of mission lands to settlers, as they belonged to the Indians, and he wrote to the Mexican capital to that effect. But, on the 17th of August, 1833, the government declared unequivocally for secularization and in November connected secularization with colonization of the frontier and use of the Pious Fund to assist in the plan. In April 1834, the government passed a law that "secularization should go into effect within four months." This was the death blow to the entire mission chain in Alta California.

Governor Figueroa, while not in favor of immediate secularization or opening the mission lands for settlement by colonists and members of the ruling class in California, was forced to proceed with the work and take the blame for the ruination of the missions and their fine work.[5]

The first regulation for the mission Indians was issued by the governor on July 15, 1833. *"Prevenciones provinciales para la emancipación de Indios reducidos."*

Indians best fitted for release to own lands were to be given small parcels of land, seeds, implements, few cattle and horses, a year's food, and other items. They could form pueblos, if enough were at one place, but all were to continue under some control of the padres. If they failed, they were to be returned to the mission population. However, only a few families left the missions and less at Sonoma.

The fatal regulation on secularization was issued by the governor on August 9, 1834. *"Reglamento Provisional para la secularización de las Misiones de la Alta California, 9 de Agosto, 1834."*

1. The *gefe político*, according to the spirit of the law of Aug. 17, 1833, and to his instru. from the sup. govt, acting in accord with the prelates of the friars, will partially convert into pueblos the missions of this territory; beginning in Aug. (erroneously printed 'next August,' it having been discussed in July) with 10 missions and continuing with the other successively. (In the original proposition the last clause was 'so far as his duties may allow,' the definite date and the specification of missions being substituted after much debate.) 2. The friars will be relieved from the administration of temporalities, and will exercise only the functions of their ministry in spiritual matters until the formal division of parishes be made and curates provided by the govt and bishop. 3. The ter. govt will re-assume the admin. of temporalities, directively, on the following plan. 4. The approval of this regl. will be solicited from the sup. govt by the quickest route.

Distribution of property and lands. - 5. To each head of a family, and to all over 20 years old, will be given from the mission lands a lot not over 400 nor less than 100 *varas* square. In common, will be given them enough land to pasture their stock. *Egidos* shall be assigned for each pueblo, and at the proper time *propios* also. 6. Among the same individuals there shall be distributed pro rata, according to the judgment of the *gefe pol.*, one half of the live-stock, taking as a basis the latest inventories rendered by the missionaries. 7. There will also be distributed to them, proportionally, half or less of existing chattels, tools, and seed indispensable for the cultivation of the ground. 8. All the remaining lands and property of every kind will remain under the charge and responsibility of the majordomo or employee named by the *gefe pol.*, at the disposal of the sup. govt. 9. From the common mass of this property division shall be made for the subsistence of the padres, pay of majordomo and other servants, expenses of worship, schools, and other objects of public order and improvement. 10. The *gefe pol.*, intrusted with the direction of temporalities, will determine and regulate after proper investigation, the expenses which it may be necessary to incur, both for the execution of this plan and for the preservation and increase of the property. 11. The missionary will choose that one of the mission buildings which suits him best for his dwelling and that of his attendants; and he will be provided with the necessary furniture and utensils. 12. The library, sacred vessels, church furniture, etc., shall be in charge of the padre, under the responsibility of a sacristan chosen by him and paid a fair salary. 13. General inventories shall be made of all mission property duly classified, account books, documents of every class, debts, and credits - all to be reported to the sup. govt.

Political government of the pueblos. - 14. The political govt shall be organized in conformity with existing laws; and the *gefe pol.* will give the proper rules for the establishment of *ayuntamientos* and holding of elections. 15. The economical management of the pueblos shall belong to the *ayunt.*; but in the admin. of justice they will be subject to the judges of 1st instance constitutionally established in the nearest places. 16. The emancipated will be obliged to aid in the common work which in the judgment of the *gefe pol.* may be deemed necessary for the cultivation of the vineyards, gardens, and fields remaining for the present undistributed. 17. They will render to the padre the necessary personal service.

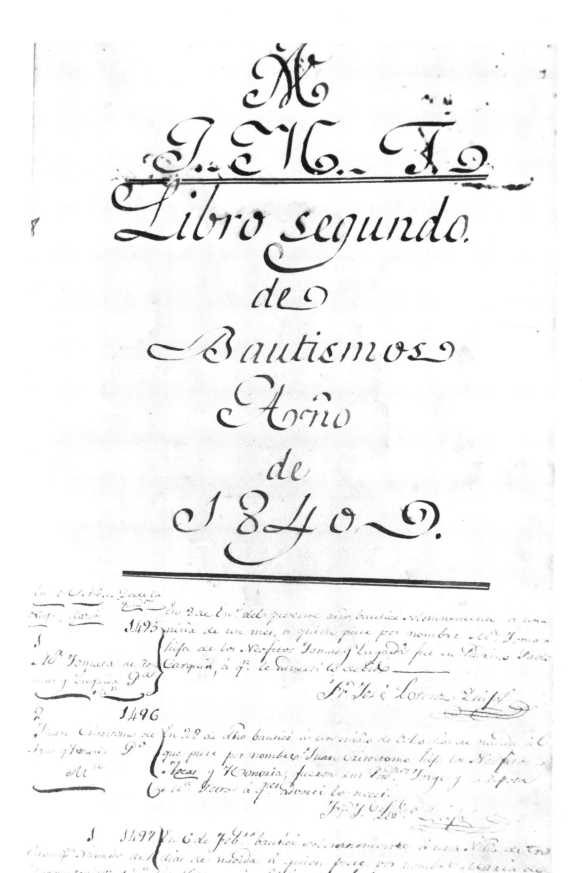

Baptismal Register, Book 2 - 1840. Courtesy St. Francis Solano Church Archives.

Restrictions. - 18. They may not sell, burden, nor convey the lands given them; nor may they sell their stock. Contracts made against these orders shall be void; the govt will reclaim the property and the buyers will lose their money. 19. Lands, the owners of which die without heirs, shall revert to the nation.

General rules. - 20. The *gefe pol.* will appoint the *comisionados* whom he may deem necessary for the execution of this plan. 21. The *gefe pol.* is authorized to settle whatever doubt or matter may arise in connection with the execution of this regulation. 22. Until this regul. is put in force the missionaries are prohibited from slaughtering cattle in considerable quantities, except the usual slaughter for the subsistence of neophytes, without waste. 23. The debts of the missions shall be paid in preference out of the common property, on such terms as the *gefe* may determine. And for exact compliance there shall be observed the following rules: 1. The *comisionados* as soon as appointed will go to their respective missions to carry into effect the plan, presenting their credentials to the friar, with whom they are to preserve harmony, politeness, and due respect. 2. At first the com. will receive all accounts and documents relating to property; then the general inventories will be formed in the order given, an estimate of two intelligent persons sufficing for the livestock. As entered in the inventory, all passes from the control of the friar to that of the com.; but no innovation is to be made in the system of work, etc., until experience proves it to be necessary. 3. The com. and majordomo are to see that all superfluous expenses cease. 4. Before making an inventory of field property the com. must explain to the Indians this regulation and the change it is to effect in their condition. Their lots are to be immediately distributed. The com., padre, and majordomo will select the place, given to each what he can cultivate within the fixed limits, and allow each to mark his land in the most convenient way. 5. The com. must pay no debts of the mission without an express order from the govt, to which a report must be made in order that the number of cattle to be distributed may be determined. 6. Implements will be distributed for individual or common use as the com. and padre may decide; but grain is to remain undistributed, and the neophytes will receive the usual rations. 7. What is known as the 'nunnery' is to be abolished at once. The girls and boys are to be given to their parents, to whom their parental duties are to be explained. 8. The com., after investigation, will propose as soon as possible one or more persons deemed fit for majordomos, with the salary that should be paid them. 9. *Rancherías* at a distance having 25 families may form a separate pueblo if they wish to do so, otherwise they will form a *barrio* or ward of the main pueblo. 10. The com. will report the population, in order to prepare for elections, which so far as possible are to conform to the law of June 12, 1830. 11. The com. will take all necessary executive steps demanded by the state of business, reporting to the govt and consulting it in serious or doubtful cases. 12. In all else the com., padre, majordomo, and Indians will act as prescribed in the *reglamento*. - Monterey, Aug. 9, 1834. José Figueroa; Agustin V. Zamorano, secretary.

This regulation of 23 rules and 12 subrules, as noted, contained instructions for turning the Mission establishments into pueblos, distributing land and supplies to the neophytes, the administration of the pueblos, the restrictions on Indians selling land or stock, and making inventories, reports, in detail. *Administradors* or *gefe politico* were to be appointed for each Mission and were the responsible agents of the government.[6]

The next cloud over Mission San Francisco Solano was the determination to settle the *Frontera del Norte* as quickly as possible. There was a Hijar colony of 250 settlers coming from Mexico and it appeared the ideal place to establish them on this land on their arrival. Sonoma was selected as a headquarters for this group which was expected late in the year 1834.

On May 1st of 1834, Governor Figueroa mentioned to the territorial legislature, then in session, his plan to establish a new fort at Santa Rosa in the *Frontera del Norte*, as he had advocated on April 11, 1833. He also sentenced a criminal to serve time at the "fort being established at Santa Rosa," on May 14th.

And, to further the settlement of the frontier, the governor granted the huge Rancho Petaluma to Lieutenant Mariano Vallejo in June of the same year and the legislature passed it without opposition. The grant extended from *Arroyo* Petaluma east to *Arroyo* Sonoma and from Bay of San Pablo north three leagues - 10 square leagues in all.[7] Mariano Vallejo, now a lieutenant, was supposed to use it to grant land to new settlers he was to attract to the valley. It also cancelled any claim that the mission at Sonoma had to that area of the Valley of the Petalumas and the western half of their own Sonoma Valley to within one league of the mission.

In August of the same year, 1834, Governor Figueroa made a tour of the Valley of the Petalumas and north to the Santa Rosa area. He decided this latter area was the desirable place to locate the Hijar colonists who were on their way from Mexico. The trip was continued on to *Fuerte del Ruso* where the Governor was courteously received by the Russians who discussed the possibilities of trade and commerce with the Mexican settlements. On his return, he left a small military force at the Santa Rosa site. He then returned to San Francisco and continued south, arriving at his capital in Monterey the 12th of September.

The governor, in September, ordered Lieutenant Vallejo to establish a settlement in the Santa Rosa area approximately at the old site of the former 1833 colony where a few huts were still standing. It was called Potquiyomi by the Indians. The new name was Santa Anna y

Farías, after the President and Vice President of Mexico. It was to be laid out as a pueblo, with plaza, house lots, public lands, and crop lands for the settlers. It was to be surveyed by Zamorano from Monterey.[8]

Lieutenant Vallejo took some Indians from Sonoma to help build housing and prepare the area for the settlers. Also, he had a modest house built for his own use. The Cooper sawmill, west of the new settlement, was built this year and used the ample redwood or Palo Colorado timber supply on the Molino Rancho.

In later October of 1834, Governor Figueroa appointed Mariano Vallejo *Comisionado* (Administrator) of Mission San Francisco Solano. On receiving this appointment, Lieutenant Vallejo moved several families, his 20-year-old brother Salvador, and Don Guadalupe Antonio Ortega to Sonoma and took over the mission property. There were 760 neophytes at the mission at this time.[9] Lieutenant Vallejo appointed Don Ortega major-domo of the mission, in full charge of its secularization, and Salvador Vallejo to be his assistant. Fr. Quijas was in possession and he was instructed to turn over all the physical property to them for distribution to the neophytes as per the rules laid down by the governor's *Reglamento*.

Lieutenant Vallejo traveled to the mission and a detailed inventory was taken of the mission buildings and all supplies and equipment in the various units under the control of Fr. Quijas. These included the following (an incomplete copy extant):

Church vessels and equipment - 3 pages
Padres' house of 27 rooms
Musica (music room)
Toolroom
Carpenter shop
Forge shop
Storeroom warehouse
Tannery
Granaries
Weaving room
Sewing room
Library
Soap factory
Orchard - 3250 trees
Vineyard
Indian *rancheria* - 27 huts, *palizada*
Cattle, 6000
Sheep, 6000
Horses and mares, 2000[10]

In addition to the above, but not listed in the incomplete inventory, was the long adobe *monjerio*, the original palisade church, some smaller buildings such as the guardhouse and soldiers' family houses; the ranchos of the mission and their buildings - over 20 items in all.

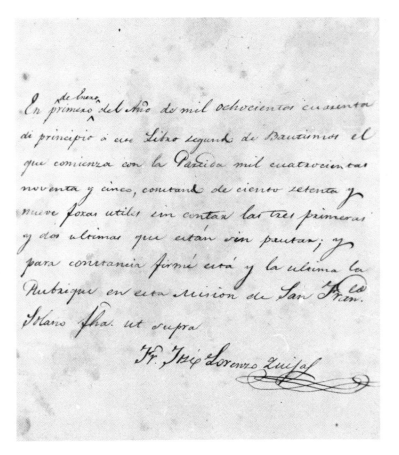

Frontispiece Bautismos - Tome II. Courtesy St. Francis Solano Church Archives.

Sonoma would become a pueblo and the mission would cease as a mission and become a parish church for the pueblo. Fr. Quijas was still to be in charge of the church with certain quarters and supplies furnished from church funds derived from part of the mission cattle and properties retained for government support. The neophytes were released from the padres' control and the young unmarried women were to be returned to their families.

This was happening up and down Alta California as the decrees of the central government in Mexico were being enforced. Some missions were being secularized by honest, efficient administrators; some by inefficient and poor managers; and others by outright plunderers who took everything they could lay their hands on for their own use and possession and allowed their friends and relatives to help themselves as well. The vast and fertile ranchos developed by the mission padres over the years were the rich plums and were soon granted and in the hands of the favorite sons and relatives. In a few locations, the desirable land was divided among the neophytes and granted to them, but they were the exception.

Frontispiece - Marriage Register, Book 2, 1840. Lettering at bottom: For El Padre Fr. Jose Lorenzo Quijas Reverend Missionero del Colegio Apostolico del Padre Francisco de Nuestra Senora de Guadalupe de Zacatecas. Made by De La Rosa. Courtesy St. Francis Solano Church Archives.

First page of Matrimonial Register, Book 2. Courtesy St. Francis Solano Church Archives.

PART III

THE MISSION DOMAIN

A MEXICAN MILITARY POST
AND RANCHOS

XI

Santa Anna y Farías Colony— Failure
El Pueblo y Presidio de Sonoma

Lieutenant Mariano Vallejo was busy with preparation for the settlement of the Híjar colonists who had arrived in San Diego and Monterey. Some houses were erected and lands laid out and the usual plaza was the center of the new Santa Anna y Farías pueblo in the valley called Santa Rosa.

In Mexico, the leaders of this band of settlers had inveigled the government into passing a decree granting them all the Alta California mission properties for a grand colonization scheme. José María Padrés, a warm friend of Mexican Vice President Farías, was to be governor in place of Figueroa, who was ill. The Pious Fund was to be used for expenses of the colonization. On arrival, their leaders José María Padrés and José María Híjar presented these demands. But the supreme power in Mexico City had changed in the meantime and the Alta California authorities and the Governor, who had recovered from his illness, had received orders by fast overland messenger from President Santa Anna not to recognize them.

The Híjar colonists arrived bag and baggage, 250 strong, on two vessels - the *Natalia* and *Morelos*. The first vessel arrived at San Diego September 1, 1834, with half the colony, and the second at Monterey on the 25th with the balance. Their destination was the new settlement above Sonoma and a majority of the members made it overland to Sonoma by late fall. Many stopped and settled at the pueblos or missions along the route north.[1]

At Sonoma, the mission buildings were used for housing the colonists and supplies from the storerooms and granaries used to feed them. Some went up to the new settlement, Santa Anna y Farías; but, as the winter progressed, they soon returned and the entire colony refused to occupy the site. It was too isolated and the hostile Indians too close.

Back at Mission San Francisco Solano things were not running very smoothly. Major-domo Ortega had taken over and had become very autocratic in his handling of the mission affairs and in his dealings with Fr. Quijas. The padre had complained that both Ortega and young Salvador Vallejo had been ordering the neophytes around and told them not to obey the padre's orders; that they also disregarded the requirements of the church attendance of the neophytes and forced them to work during their Mass periods, etc. His privacy was being abused and the living quarters being restricted. His complaints to Lieutenant Vallejo received no attention; conditions were not improved, but continued to worsen.

Neophytes were being given their allotment of animals, tools and food, and also plots of land suitable for their use. However, many were unable to handle their own affairs and left, after disposing of their possessions, for the life of the wild gentile tribes. The 760 neophytes at the mission, before secularization, were drifting away. Others returned later and requested Lieutenant Vallejo to care for their cattle on a share basis and soon the Mariano Vallejo herds took the place of the mission herds on the ranchos and pastures formerly operated by the padres.

The buildings of the mission were being used by the major-domo and the new arrivals, and also by the settlers of the Híjar colony. These latter arrivals increased in number as winter arrived, with the members who had started Santa Anna y Farías moving back to Sonoma.

So the Governor sent word for Lieutenant Vallejo to abandon the Santa Anna y Farías settlement and allow the colonists to select their own residences in California. Lieutenant Vallejo moved his soldier escort back to the Presidio at San Francisco and other workers were returned to Mission San Francisco Solano.

Governor Figueroa had issued on October 30, 1834, a resolution passed by the *diputación* that, while a former mission community or Indian town still was using the old designation, namely, Mission San Jose, it was not lawfully a church Indian mission but, after secularization, was a town of the Republic. It was subject to the laws as other towns and was under the civil authorities of the head town of their district. Sonoma was to be a Pueblo First Class.[2]

On November 3rd of 1834, Mission San Francisco Solano was designated as a First Class Parish. The curate's salary was $1,500 a year and the church was allowed $500 a year for its expenses. These payments were to be made from the funds of the church and its common property. And Mission San Francisco Solano ceased to exist as a mission - it was now a parish church.[3]

These regulations were issued after consultations with President Durán of the Missions, as follows:

Reglamento de Misiones secularizadas, aprobado por la Diputación en 3 de Nov. 1834. Art. 1. Conformably to the law of Aug. 17, 1833, salaries of $1,500 are assigned to curates of first-class parishes, and $1,000 to those of the second class. 2. Parishes of the first class shall be, S. Diego and S. Dieguito; S. Luis Rey, Las Flores, and annexed settlements; S. Gabriel and Los Angeles; Santa Barbara Mission and presidio; S. Carlos and Monterey; Sta. Clara and Jose de S. Guadalupe; and S. Jose, S. Francisco Solano, S. Rafael, and the colony (7 in all, incorrectly grouped in Halleck's and other translations). Parishes of the second class, S. Juan Capistrano, S. Fernando, S. Buenaventura, Sta Ines and Purisima, S. Luis Obispo, S. Miguel, S. Antonio and Soledad, S. Juan Bautista and Sta Cruz, S. Francisco Mission and presidio. In parishes of more than one place, the curate will reside at the first named. 3. The *comisario prefecto* Garcia Diego will reside at this capital. The *gefe pol.* will ask from the bishop in his behalf the faculties of *vicario foranco.* His salary shall be $3,000. 4. In all other respects the vicar and curates are to conform to the law of Aug. 17th. 5. Until the govt shall provide regular curates, the prelates will do so (from the friars) provisionally, by consent of the *gefe pol.* 6. $500 per annum shall be paid in each parish for church expenses and servants. 7. All these salaries and expenses of worship shall be paid from the common property of the extinguished missions, in money if there be any, or in produce at current rates - the *gefe pol.* to give the necessary orders. 8. Art. 17 of the regl., requiring the Ind. to render personal service to the friars, is abrogated. 9. The *gefe* will cause to be assigned buildings for the residence of curates, *ayuntamientos*, schools, etc. according to art. 7 of the law. 10. Other points of Durán's recommendations may be attended to by the *gefe pol.* under art. 17 of the regl. 11. All to be communicated to the prelates and by them to their subordinates.[4]

The end of the year 1834 found that the neophytes had begun to leave the mission control as they now numbered 650, a hundred less than when secularization started in the summer. Other activities and harvests were in the same trend due to the change in the management.

With the failure and closing of the Santa Anna y Farías settlement, Governor Figueroa decided that the Valley of the Sonomans was a good location and instructed Lieutenant Vallejo to establish the presidio and pueblo in that valley - June 24, 1835.

POLITICAL GOVERNMENT OF UPPER CALIFORNIA
Monterey, June 24, 1835.

Don M. G. Vallejo, Military Commandante:
In conformity with orders and instructions issued by the Supreme Confederation respecting the location of a village in the Valley of Sonoma, this commandancy urges upon you that, according to topographical plan of this place, it be divided into quarters or squares, seeing that the streets and plaza be regulated so as to make a beginning. The inhabitants are to be governed entirely by said plan. This government and commandancy approves entirely of the lines designed by you for outlets - recognizing as the property of the village and public lands and privileges, the boundaries of Petaluma, Agua Caliente, Rancho de Huichica, Lena de Sur, Salvador, Vallejo and La Vernica, on the north of the city of Sonoma, as the limits of its property, right and privileges - requesting that it shall be commenced immediately around the hill, where the fortification is to be erected, to protect the inhabitants from incursions of the savages and all others. In order that the building lots granted by you, as the person charged with colonization, may be fairly portioned, you will divide each square (*manzana*) into four parts, as well for the location of each as to interest persons in the planting of kitchen gardens, so that everyone shall have a hundred yards, more or less, which the government deems sufficient; and further, lots of land may be granted of from one hundred and fifty to two hundred yards, in opening for outlets, for other descriptions of tillage, subject to the laws and regulations on the subject, in such manner that at all times the municipality shall possess the legal title.

This government and commandancy-general offers you thanks for your efforts in erecting this new city, which will secure the frontier of the republic, and is confident that you will make new efforts for the national entirety.
"God and Liberty."
José Figueroa.[6]

Governor Jose Figueroa's second letter of June 24, 1835 to Don M. G. Vallejo advised that the reason for the new establishments in the Valley of Sonoma, especially a center for Mexican settlement of the Northern Frontier, was to arrest the advance of the Russians from their present Port Bodega and Ross bases. It gave Vallejo authority to grant lands, which would be confirmed, to settlers - a majority to be Mexican. The letter was very confidential and praised Lieutenant Vallejo most highly.[5]

Mission San Rafael, circa 1830. It was founded December 14, 1817, as a sub-mission across the bay from Mission San Francisco, to be used as a sanitarium for convalescent neophytes. From a wash drawing by H. Chapman Ford.

Sonoma was an attractive site for the new military headquarters in the Contra Costa del Norte. The mission padres had developed a prosperous settlement with many buildings and improvements; the lands in all directions were fertile and had been set up as rancho units. It was near the Bay of San Francisco by water and other transportation. It was also within military operating distance of the Russian settlements at Port Bodega and *Fuerte del Ruso* on the Pacific Ocean.

The mission was now being secularized and turned over to the control of the government so the troops could use the mission buildings until permanent barracks could be built. Lieutenant Vallejo began preparations at Presidio of San Francisco for moving all the troops and headquarters to Mission San Francisco Solano.

The new year of 1835 found a busy settlement at Sonoma. The secularization was in full swing with the neophytes receiving their allotments of cattle, seed and food and, those that desired them, small ranchos to care for their possessions. However, a large part of the mission's cattle herds and lands still remained under the control of the major-domo, Antonio Ortega, and his assistant, Salvador Vallejo.

The village was full of the Híjar colonists who had wintered there and few did any work to help the crowded situation. The stock of food had been heavily drawn on and trouble over short rations loomed ahead - unless a solution was found.

Plans for the transfer of the military headquarters were being made and building sites laid out for the new presidio. Lieutenant Vallejo made trips up from San Francisco to keep both ends running. On January 5th he petitioned the Governor for a 150 *vara* lot, next to the mission buildings, where he wanted to build a home and barracks.

Relations between Fr. Quijas and Majordomo Ortega and Salvador Vallejo were becoming very strained as Ortega, who appeared to take his authority too seriously, gave Fr. Quijas little consideration and no authority.[7] Appeals to Lieutenant Vallejo did not correct the situation as he was busy elsewhere.

Fr. Quijas was a refined, educated gentleman and a good administrator and resented being treated this way by one who was far his inferior. Further complaints from the padre to his superiors were forwarded to the Governor. Soon a letter was received by Lieutenant Vallejo from the Governor advising that he must furnish the padre free use of furniture and utensils, in addition to his allowance. He may also furnish horses and boats for the padre's use.[8]

The unrest among the idle Híjar colonists was being stirred up by one of their leaders, Padrés, who had seen his dream of an empire collapse. The Governor had received word of a similar unrest in the south among a portion of the colonists who had remained there. He warned Lieutenant Vallejo to watch them closely. In March of 1835 the colonists were very discouraged and became restless. It finally came to a crisis when they realized they were not to receive the mission properties, as promised. Their leaders issued their large stock of arms at Sonoma and an uprising threatened. However, Lieutenant Vallejo discovered their plans and arrested the leaders and disarmed the settlers. The leaders, Híjar and Padrés, were banished from California and sent back to Mexico.[9]

After their leaders were banished, most of the colonists left Sonoma for other parts of the coast. A few stayed in the Contra Costa - one, Victor Prudon, a Frenchman who was well educated and a good speaker. He later became a secretary to Lieutenant Vallejo and lived in Sonoma many years.

One of Vallejo's first acts was to grant the pueblo, on June 24, 1835, four square leagues of land, the usual amount given all pueblos in California when they were founded. July 5th, the Governor granted Lieutenant Vallejo the pueblo 150 *vara* lot for which he had petitioned. The mission quadrangle and his 150 *vara* lot were about the center of the pueblo area.[10]

Early in July Lieutenant Vallejo had 30 soldiers and their families ready to move to Sonoma. Two schooners, owned by William A. Richardson of Yerba Buena, were rented and loaded with the people, baggage and household effects. Sailing across the Bay, they were subject to a shower of Indian arrows at Punta Novato (Corte Madera) and finally landed at the embarcadero of Mission San Rafael.

Here, Fr. Quijas was the padre in charge as well as at Sonoma. A Licatiut tribe of Indians who lived in the San Rafael area were peaceful and Lieutenant Vallejo made a treaty with them, all agreeing to live in peace and respect each other's rights.

Embarking, the large party sailed to the east and entered a wide estuary that led to the north. They followed it for a distance and found that they were in the Plain of the Petalumas. A large party of Indians from this valley met them and Lieutenant Vallejo also made treaties with them in the name of Commander of the *Frontera del Norte*. Shipping out again, the two schooners sailed east and, after various tries as they were not familiar with the many sloughs and swamps, finally anchored at Punta Tulai (Midshipman's Slough). Exploring further, they found there was no suitable route overland to Sonoma as it was all tule swamp.

The next day, they sailed up *Arroyo* Sonoma to a landing at the *ranchería* of Captain Pulpula, near where the party pitched their tents and made camp on the higher ground. Their location was a short distance downstream from the mission embarcadero. Word of their coming

had reached the mission and Chief Solano of the Suisuns was on hand with hundreds of Indians from his Suisun tribe as well as many from the mission and nearby *rancherías*. Lieutenant Vallejo sent word to other tribes to send envoys to make treaties with him as the representative of the Mexican Government. It was a week of feasting, dancing, and Indian games; and of presents given the Indian Chiefs and their offerings in return. Treaties were signed by many of the chiefs, one having arrived from the Petaluma Valley with many of his Licatiuts. The party moved up to the Sonoma Mission on the many horses that had been sent down with the latter band of Licatiuts. They camped beyond at some fine springs against the hills, the source of the Arroyo Chiucuyom. However, Lieutenant Vallejo always kept his men on guard no matter how friendly the Indians appeared.[11]

Now it was time to lay out the proposed pueblo and, with A. Richardson who had come up from Yerba Buena, Lieutenant Vallejo began to survey the area. With the mission as a starting point, they extended the *calle* (street) in front of the padres' house and the church to the west along the front line of the 150 *vara* lot granted Lieutenant Vallejo during July. From the corner of the old wood church another *calle* was extended south past the *cuartel*, or guardhouse, and houses of the retired soldiers. Between these two streets, the pueblo plaza was laid out, about 200 *varas* square. On the south and west sides of the plaza, *calles* running east-west and north-south were laid out, completing the square. All the *calles* were to be extended beyond the plaza as they were needed. Each *calle* was 20 *varas* wide, except around the plaza where 28 *varas* was the width to allow for animals at hitching posts. On the south side of the plaza at the central point, a wide *calle* 40 *varas* wide led due south towards the embarcadero.

As additional streets were added, they were to be 217 *varas* apart parallel to the original plaza streets extended. These blocks were 47,000 square *varas* and each were to be divided into four lots. These *calles* were known as *Calle* Vallejo, alongside and west and east from the north side of the plaza. *Calle Huerta* (orchard) was on the west side of the plaza, while *Calle Cuartel* (guardhouse) was on the east side. *Calle* Napa on the south side led off east towards the old route to Rancho Napa. The wide *calle* leading south from the center of the plaza was called *El Calle*.

A barracks for the soldiers was necessary and erection of a large two-story adobe building was rushed. It was 45 *varas* long and 17½ *varas* wide with a balcony along the front which faced on *Calle* Vallejo, just 28 *varas* west of the old mission wooden church. Tiles for the roof came from the mission tile kilns and some of the lesser buildings of the quadrangle which were being dismantled.

Also, a large residence for Lieutenant Vallejo was started 21 *varas* west of the barracks and fronting on the same *calle*. It was two stories high with balconies on the front and rear. This "Casa Grande" was 40 *varas* long and 18 *varas* wide. It was also built by the Indians of adobe bricks and roofed with tile. Both the barracks and residence were on his pueblo lot.

While laying out the pueblo, Lieutenant Vallejo stated: "I left the small edifice that had been constructed for the church to the east of the plaza." Presumably the first wooden chapel.[12]

While the residence was being built, Lieutenant Vallejo brought his wife, Doña Francisca Benicia to Sonoma in July. They used rooms in the mission padres' house for temporary quarters and it was there, on August 4th, that their first daughter, Epifania Gertrudis, was born.

West of the new house being built for Lieutenant Mariano Vallejo, near the end of the 220 *vara* block and facing the plaza, Salvador Vallejo built a small adobe house for himself - 21 *varas* long by 15 *varas* deep. On the southeast corner opposite the old wooden church, a small adobe building was built for the soldiers to use as a recreation room. It faced the plaza and was called *Casa del Billar* or billiard parlor. It was 17 *varas* long by 11 *varas*, but room was allowed for future extensions to the south.

With the establishment of the Pueblo of Sonoma and changing the mission to a parish church, Fr. Quijas recommended a new cemetery separate from the mission area. He requested the new burial ground from Lieutenant Vallejo who was laying out and alloting the pueblo lots to the new settlers.

In 1835 a plot approximately 75 *varas* square on *El Camino para* Napa, 1,060 *varas* east of the plaza, was granted the church. It was enclosed with a fence and consecrated, and burials of the deceased of the pueblo began at this new *campo santo*. This conforms to a provision of the decree - Mexican Congress, November 20, 1835.[13]

XII

Father Quijas Moves Residence to Mission San Rafael Arcangel

In the meantime, relations between Fr. Quijas and Major-domo Ortega and Salvador Vallejo had become unbearable to the padre and he had declared that he could not remain in residence at Sonoma as long as Ortega was in charge. Nothing was being done to correct the situation so he moved his belongings, in the month of June, to Mission San Rafael Arcangel where he had also been priest-in-charge for the last year.

Padre Quijas advised his superior, Commissary Prefect García Diego, of his move and of his determination not to reside at Sonoma as long as Ortega was major-domo and in control. He sent Fr. García Diego the following letter on the situation there in support of his action:

Very Rev. Fr. Comisario Francisco García Diego.

San Rafael, August 2nd, 1835.

My very esteemed Prelate, Father and Superior:

I did not mean to open my lips for any complaint whatever concerning the things inflicted upon me, but as day after day grievances are multiplying and even developing into public anti-religious and indecent acts, I cannot but lay before Your Paternity some incidents which, if I should allow them to pass in silence, would burden my conscience, and I should not comply with the duties of my ministry.

Almost from the very day when the administration of the spiritual and temporal affairs of Mission San Francisco Solano was divided, there has been mute but continuous dissension, which, I believe, has proceeded from the *comisionados* Guadalupe Vallejo, Antonio Ortega, and Salvador Vallejo; from the first-named not in so blunt a manner, from the second with the greatest coarseness, incivility, and irreligion; from the third with boldness, insolence, and impudence.

In order to inform Your Paternity the better, it will be necessary to begin at the time when I surrendered my charge. I had not yet made the transfer of the land or of its belongings, when they began to give orders to the mayor-domo, laborers, etc., so that when on one occasion I told the mayordomo (predecessor of Antonio Ortega) to take out two yoke of oxen, he replied that the *comisionado* (Mariano Vallejo) had given orders not to obey me any more in anything I commanded in the future. To avoid trouble I had to bear this and leave the matter as it was. The same happened concerning the property in the field, for he disposed of it as though he had already obtained control before I had made the transfer.

The small launch, which I used with the consent of Your Paternity and the permit of the governor, who told me that I could keep it till he should determine otherwise, has in a manner been taken away from me. At all events, I have not been considered worthy of being notified in the least regarding the many and continuous trips it is making. On the contrary, I am compelled to go around begging to let me have it when sometimes I need it. Then they loan it to me with bad grace.

When the governor charged me to select some black colts, I informed him that I should like to take on account of any stipend about twelve horses or colts. He agreed to it; but as I deferred till after the transfer in order to avert slanderous talk, they have flatly refused to let me have them, notwithstanding that I asked for them as part payment of my allowance.

The Honorable General has given orders that the apartments should be divided, that three horses should be assigned for my use, and that work on the church should continue. Nothing of this has been executed. I have asked that the herd belonging to my house be divided, that four cows be given me on account of my allowance, and to the same account one cow a week for slaughter in order to have enough meat and fat to pay the expenses of the week, and also to derive some gain from the hide. All these three requests have been refused; and if at some time the last was granted, Ortega told me it was as a favor from him. For being deprived of the yard and porch I am obliged to suffer not little. It really seems as though I am living in a stranger's house, as everything is closed up and I am forced to have even my little reception room turned into a passage way so that whoever wills may go in and go out, because the ordinary passage way is continually closed. For this reason some disagreements have risen much as the following.

I sent some one to ask Antonio Ortega for the key to the hallway in order to bring water and two sheep, and, since on the preceding day other reasons had turned up, I sent word to him as follows: 'that he

Yerba Buena [now San Francisco], circa 1837, showing Jacob P. Lees's house on hill [left center]. Lithograph from original drawing by John J. Vioget. Courtesy Society of California Pioneers.

should send me the key to the passage way; that if others allowed their apartments to serve as a passage for everybody I would not, because the hallway was for the common use of all who lived in the house, and more especially for those who like myself had something to say there; that he should obey or give orders to execute what pertained to him, because I was not in the mission to carry out the will and orders of every one.' For this message, Salvador Vallejo, (who, as I believe, has no other connection with the mission except that he is the brother of the *comisionado*), presumed to come to me with the greatest boldness and impudence. Reproaching me for sending such a message to Ortega, he raised his hand as if to strike me, uttered many shameless words, and pulled me by the sleeve of the habit as if he would defy me. If it had not been for the holy habit, and the sacred character of a priest which I though unworthily bear, I would not have gone very far for the reply. However, I suffered it all, but in a dignified manner I reproved him to his face in somewhat strong words for his audacity and effrontery, and for his meddling with things that did not concern him.

Yet all this is as nothing, and I have not even thought of complaining; but I am bound to do so by reason of the many and abominable deeds of Ortega who in an unbridled and barefaced manner has given free rein to the infamous vice of lust. He spares neither young girls nor married women or widows, neither heathen nor Christian, as is affirmed by the majority of the inhabitants of San Solano, soldiers as well as paisanos and neophytes, but especially by Sergeant Pablo Pacheco, Ignacio

Azevedo, Nicolás Higuera, a number of carpenters and shoemakers, and other neophytes, men as well as women, who have told me personally, and even to Fr. Pérez they have related it. (We do not dare translate what follows in the text, where Fr. Quijas gives names and facts. In a footnote the student will find the story. Only the names are suppressed for the sake of the descendants of this monster's innocent victims.) (See Note 1)

One day, whilst Fr. Pérez was celebrating holy Mass, and I was reciting the Divine Office, the said Ortega talked in front of the military quarters with Nicolás Higuera, Nicolás Juárez, Jacinto García, Olivas and others. He told them, and I heard it, 'that fornication was not forbidden: that formerly - it would be necessary.' (Fr. Quijas puts in here,) to write too much if I should relate all the obscenities that he makes use of in his speech whenever he gives orders or speaks to the neophytes. He not only utters them himself, but makes the neophytes repeat them, as Ignacio Azevedo relates, and I myself have heard. The following is a sample: He made a recent convert named Christophoro first say 'Gracias á Dios' and then he added something shameless; he also told him that a man should know everything. In short, he has taught these poor people such bad words that many of them do not mention him among themselves in any other way than as - 'That Fellow.'

(The narrative now takes another course.) One day, after I had celebrated holy Mass, while the people were saying their private prayers as was customary, before they finished their devotions Ortega ordered them to stop and to go to work. I pretended not to have noticed it at the time, but this only emboldened him. On the 15th of last month, on which day began the Novena of San Francisco Solano, the patron saint of the mission (I had told him in advance on the preceding day that on the morrow the Novena would begin, and that I intended to finish early in the morning, so that the people might be ready to perform their work through the day), he assumed such an inconsiderate manner and was guilty of such want of respect and reverence that, just as I had concluded holy Mass and was about to kneel down to say the prayers of the Novena, he commanded all the Indians to go out of the church, thus leaving me alone with the two servers, the sacristan, Pablo Pacheco, and one woman. He thus prevented solemnizing the Novena as far as possible, as has always been the custom not only at this mission but in the whole Christian world for the honor of the holy patrons.

When I took him to task for this, he replied that it did not concern him whether the Indians prayed or not; that it was his business to make them work; that for this the government had placed him there; that the Indians were free; that nothing of this was binding upon the Indians with the exception of holy Mass on Sundays; and that if they went to church on work days it was because he would have it; for even Guadalupe Vallejo had warned him that, since the feast of San Solano was at hand it was likely that the Father would want to cause delay with his Novena, as he had done at Dolores; but that in such a case he should drive the Indians out to their work as soon as Mass was finished. This in effect he did, notwithstanding that I concluded holy Mass and the Novena devotions before six o'clock in the morning!

From all this Your Paternity will understand the present situation in which the poor neophytes find themselves, of the religious, civil, and political training which they are receiving, and the harsh and merciless treatment which they suffer to such a degree that this has been the cause why the majority of the gentiles, who had come last year, has fled as well as many of the old Christians. I also believe that they will continue to run away if the treatment is not changed. These are facts upon which we cannot look with indifference, for, inasmuch as our chief aim is to increase the flock of Jesus Christ, this is not only frustrated, but even what has been gained is being destroyed. In fine, as I am not able to bear this any longer, I have resolved, with Your Paternity's consent, to withdraw to this Mission of San Rafael until Your Paternity succeeds in obtaining a remedy along the line of the following articles, subject to your approval.

Fr. Quijas under ten heads then offers certain propositions which in his opinion would effect a decided improvement. Several of them had already been presented in Fr. García Diego's "Suplica," and as no notice was taken by the government of any of them any way, it is unnecessary to reproduce them. The last one, however, demanded 'that Antonio Ortega, the mayordomo, should be removed in punishment for his many abominable and scandalous misdeeds in the mission to the dishonor of the holy Religion of Jesus Christ.' In case he is not re-

moved, Your Paternity may hold for certain that I will not go back there, not even by force; for, even though others can witness all this with cold indifference, I am not of that class. I shall rather flee to my College than return there before everything has been entirely set aright. May Your Paternity be pleased to excuse my long letter, overlook my mistakes, and command me, your least subject and son, who humbly kisses your hands.

Fr. José Lorenzo Quijas.[1]

Fr. Garcia, on receipt of Fr. Quijas' letter, sent it on to Governor Figueroa on August 12th with a demand for some action in the case of Major-domo Ortega. But the Governor was critically ill and died suddenly at Monterey on September 29th. Acting Governor José Castro had many more important problems then and there was no action by his office. So conditions continued as they were at Sonoma but without a resident priest.

Also, after visiting the missions as far north as Mission Santa Clara, Fr. Commissary Prefect García Diego returned to Mexico on November 17th of the year 1835.

Lieutenant Vallejo did not object to Fr. Quijas' move but on October 20th wrote the Governor's office that, since the Father had moved to Mission San Rafael and was in residence there, Mission San Francisco Solano should be relieved of paying him a salary and that Mission San Rafael should assume same.[2]

During the fall, Lieutenant Vallejo had an encounter with the Suscol tribe of Indians to the east in the lower Suisun Valley. After a short engagement with his soldiers and Indian allies near the Strait of Carquinez, they were subdued and peaceful again.

To reduce the expenses of secularization, which was well along at many missions, the Governor issued an order to all the missions combining the offices of *administrador* and major-domo. So, Lieutenant Vallejo resigned his *comisionado* on December 14, 1835. Don Antonio Ortega was appointed Acting Commissar at a salary of 500 *pesos* a year notwithstanding the serious complaints of Fr. Quijas. Cayetano Juárez was acting major-domo at 240 *pesos*, and Ignacio Acedo, assistant at 120 *pesos*.[3]

This gave Don Ortega full charge of the mission establishment and all the Indians, as well as the extensive ranchos well stocked with livestock. These were what remained after the neophytes had received their allotments, though few qualified for much land. Lieutenant Mariano Vallejo had been kept busy with political affairs in the north and at the capital at Monterey as well. The year of 1835, under the supervision of Antonio Ortega, ended with 550 neophytes still at the mission.

XIII

El Pueblo—Indian Tribes
Mission Ranchos Granted

The Cainamero Indians of the Santa Rosa Rancho area had been friendly for a long time and Lieutenant Vallejo used their Chief Daniel to help stop the horse stealing from the ranchos in the vicinity and from the Petaluma Rancho. Early in 1836, one of their chiefs, Santiago, recovered four, or half of a drove, that had been stolen and sold to Colton, a chief of the Guapos or Satiyomi tribe. A few days later, Santiago and his tribe were fishing and gathering seeds near Santa Rosa Rancho and were attacked by a large party of Guapos under Chief Colton. Twenty were killed and 50 wounded.

Wet spring weather delayed action but, on April 1st, Lieutenant Vallejo with Salvador Vallejo, 50 soldiers and a hundred Indians, aided by the Cainamero tribe warriors, attacked the Guapos and drove them into the rough country of the Geysers. They drove in from two sides and killed most of the Indians in a battle on the 4th with no serious loss to their troops. Lieutenant Vallejo returned with his troops to Sonoma on the 7th of April.

That day chiefs of seven tribes, Yoloytoy, Guilitoy, Ausactoy, Liguaytoy, Aclutoy, Churuptoy and Guapos voluntarily arrived at Sonoma and concluded a treaty of peace. The treaty provided:

That there should be friendship between the tribes and the Sonoma garrison;

That the Cainameros and Guapos should live at peace and respect each other's territory;

That the Indians should give up all fugitive Christians at the request of the Comandante;

That they should not burn the fields.

Lieutenant Vallejo did not promise anything but friendship, and the usual gifts were exchanged between Vallejo and all the chiefs. A copy of the treaty was sent to Governor Chico who signed it on the 27th of April.[1]

At the new Pueblo of Sonoma, building was the main activity in 1836. Commisar Ortega and Salvador Vallejo had a large crew of the ex-neophytes from the mission at work on the barracks and the new house for Lieutenant Vallejo, just beyond. Some buildings and walls of the mission supplied many of the adobe bricks, timbers, doors, window frames and roof tiles. Erection was speeded up so that by late 1836 the troops could use their new barracks. Lieutenant Vallejo could also move into his new house, called the *Casa Grande*. A servants' building 6¾ *varas* by 37 *varas* of adobe, with a second story and balcony, was also built in the rear.

Back and 22 *varas* north of the barracks, a second barracks building was started as additional room for the soldiers. An adobe wall connected these two buildings on their east sides.

Fronting on the plaza at the west end of the *Casa Grande*, foundations were laid for a tall three-story watchtower, 12 *varas* square, with balcony that would allow sentries to see for many leagues over the vast plain of the Valley of the Sonomans.

Sixty *varas* beyond the tower site Salvador Vallejo was building his house, also of adobe, two-story with a tile roof. It fronted 21 *varas* on the plaza and was 14½ *varas* deep.

Adobe walls with portholes connected the houses and also the barracks with *Casa Grande*. And, when the walls in the rear were finished, the buildings and walls formed an enclosed court or large patio. This was for security from thievery and loose cattle and for defense in case of an Indian uprising.

Opposite the padres' house at the mission, a small adobe house was built on the street for Antonio Ortega and also used for guests.

Fr. Quijas made occasional trips to San Francisco Solano from Mission San Rafael Arcangel and conducted services when necessary. He still refused to deal with the *administrador*, Ortega.

On one visit he baptized the new daughter in the Vallejo family, Epifania Gertrudis.

However, Don Ortega was in full charge of the mission and its properties and he and Salvador Vallejo handled the few hundred neophytes that they could keep at the pueblo. It was not a pleasant sight for the padre to see the hard work of 10 or more years of the mission Fathers being confiscated and ruined so quickly both materially and spiritually.

Secularization was also being accomplished at Mission San Rafael Arcangel where Fr. Quijas was residing; the *administrador* Ignacio Martinez was cooperative and they became fast friends. He took good care of the neophytes and their rights and was handling the secularization of the mission to their advantage as much as possible. John Read was the major-domo.

Near the end of October, Juan B. Alvarado visited the Pueblo of Sonoma while organizing the northern Californians against the unpopular Governor N. Gutiérrez. As Lieutenant Vallejo was leaving for the Napa country where the Napajos were honoring Chief Solano with a big feast, Alvarado joined him and, after attending the Napa festivities, continued on to San Jose with friends and an escort furnished by Lieutenant Vallejo.

The balance of the soldiers from the Presidio of San Francisco was now at the Sonoma barracks and all operations were directed from there.

Mariano Vallejo was advanced to the rank of Colonel by the California authorities and, on November 29, 1836, took his new office of Commandante General of California also. He was now called General Vallejo.[2]

With secularization accomplished, the vast domain of Mission San Francisco Solano was a rich plum for the many members, relatives and in-laws of the Vallejo family, as well as some of the members of the military units stationed at the pueblo. Land grants were in order and the former mission ranchos were soon granted *in toto* or divided into smaller though ample units.

The status of the Contra Costa del Norte Este changed from a vast mission-controlled domain to a large Mexican rancho area with its central pueblo and military post, Sonoma.

Some pueblo lots were being granted by General Vallejo and one, on the corner opposite the northwest corner of the plaza, was received by Salvador Vallejo. He began construction of a large one-story adobe house facing the plaza and extending 70 *varas* along *Calle Huerta*.

A nearby mission rancho, Agua Caliente (hot water), just beyond the pueblo to the north, had been granted by Governor Figueroa to Ignacio Pacheco, a sergeant of the San Francisco Company. However, his grant was unsuitable and was allowed to lapse in the years following as the sergeant received another grant, Rancho San Jose north of Mission San Rafael Arcangel, in its place.

Over in the Valley of the Napas, seven leagues by trail from Sonoma Pueblo, a rancho of two square leagues was granted in March to George Conception Yount, a converted trapper from North Carolina. He had been supplying Sonoma with hand-riven shingles for some time. Next to the Rio Napa, halfway up the valley, Yount built a log block house typical of the Eastern United States frontier. The house was for protection against Indian attacks, though he was successful in handling them, having lived with them during his trapping days. An adobe house was planned for the next year on his Rancho Caymus.

Another mission rancho in the Valley of the Napas was being cut up and given to local men. Nicolas Higuera, a soldier of the San Francisco Company was granted Rancho Entre Napa. It was three-fourths of a square league of fine land on the west side of the Rio Napa. Farther down where Arroyo Carneros met Rio Napa, Nicolas Higuera received another half league, Rancho Rincon de los Carneros.

As the year 1836 closed, the neophytes had all been released by the mission as there was no padre in residence there. They had returned to their *rancherías*; some on a few plots of allotted land with their allotted cattle, and others held as workers under Salvador Vallejo and Antonio Ortega at the pueblo. Many of the women were servants of the pueblo families.

The herds of cattle and sheep, some belonging to the ex-neophytes, others to the mission accounts, and the balance to General Vallejo and other residents, were multiplying on the ranchos that the mission had claimed but which were now considered government property -- except the large Rancho Petaluma of the General. Up in the Rio Ruso Valley, northwest of Santa Rosa, Don Juan Cooper's water-powered sawmill, finished in 1834, was operating on the bank of the stream producing lumber for the new pueblo to the south, brought down by *carrettas* and pack train.

The new year of 1837 found Fr. Quijas still in residence at Mission San Rafael Arcangel which was being secularized now by *Administrador* Timothy Murphy, a good friend of the padre. His trips to the Pueblo of Sonoma were growing fewer, only being made when necessary. Services were still conducted in the large adobe church which was still intact as was part of the padres' house next to it.

The balance of the buildings and walls of the quadrangle were melting away under demolition and neglect, especially as the tiles were

Sonoma, circa 1840. Earliest painting of north side of plaza, showing original Palizada Church and completed adobe church at far right. Reproduced from San Francisco Call.

removed and the soft adobe walls left to the mercy of the elements. The tiles, timbers, woodwork, and salvaged adobe bricks were being used for the buildings taking form around the plaza to develop the new pueblo and house the new arrivals. The neophytes who were skilled were kept busy building and making new bricks and tiles for the roofs and floors, and in the many duties that they performed formerly for the padres.

A small vineyard was planted along with some orchard trees on the rear of General Vallejo's residence area, enclosed with a protecting wall. The second or north barracks was finished. It was 15 *varas* by 45½ *varas* and filled the north side of the courtyard or quadrangle of the military unit, with adobe walls between the buildings.

The pueblo Lot No. 35, 109 *varas* square opposite the churches and the padres' house, was granted by General Vallejo during the year to Antonio Ortega, Antonio Pina, and Dons Alviso and Davilla. This lot included Ortega's house and the *Casa el Billar* on the corner. Other plaza lots were granted to newcomers who were settling in the area also.

At the northern end of the valley ex-Mission Rancho Guilucos, four square leagues, was granted to Juan Wilson, brother-in-law of the General. His wife was Ramona Carrillo.

Far to the west, a few leagues inland from the Russian settlement and harbour at Port Bodega and the Rancho Estero Americano, two square leagues, had been provisionally granted by General Vallejo to Edward M. MacIntosh and James Dawson -- two sailors who had been recommended by Don Juan Rogers Cooper of Rancho Molino, General Vallejo's brother-in-law.

On April 12th, Doña Rosalia Vallejo, sister of the General, was married to Jacob P. Leese, a merchant of Yerba Buena. He later spent much of his time in Sonoma.

Another new arrival at the pueblo was Doña Maria Ignacia López de Carrillo. Mother of Benicia, the General's wife, Doña Carrillo was accompanied by her numerous unmarried children and had moved up to Sonoma from their old home in San Diego. Late in the year of 1837, Doña Carrillo petitioned for a two-square-league rancho in the Santa Rosa area, naming it Cabeza de Santa Rosa. Permission to occupy it was given. Later, the General and brother Salvador had an adobe house built alongside a good stream of water.[3] Here the family settled, their nearest neighbors being at the Cooper's Rancho Molina 10 miles to the northwest. Cattle from Sonoma soon were pastured on the verdant land in the surrounding plain of Santa Rosa.

Over in the Valley of the Napas, to the east, Antonio Ortega had obtained permission to occupy five square leagues, more or less, of the ex-mission large Rancho Napa in the middle of the valley. Here he was building a ranch adobe and stocking the fields with cattle from Sonoma. To the east and south of Rancho Napa, another section of the mission rancho was granted to Cayetano Juarez, a sergeant of the Sonoma garrison. He called it Rancho Tulucay and it covered two square leagues.

Farther east in the Valley of the Suisuns, four square leagues around the old Indian *ranchería* of his younger days was granted to Chief Francisco Solano. It was also part of Rancho Santa Eulalia established in 1824 by Fr. Altimira.

In the early summer of 1837, Antonio Ortega was removed as *administrador* of Mission San Francisco Solano because of his newer scandals

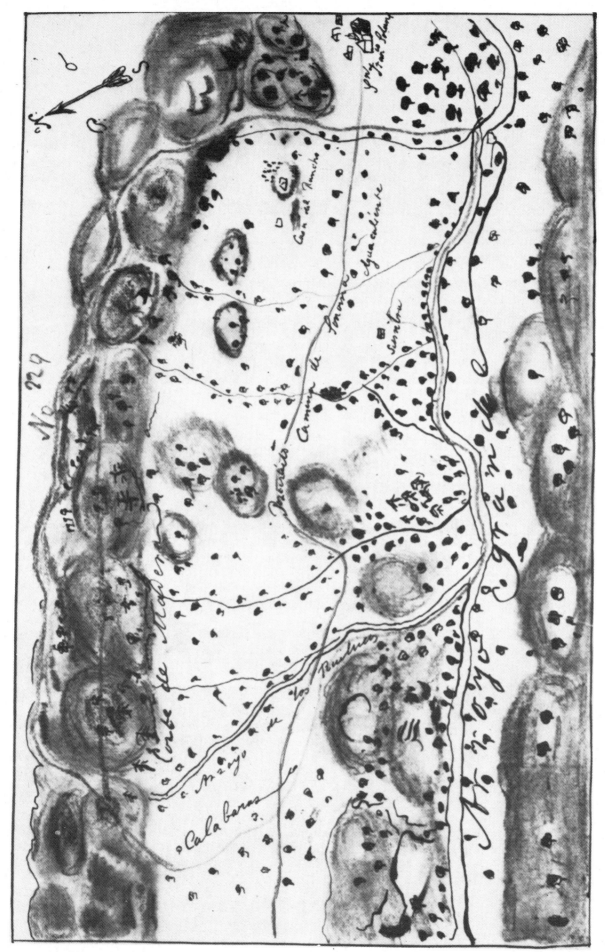

Diseño Rancho Agua Caliente. *Courtesy California State Archives.*

Diseno Rancho Guilucos. Courtesy California State Archives.

and unsatisfactory accounts. Don Pablo Ayala was appointed to take his place. However, there was little left of the mission except some buildings, some small parcels of land and few cattle. The buildings, those that had not been dismantled for use in other pueblo construction, were fast falling into ruin for lack of care. The orchard and vineyard were sadly neglected, their crumbling adobe walls offering little protection from the loose cattle and the elements.[4]

The large adobe church was still used as a parish church and occasional services were conducted by Fr. Quijas whenever he came to the pueblo from Mission San Rafael Arcangel.

The previous year, Chief Zampay had led his tribe in horse stealing raids and killing some friendly chiefs, but no campaign was sent against him then. But, again, the Yoloitoy Indians had begun to make trouble and their Chief Zampay was trying to arouse the Satiyomis. So, in July, Captain Salvador Vallejo with Chief Solano led an expedition against the Yoloytoys and Chief Zampay which ended in the Clear Lake area. Chief Zampay was captured and brought to Sonoma where he was to be tried and, no doubt, shot. However, Chief Solano asked for his release as a favor as he was more valuable alive. So he was paroled and became a peaceful citizen under the watchful eye of Chief Solano.

Envoys from Chief Succara of the Satiyomi tribe called on General Vallejo wanting a hearing between him and their chief and to arrange a truce. It was decided to meet at the old mission rancho on the west side of the Sonoma Valley (Nicholas Carriger's Creek). Here, Chief Succara and General Vallejo drew up the following terms of a peace treaty:[5]

The treaty provided that the truce should last one year, during which time Vallejo was to deliver eight steers and two cows weekly to Chief Succara; Succara was to furnish two bears large enough to fight bulls, every new moon; Succara was to give his brother and two sons as hostages, who, during good behavior, were to be "treated like Russian officers;" Succara aceed to surrender fugitive Indians of his tribe who committed theft or murder; not more than thirty Satiyomi warriors were to come to Sonoma at a time, but as many as a hundred of their wives might come, provided they carried no concealed weapons; Vallejo was to send no armed expedition into the Satiyomi country without permission from their leaders; the Satiyomis promised to deliver all captive children of the neighboring tribes taken during the past three years; Vallejo was to give Succara a saddle horse with harness; and Chief Succara and General Vallejo pledged mutual responsibility for damages inflicted by their followers upon the other contracting party.[6]

This was followed by the usual exchange of gifts, with feasting and Indian dancing.

Yet a month later, Chief Succara aroused the Cainamero tribe (which was supposed to be loyal to the General) to join in raiding ranchos. Lieutenant Pina led a small party, mostly Indians, against Succara but his Indians turned traitor, laying down as if all wounded, so the campaign was called off for the present.

During July, eight prominent men were brought as prisoners to Sonoma to be detained by General Vallejo because of revolutionary activities in the capital. After a few days they were given the freedom of a *Casa Grande* room and remained until released in September.

In July of 1837, the General moved the only printing press and type in Alta California from Monterey to his headquarters in Sonoma. The press had been brought from Mexico in 1825 by Agustín V. Zamorano, the secretary of Governor Micheltorena. The Mexican, José de la Rosa, who had arrived in Sonoma earlier with the Híjar colonists, was a printer by trade and was soon printing the General's proclamations and other public papers.

Most of the neophytes who had received their share of cattle had found it hard to care for them in small herds and had made arrangements with General Vallejo to add them to his herds of cattle on a share basis. So the herds of cattle on the ranchos and plains were large and well fed. The large Rancho Petaluma was operating with many Indians, both in the fields and on the ranges. The large rancho adobe, begun in 1834, was being added to each year as new wings, storerooms and workshops were needed. The rancho occupied the entire east side of the Valley of the Petalumas and the west side of lower Sonoma Valley, and was well stocked with fat cattle and had large fields of grain.

XIV

Smallpox—A Plague
Inspector William Hartnell—Johann Sutter

In the winter of 1837-38 one Mexican soldier, Miramontes, visited Port Bodega and contracted smallpox. On his return to Sonoma it slowly spread, especially among the Indians. They appeared to be easy prey to the disease and soon it appeared in the nearby *rancherías*. Later, local Indians and whites were vaccinated and some control was possible; but Indians returning to their *rancherías* spread the malady through their many settlements north and east, where no help was available.

During 1838, the plague spread rapidly throughout the *Frontera del Norte Este* and the squalid and unsanitary living conditions in the *rancherías* of the gentiles were fertile ground for the pestilence. By the next two years some *rancherías* were completely wiped out; in others only a few survived. It was estimated that between 60,000 and 70,000 Indians in the *Frontera del Norte* died from the disease. As a result, for many years there were few Indians and little trouble in the north Bay areas.[1]

The year of 1839 found Mission San Francisco Solano nearly a ruin. The adobe church was in poor shape though the padres' house still had some livable sections. The rest of the buildings and walls had been taken down and used in the pueblo or had been left to the mercy of the weather. Some of the lesser buildings south of the church around the *calabozo*, or guardhouse, were occupied by residents and their families and some retired soldiers. These had been maintained and were usable. The orchard had been taken over by a settler and many of the trees had begun to bear fruit. The vineyard, to the east, had been neglected and the broken-down walls did not keep the loose cattle and horses from destroying the vines.

Some Indians were still giving trouble. In March, Tobias, Chief of the Guilucos tribe and a companion were sentenced to the chain gang for killing two Indian fishermen. And the Moquelumnes from the Sacramento Valley drove a herd of tame horses to Rancho Suscol to drive away the tame horses pastured there. General Vallejo sent troops after them, killing 35 Indians and bringing the remainder back to Sonoma. Their chief, Cumuchi, was tried and executed.[1]

Another group of political prisoners was sent to Sonoma by Governor Alvarado to be held by the General. They were mixed in a plot to overthrow the Governor. The eight were José Carrillo, Gil Ibarra, Narciso Botello, Ignacio Palomares, José Mariá Ramírez, Andrés Pico, Ignacio de Valle and Roberto Pardo -- all prominent in Southern California. They arrived June 3rd and were released at the end of September. However, their confinement was not too strict.[1]

On April 23, 1838, Governor Alvarado confirmed that Lieutenant Mariano Vallejo would now be recognized as Commandant General of Alta California. He was also advanced to Captain of the San Francisco Company and confirmed as *Comandante* by orders from Mexico which arrived on November 15, 1838.[2]

Chief Solano, the big Indian chief from Suisun who was head of the Indian troops at the pueblo and much respected and trusted, became mixed up in a slave trade of young Indian children taken by other tribes. He was tried and found guilty. However, General Vallejo interceded and had him freed on parole (probation), with his apology and naming the members of the gang -- who were also tried and put on parole. The children were all returned to their families as a result.[3] Solano II, the Chief's younger brother, was in charge while the Chief was unable to care for pueblo or army affairs.

Over in the Valley of the Petalumas, on the west side of Rio Petaluma beyond the Rancho Petaluma, Antonio Ortega, the ex-*administrador* of Mission San Francisco Solano, was given permission to occupy and request a grant of three square leagues -- named Rancho Arroyo de San Antonio. It was west of the Punta

Inventory, approximately 1832. "Fabricas." The principal [padre] house is constructed with 20 and 7 rooms with different dimensions... including that which belongs to the new church... Courtesy Santa Barbara Mission Archives.

TABLA PARA LOS NIÑOS QUE EMPIEZAN Á APRENDER Á CONTAR.

VAN AÑADIDAS CUATRO TABLAS MUY PROVECHOSAS.

2 veces 1. 2.	6 veces 1. 6.	10 veces 10...... 100.		
2 veces 2. 4.	6 veces 2. 12.	10 veces 100...... 1000.		
2 veces 3. 6.	6 veces 3. 18.	10 veces 1000..... 10000.		
2 veces 4. 8.	6 veces 4. 24.	10 veces 10000.... 100000.		
2 veces 5. 10.	6 veces 5. 30.	10 veces 100000... 1 cuento.		
2 veces 6. 12.	6 veces 6. 36.			
2 veces 7. 14.	6 veces 7. 42.	Unidad.		
2 veces 8. 16.	6 veces 8. 48.	Decena.		
2 veces 9. 18.	6 veces 9. 54.	Centena.		
2 veces 10. 20.	6 veces 10. 60.	Millar.		
3 veces 1. 3.	7 veces 1. 7.	Decena de Millar.		
3 veces 2. 6.	7 veces 2. 14.	Centena de Millar.		
3 veces 3. 9.	7 veces 3. 21.	Cuento.		
3 veces 4. 12.	7 veces 4. 28.	Decena de cuento.		
3 veces 5. 15.	7 veces 5. 35.	Centena de cuento.		
3 veces 6. 18.	7 veces 6. 42.	Millar de cuento.		
3 veces 7. 21.	7 veces 7. 49.	Decena de millar de cuento.		
3 veces 8. 24.	7 veces 8. 56.	Centena de cuento de cuento.		
3 veces 9. 27.	7 veces 9. 63.	Millar de cuento de cuento.		
3 veces 10. 30.	7 veces 10. 70.	Decena de millar de cuento de cuento.		
4 veces 1. 4.	8 veces 1. 8.	Centena de millar de cuento de cuento.		
4 veces 2. 8.	8 veces 2. 16.			
4 veces 3. 12.	8 veces 3. 24.			
4 veces 4. 16.	8 veces 4. 32.			
4 veces 5. 20.	8 veces 5. 40.			
4 veces 6. 24.	8 veces 6. 48.			
4 veces 7. 28.	8 veces 7. 56.			
4 veces 8. 32.	8 veces 8. 64.			
4 veces 9. 36.	8 veces 9. 72.			
4 veces 10. 40.	8 veces 10. 80.			
5 veces 1. 5.	9 veces 1. 9.			
5 veces 2. 10.	9 veces 2. 18.			
5 veces 3. 15.	9 veces 3. 27.			
5 veces 4. 20.	9 veces 4. 36.			
5 veces 5. 25.	9 veces 5. 45.			
5 veces 6. 30.	9 veces 6. 54.			
5 veces 7. 35.	9 veces 7. 63.			
5 veces 8. 40.	9 veces 8. 72.			
5 veces 9. 45.	9 veces 9. 81.			
5 veces 10. 50.	9 veces 10. 90.			

TABLA PARA REDUCIR MARAVEDISES Á REALES

Adviertase que el real de plata tiene 34 maravedis; como asimismo tiene el real de vellon 34 de vellon.

1 Real....	34 maravedis
2 Reales...	68 maravedis
3 Reales...	102 maravedis
4 Reales...	136 maravedis
5 Reales...	170 maravedis
6 Reales...	204 maravedis
7 Reales...	238 maravedis
8 Reales...	272 maravedis
9 Reales...	306 maravedis
10 Reales...	340 maravedis

TABLA Para reducir tomines á granos.

1 Tomin....	12 gran.
2 Tom.....	24 gran.
3 Tom.....	36 gran.
4 Tom.....	48 gran.
5 Tom.....	60 gran.
6 Tom.....	72 gran.
7 Tom.....	84 gran.
8 Tom.....	96 gran.
9 Tom.....	108 gran.
10 Tom....	220 gran.

TABLA Para reducir pesos á reales.

1 Peso....	8 rs.
2 Pesos...	16 rs.
3 Pesos...	24 rs.
4 Pesos...	32 rs.
5 Pesos...	40 rs.
6 Pesos...	48 rs.
7 Pesos...	56 rs.
8 Pesos...	64 rs.
9 Pesos...	72 rs.
10 Pesos...	80 rs.

TABLA Para reducir centavos á reales, que es tanto como decir que un peso vale ciento.

Reales.	Centavos.
1 Real vale	12
2 Reales. valen	25
3 Reales. valen	37
4 Reales. valen	50
5 Reales. valen	62
6 Reales. valen	75
7 Reales. valen	87
8 Reales. valen	100

1 Quintal	4 arrobas.
1 Arroba	25 libras.
1 libra	16 onzas.
1 Onza	16 adarmes.

El marco de oro tiene 50 castellanos, el castellano 8 tomines, y el tomin 12 granos.

IMPRESO EN SONOMA: DE LA ALTA CALIFORNIA, EN LA IMPRENTA DEL GOBIERNO.

(La Rosa.)

Tables for teaching children to count, including multiplication and money conversion. Bottom line: Printed in Sonoma, Alta California, in the press of the Government by De La Rosa. Courtesy Fr. Arthur D. Spearman, S.J., University of Santa Clara.

de los Esteros. Ortega had some planting done and settled his father-in-law Juan Mirando and family on it to operate for him.[4]

Early in the year 1838 General Vallejo, in a letter to the Zacatecan Friars in charge of the northern missions, proposed the founding of four or five new missions to the north and east of the Pueblo of Sonoma. Settlement had been tried twice by military forces during the last five years, as previously related, without success.

Fr. Quijas answered on March 19th that he would be interested in founding a mission in the Santa Rosa area providing his superior, President Gonzáles Rubio, consented. However, President Rubio had no extra priests for any new missions and not enough for the present ones, so would not consent to any expansion at this time.[5]

On May 14th, General Vallejo appealed to Governor Alvarado urging a mission be established at Santa Rosa to care for the Russian River and Clear Lake areas. But the Governor was not interested in the proposal for the present.[6]

William Edward Petty Hartnell, an educated Englishman who had conducted the El Colegio de San Jose near Natividad in the Monterey district, was appointed *Visitador General de Misíones* by Governor Alvarado on January 19, 1839. He was to act as an inspector and regulator of the missions under the direct authority of the Governor. From the Governor, William Hartnell received instructions concerning law enforcement and investigation of the conditions at each mission. His duties were in substance as follows:

1. To methodize the matter of accounts and reports, instructing the admin.
2. To make an inventory of property at each mission.
3. To have an assistant at a reasonable compensation.
4. To show the laws to each admin. and explain the object of his visit, so as to avoid pretexts for not obeying.
5. To remedy actual and urgent needs reported by admin., using mission produce for that purpose.
6. To decide regarding complaints of padres and employes against admin. and to promote harmony between all classes.
7. To enjoin upon admin. all possible economy so as to promote the increase of the estates.
8. To regulate the weekly and annual slaughter of cattle in such a manner that the live-stock may not decrease.
9. To recommend to the admin. to treat the Indians kindly, inflict but moderate punishments, and see that they attend faithfully to their religious duties.
10. To report to the govt. any failure of the admin. to perform their duties, and even to suspend them temporarily from office if necessary.
11. To be diligent, to collect all kinds of information, and to make suggestions for the formation of police regulations.

The missions were to pay the annual $2,000 salary of the inspector; Mission San Francisco Solano's share was $200 a year.[7]

During May, Hartnell started on his first inspection trip at Mission San Diego and the other missions were advised of his arrival in advance.

At Mission San Francisco Solano Pablo Ayala was still *administrador*. On May 7th of 1839 Salvador Vallejo was appointed in his place by Governor Alvarado but Salvador was never placed in possession of the properties.

El Visitador (Inspector) Hartnell arrived in Sonoma in late August and was received by General Vallejo. The General would not open the mission records for inspection and would not allow Hartnell to inspect the mission properties. After heated arguments, a report prepared by Vallejo was accepted.

Salvador Vallejo protested to *el Visitador* that he had not been placed in possession of the mission when he had been appointed *administrador* by the Governor; but as nothing could be done, the General not being in favor of relieving Pablo Ayala, Salvador resigned. General Vallejo claimed all the property that belonged to the Indians had been distributed and wanted *el Visitador* to take over and administer what was left of the mission. But things were in such a mess and the accounts so deplorable that Hartnell was not interested.[8]

Pablo Ayala was left in charge of what little remained, being under direction of the General. Later in the year, *el Visitador*, having received no reports from Sonoma, wrote the General: "I reproach the administrator because this office has not received any notice of entries and expenditures since I passed by for inspection . . . . . I warn him that if he does not give complete satisfaction and explanation of the causes that have motivated his disobedience to superior decisions the government will demand the strictest accounting." However, no answer was recorded.[9]

Johann Augustus Sutter, born February 23, 1803, in Kardeon, Baden, Germany, later a Swiss Army officer, arrived in the United States in 1834. He entered the Santa Fe Trail trade before coming to California in July 1839 looking for a large tract of land. He had applied for Mexican citizenship to Governor Alvarado who had promised him a land grant in the interior when the citizenship was completed.

While preparing for an exploration trip to the interior valleys, he made a trip to Sonoma in July of 1839. Leaving Yerba Buena by boat with Juan Wilson and William Richardson, they crossed over to the north shore. Here, they secured horses and rode over the dry hills to the pueblo, as described by Sutter.

"The church, *calabozo* and a dozen detached buildings flanked the central square. It was a drowsy scene, still lethargic from the lingering heat of the midday........

"Vallejo's home was the focal point of the settlement: its wings faced each other, a billiard hall in one; Jacob Leese's house in the other. Flanking the central building stood Don Salvador Vallejo's quarters and a large barracks.

"Vallejo had ordered the erection of the church (chapel), *which supplanted a still larger one.* (Emphasis by author.) The *calabozo* -- every mission had its cage for refractory converts -- had been part of the original establishment. But the church and *calabozo* were empty -- Fr. Quijas, the resident friar, had chosen to move to San Rafael."[10]

Captain Sutter was given the usual salute of two cannon when his party arrived at the plaza and was met by Jacob Leese at the General's house. They were dined and entertained at a grand ball at night. The General suggested that Captain Sutter settle in the Sonoma area where there was lots of new land but it was not considered seriously by the Captain as he wanted his own domain.

The mission orchard was again producing peaches and pears, and a replanting of the mission vines was beginning to supply a quantity of grapes for their winemaking. The barracks housed 15 *soldados*, and several small field pieces and *carronades* (short light cannons) were on hand.

Captain Sutter planned a trip to the Russian settlements and the General supplied a passport and *vaquero* guide the next day. The Captain rode over the hills past the Petaluma Rancho headquarters and on the well traveled route to Port Bodega.

Stopping at Rancho Estero Americano for fresh mounts, they noticed that the two owners, Edward McIntosh and James Dawson, while pleasant to them, were at outs. Dawson was sawing the house into two parts also. He learned later that the two men had received the land grant a few years previously; that McIntosh had gone recently to Monterey to have the grant confirmed; however, he had it confirmed to himself, leaving Dawson out of the final grant. Dawson, on finding out about it, roundly thrashed McIntosh, sawed their new wooden house in half and moved his half to adjoining land to which he obtained title later.

Continuing on to Port Bodega and north to Ross the next day, Captain Sutter was well received by the Commander, Governor Rotscheff and his wife, Princess Helena. After a pleasant visit, the Captain returned to the Pueblo of Sonoma via the Rancho Estero Americano and Rancho Petaluma. Leaving the pueblo the next morning, the Captain and William Richardson and Juan Wilson retraced their route back to Yerba Buena.[10]

During the year, Captain Salvador Vallejo had been commander of troops at Sonoma headquarters. Ensign Lazero Pina and Ensign Prado Mesa acted as commanding officers in Salvador Vallejo's absence. The infantry company of native Indians was armed with muskets and wore light uniforms and received a little pay. General Vallejo was recognized by Mexico as *Comandante Militar* of California this year.[11]

At the mission, the records showed:
Baptisms - No. 1494, Oct. 1, 1839 (to) No. 1518, Dec. 31st.
Burials - No. 875, Oct. 7, 1839 (to) No. 876, Dec. 31st.[12]

During the year 1839 the local printer, José de la Rosa, printed elaborate frontpieces for the new set of mission records for Fr. Quijas, as well as forms for the annual *Informes* which were sent into the Mission Presidente's office. The frontpieces were works of art of the printer trade of the time and added to the decoration of the important mission books. The printing press, which had been brought up from Monterey in 1837, was returned to the capital early in the following year and Sonoma was without a press until a second one was obtained in later years when José de la Rosa could then open his own print shop on the plaza.

The deadly scourge of smallpox was still raging throughout the *rancherías* of the gentile Indians to the north and northeast, especially where vaccination had not been possible.

In December, the pueblo received a visit from William Heath Davis of Yerba Buena who, with Jacob Leese and Thomas Shaw, (super cargo or owner's clerk of the ship *Monsoon* of Boston) arrived at the embarcadero in the schooner *Isabel*. They were entertained at the General's house and the next day returned down the Bay.[13]

XV

The New Chapel
The Russians Sell Out

Mission Presidente José María de Jesús Gonzáles Rubio, now Vice *Comisario* as well, wrote in one of his letters in 1840 that the large adobe church at Mission San Francisco Solano was nearly a complete ruin.[1] It was during the previous year that the General, no doubt at the insistence of his wife Benicia, ordered the erection of a smaller church or chapel built on the site of the original wooden church at the southwest corner of the mission quadrangle. The original wooden church, which had been used as a small store, was being torn down. The new chapel would care for the spiritual affairs of his large family and the growing pueblo, replacing the large adobe church at the east end of the padres' house.[2]

Across the street from the large adobe church and padres' house, the small house of adobe bricks was offered for use of visitors and travelers who might stop in the pueblo. It was 11 *varas* wide and 12 *varas* long, facing the street. This building was on the pueblo lot, 109 *varas* square, deeded to Antonio Ortega (then major-domo), Antonio Pina, Dons Alviso and Davilla in 1837, and which contained *Casa del Billar* (billiard hall).[3]

Fr. Quijas still visited the pueblo and held church services when necessary but he now had to care for Mission Dolores as well as Mission San Rafael Arcangel. Relations between the padre and the General and his staff at the pueblo were still strained at best; however, he was very interested in the construction of the new chapel.

On the 18th of March 1840, Governor Alvarado issued an order to all administrators to turn the mission properties over to *el Visitador* Hartnell. In addition, the major-domos would take the place of the administrators and report to *el Visitador* direct, per a March 1st order. *El Visitador* Hartnell was ordered on March 18th to begin his second visits immediately.[4]

When *el Visitador* Hartnell arrived on his visit of inspection to Mission San Rafael in April, all possible obstacles were put in his way. On hearing that he was inspecting at San Rafael, General Vallejo went over at once but found that Hartnell had finished and returned to Yerba Buena.

The General followed him to Yerba Buena and arrested him "for having ventured to interfere in matters concerning the northern frontier" and brought him back. He kept him a prisoner until Hartnell agreed that "Vallejo's views in this particular case were correct." On May 14th Hartnell advised Governor Alvarado "that General Vallejo would not permit occupation of San Rafael in pursuance of your instructions" and, of course, *el Visitador* could not inspect or report on conditions at San Francisco Solano.

Later, in September, Hartnell resigned as the position was too demanding, and while some missions were well managed, others were in a deplorable shape with unsatisfactory men in charge. No replacement was appointed and major-domos were ordered to report directly to the government in the future.[5] Also, ex-Presidente García Diego was made Bishop of both Baja and Alta California, with the Pious Fund to help finance the missions.

Captain Salvador Vallejo brought his bride, Maria de la Luz Carrillo, to the Sonoma pueblo in September to occupy his house on the north side of the plaza - a short distance west of the General's *Casa Grande*. They were married on the 8th, No. 355, by Fr. Quijas. Maria Carrillo was a sister of the General's wife Benicia.

The Captain applied in 1840 for a land grant in the Lake region to the north. It covered 16 square leagues and included most of the grazing lands around the lake. He included a brother, Juan Antonio, in his application for this large grant called Lup-Yomi. Governor Micheltorena granted the rancho to both on September 4, 1844.

IGLESIA DE SAN FRANco SOLANO DE SONORA.

Informe anual.

BAUTISMOS ADMINISTRADOS en el año de 1840.						CASAMIENtos en dicho año.		CUMPLIMIENTO de iglesia en dicho año.			DIFUNTOS en dicho año.		ECSISTENTES EN fin de dicho año.		
Adultos.	Parvulos de Gentiles.	Hijos de gentiles catecúmenos.	Idem de gente blanca ó de razon.	Idem de los neófitos antiguos.	Son por todos.	De los indigenas.	De Gente blanca.	Confesiones.	Comuniones.	Santos Viaticos.	De los indigenas.	De Gente blanca.	Hombres.	Mugeres.	Son por todos.
0.0.0	0.3.0	0.0.0	0.0.6	0.36.0	0.45.0	0.8.0	0.0.0	0.19.0	0.12.0	0.0.0	0.19.0	0.0.0	0.89.0	0.75.0	144

Bautismos desde la Fundacion. . . . . . . ₥1563.

Matrimonios celebrados desde la Fundacion. . . . . ₥359.

Los que han fallecido desde la Fundacion. . . . . ₥896.

NOTA.

Se ha levantado una Yglesia de cuarenta varas de largo seis de ancho, seis y media en alto con su Sacristia, Baptisterio y Coro con sus Tribunas; se ha enlucido blanqueado y pintado el Presbyterio se le ha puesto sus Varandillas, y con el favor de Dios se concluira en el año entrante

S. Fran.co Solano Dbre. 31 de 1840

Fr. Jph Lorenzo Quijas

Informe - 1840, Fr. Quijas. "Note. There has been built a church 40 varas long, 6 varas wide and 6¾ varas high together with its sacristy, baptistry and choir with its tribunes [screen]. [The Present Chapel, 1841: The sanctuary has been covered with wooden flooring and whitewashed and painted. Its balustrades have been placed and with God's favor the church will be finished in the coming year.]" Translated by Fr. Maynard Geiger, O.F.M. Courtesy Santa Barbara Mission Archives.

Over in the Santa Rosa area Don Marcus West, an English sailor and carpenter, was granted Rancho San Miguel (six square leagues) including the old abandoned Santa Anna y Farías settlement site.

Closer to the pueblo, on its northern border, Rancho Agua Caliente had been granted earlier to Ignacio Pacheco but he had not completed his possession. On July 13, 1840, Lazaro Pina, artillery officer at Sonoma, was granted the rancho by Governor Alvarado. Pina built an adobe on the rancho but later left for Mexico and sold his property to the General.

The effect of the smallpox plague was evident at the pueblo as the Indians were not very numerous, there being only a short 134 left from the mission's earlier population at the end of 1840.

Fr. Quijas' report for Mission San Francisco Solano at the end of the year 1840:

For the year	Total
45 baptisms	1563 to date
9 marriages	359 to date
20 burials	896 to date

Also, there were 89 male and 45 female Indians around the mission.

Fr. Quijas also noted - (The new chapel) "There has been built a church 40 *varas* long six *varas* wide and six and one-half *varas* high together with its sacristy, baptistry and choir with its screen. The sanctuary has been covered with wooden flooring and whitewashed and painted. Its balustrades have been placed and with God's favor the church will be finished in the coming year."[6]

Word was received that Fr. Buenaventura Fortuny, the former padre who built Mission San Francisco Solano to its greatness and prosperity during the years 1826-33, passed away at the age of nearly 66 years at his last station, Mission San Buenaventura on December 16, 1840. He was buried in the Mission Santa Barbara on the 18th of December of that year. After leaving San Francisco Solano, he had served well at Missions San Diego de Alcalá, San Luis Rey and, finally, at San Buenaventura.

Over on the Pacific Coast conditions in the Russian colony at Ross were changing. The rich harvest of furs, especially the seal and sea otter pelts, had declined as the rookeries were hunted out. The grain and food harvests were not ample to feed the northern Alaskan settlements and the Mexican government blocked any further expansion or additional land. Also, treaties with the United States prohibited settlements below 54° 40' latitude.

In 1836 Baron Wrangel, Russian governor of its American colonies, wished to extend Russian holdings south to the Bay of San Francisco, east to the Sacramento Valley and north to the English holdings in Oregon. He proposed the purchase of Missions San Rafael Arcangel and San Francisco Solano to his Russian company and received their approval. However, the Russian government would only give him authority to negotiate a commercial treaty with Mexico. The Baron resigned his position and traveled to Mexico City where he proposed the sale of the area desired, and the missions, to Vice President Barragán and others. However, the Mexican authorities would not consider any such proposition or sell or cede on any terms.

The Russian company and government then decided to abandon the settlement and in 1840 offered it to the Hudson's Bay Company for $30,000. But that company did not wish to antagonize the Mexicans or the United States, who had declared the Monroe Doctrine in effect in 1823. Also, Hudson's Bay Company claimed the Russians owned only the improvements and inventory at Ross and Bodega -- not the land.

Next it was offered to Governor Alvarado but he stalled with long correspondence, expecting he would get it for nothing if he waited. General Vallejo was contacted and terms made favorable, but he had to consult and get permission from the Governor.

Finally, they offered it to Captain Sutter who, on the second offer, accepted and bought all improvements, stock and inventory for $30,000, to be paid in installments -- partly in produce. The contract was signed in Yerba Buena on December 13, 1840.[7] And San Francisco Solano and the Pueblo of Sonoma were safe again.

The completion of the new adobe chapel was the important event at Mission San Francisco Solano in the year 1841. Standing on the site of the first wooden plank church on the corner opposite the military barracks, it added a lot to the fast-growing pueblo. The materials for its construction were obtained mostly from the older mission buildings which, except for the padres' house and the large adobe church, were fast being dismantled and used again. And the ex-mission Indians were still being used by the major-domo and others for general use around the pueblo. The new church would care for the spiritual needs of the soldiers and families and other settlers in and near the pueblo. Though there was no padre in residence now, Fr. Quijas came over from Mission San Rafael Arcangel on occasion and held necessary services.

The new chapel was 8 *varas* wide by 40 *varas* long outside, with 6½ *vara* walls.[8] The front facade was one *vara* thick as were the balance of the walls, and all were built of plain adobe bricks. All had been plastered and white-

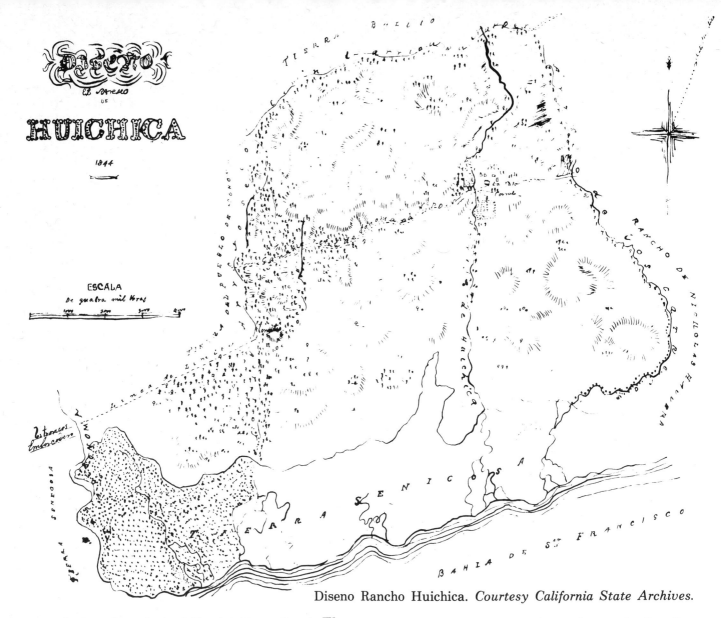

Diseno Rancho Huichica. *Courtesy California State Archives.*

washed a gleaming white, inside and out. The wide front door led into the baptistry, or vestibule, 4½ *varas* deep with its font and stairs to the choir loft above. The doorway into the nave was in the *vara* wide wall. The wide nave, 6 *varas* by 26 *varas* long, extended to the sanctuary, 5 *varas* deep at the far end. Along the left or west side, three large windows reached near the ceiling, while on the opposite or east side were two large high windows in addition to the door from the sanctuary which led to the sacristy in the quadrangle on the outside of the chapel. It was a small sacristy, 4 by 8 *varas*, built against the wall for the storage of the church vestments and other items.[8] Tiles covered the floor of the chapel, and a small cross surmounted the peak at the front.

On the heavy beam, now set up beside the front of the new chapel, hung the two large mission bells pealing out their daily message over the valley. The bellringer, who had been retained throughout the years, filled an important position in the pueblo as a timekeeper for the populace; this, besides his duty of calling the worshipers to services, the peals for the marriages, and tolling the slow message of the burials.

With the Stations of the Cross on the walls and the elaborate altar and paintings from the adobe church in the sanctuary, the new chapel was ready for dedication. After it was dedicated by Fr. Quijas in 1841 with the usual ceremonies, the chapel became the new house of worship for the parish and the pueblo.

The padres' house was still habitable and an apartment was reserved for the use of any padre who might be in occasional attendance at the mission. The other rooms, those still usable, were occupied by pueblo citizens, with one reserved for guests.

The new Bishop of California, Francisco Garcia Diego, found on taking office that his funds were very low. The large Pious Fund, the main source of mission revenue, had been taken over by the Mexican government for their own use and that left the Bishop and his flock of padres only the little income still available from the poverty-stricken secularized missions.

XVI

Visitors—Sir George Simpson, Edward Vischer, Commander Jones

In the summer of 1841, Commander Wilkes, U.S.N., in command of the U.S. Exploring Expedition with the sloop of war *Vincennes*, was at Yerba Buena. He sent Lieutenant Cadwalter Ringold and a party to visit Sonoma and the upper Bay -- and report on the area. Lieutenant Ringold's description was typical as of that period:

In Sonoma is situated the town of the same name, the residence of General Vallejo, and the mission of San Rafael (San Francisco Solano). The fertile country extends across to Ross and Bodega, the two Russian settlements. Sonoma is the seat of the government, and is situated in an extensive plain, with some high hills for its southern boundary. The plain is covered with fine oaks, and there is a never-failing stream of water passing through it. There is, besides, an inlet from the Bay, which allows a boat navigation to it of about twelve miles.

Upon paper Sonoma is a very large city, and laid out according to the most approved plan. In reality, however, it consists of only the following buildings: General Vallejo's house, built of adobe, of two stories, which fronts on the public square, and is said to be one of the best houses in California. On the right of this is the residence of the General's brother Salvador, and to the left, the barracks for the accommodation of the guard for the General, consisting of about twenty fusileers. Not far removed is the old dilapidated mission-house of San Francisco Solano, scarcely tenable, though a small part of it is inhabited still by Padre Quijas, who continues, notwithstanding the poverty of the mission, to entertain the stranger and show him all the hospitality he can.

Besides these buildings just enumerated, there was in the course of construction in 1841, a neat little chapel, and a small building for a billiard-room. There are also three or four houses and huts which were tenanted, and at some future day may boast of some further additions.[1]

The billiard room referred to was the adobe building on the corner opposite the new chapel and facing the plaza -- the recreation room for the soldiers of the barracks.

Jacob Leese, brother-in-law of General Vallejo, and his wife Rosalía had moved to Sonoma pueblo from Yerba Buena and planned to erect a new house on the plaza. He had applied for the land of Rancho Huichica, just south and southeast of the pueblo, and now received permission to occupy the fine two-square leagues from acting Governor Manuel Jimeno. He also requested an additional 3½ square leagues of the same rancho which he hoped to receive later on.

In the Santa Rosa area, Señora María Ignacio López de Carrillo, the General's mother-in-law, received her two-league grant of Rancho Cabeza de Santa Rosa. She was now established there with her unmarried children in the adobe house beside Arroyo Santa Rosa.

And farther north, in the lands of the Satiyomis, Henry D. Fitch, the General's brother-in-law, was granted the three-square-league Rancho Satiyomi. He did not reside there but sent Cyrus Alexander to take charge of the rancho and its extensive cattle herds which were soon grazing on its many meadows.

Over in the Napa area, Damaso Antonio Rodriquez, a retired soldier from Sonoma, had requested land called Yajome and was granted one and one-half square leagues along the upper Rio Napa and including the principal Napa Indian *rancheria* of the area.

Farther up the Valley of the Napas, where an arroyo of ample water flowed in from the western hills, Dr. Edward T. Bale had been occupying a rancho called Carne Humane. After requesting the rancho, he was granted it on March 14, 1841, by Governor Alvarado. His wife, María Sobranes was a niece of the General.

M. Duflot de Mofras, a French explorer, visited Mission San Francisco Solano and the pueblo and spent a few days in the area in the Fall of 1841. He had arrived at Yerba Buena on the ship *Nina* after touring the Mexican settlements and missions from San Diego to Yerba Buena. The route and impressions are as written in his report published in Paris in 1844:

After leaving San Rafael and passing the extensive salt marshes and Rancho del Indio, a farm run by a few liberated Indians, San Francisco Solano, 13 leagues from the preceding mission is reached.

Mission San Francisco Solano, founded August 25, 1823, by the Reverend Father Amorós (see Note 2) a Spanish Franciscan, is the last and most northerly of these religious establishments that so richly deserve to have been preserved. San Solano is delightfully situated, and the vast fields surrounding it are extremely fertile. The mission lies only a few miles from the end of San Pablo Bay and at least 12 leagues from the Russian settlements. Two chains of parallel hills shelter the mission from stiff ocean winds as well as those from the north. So rapid was the expansion of this mission that in less than ten years Solano had attracted 1,300 neophytes and owned 8,000 cattle, 700 horses, 4,000 sheep, and harvested 3,000 *fanegas*. Today none of this wealth remains. The buildings, except for one chapel and a small sleeping-room for the priest, have been destroyed, the materials having been used by Don Mariano Vallejo to erect a fine house. Vallejo also confiscated livestock, vines, and gardens, taking into his employ as servants the 50 Indians who remained at San Francisco Solano.

Around a large square near the mission, Commandante Vallejo founded a pueblo which he named Sonoma de Vallejo. This first word is the name bestowed by the Indians on this locality. In time this settlement will undoubtedly expand. In fact, recently the population has increased 150 persons, among whom are 20 foreigners. San Solano is the main residence of an intelligent Frenchman, M. Victor Prudon, who has established a local school and also supervises a small rancho. At one time M. Prudon hoped to locate at Monterey as secretary to the governor, an office he has already filled.[2]

During the winter, unusually high waters in the *Rio Ruso* area destroyed the sawmill of Don Juan Cooper on Rancho Molino.

January of the next year had just arrived when Sir George Simpson, Governor-in-Chief of the Hudson's Bay Company's territories in North America, in Yerba Buena with the bark *Cowlitz*, made plans to visit the Pueblo of Sonoma in the *Frontera del Norte Este*. He left an entertaining and descriptive record of his trip which included a camp near Mission San Rafael Arcangel, as follows:

Having celebrated New Year's Day to the best of our ability, we made preparations for starting on Monday, the 3d of the month (1842) to pay our respects to General Vallego, who was residing at the mission San Francisco Solano.[3]

Leaving in the long boats of the *Cowlitz* at nine with Mr. Rae and Mr. Forbes, their agent in Santa Clara, the heavy tide and wind forced them to land at Point San Pedro for the night --

on former Mission San Rafael property now owned by Timothy Murphy. Sir Simpson continues:

Timothy Murphy, who unconsciously played the part of so inhospitable a landlord on this occasion, resides at the mission San Rafel as *administrador* in behalf of General Vallego, to whom, as one of the prime movers in the revolution of 1836, there fell the lion's share or prize-money in the shape of two nice snuggeries of San Rafael and San Francisco Solano. The general, who shows his sagacity by systematically allying himself with foreigners, selected Mr. Murphy as a fitting mate for one of his sisters, the prettiest girl of the family, giving him in advance, as an earnest of the bargain, the management of San Rafael, with a good slice of the booty for his own private use. The lady, however, could not, or would not, fancy Timothy; and the matter ended by the general's acquisition of two foreigners instead of one, Mr. Leese having obtained the donna's hand, and Mr. Murphy having kept her dowry.

But the jilted *administrador* is not without his share of pleasant society in the person of one of the few priests who remained in the country after the confiscation of their establishments. Father Quigas is one of those jovial souls who show, that, in the New World as in the Old, power and wealth are more than a match for monastic austerities; nor has the removal of the corrupting influences, rendered his reverence a more rigid observer of his vows, excepting always (thanks to Murphy and Vallego), the single article of poverty. The two friends lately led each other into trouble in a way which forcibly illustrates the state of government in general and the character of Vallego in particular.

As the Bay of San Pedro (San Pablo) is separated only by a ridge of green hills from the valley of Santa Rosa, in which are situated the settlements of Bodega and Ross, Murphy and Quigas, whether it was that the former was in search of stray bullocks, or that the latter wished to ease the schismatics of a little of their brandy, fell into the snare of visiting the Russians, against all rule and precedent. The treason soon came to the general's ears, and, on the very evening after their return, the delinquents were politely invited to attend at headquarters, by a serjeant and five troopers. As the night was wet and stormy, they tried to bribe the soldiers with their best fare into a respite of a few hours, pleading at the same time the want of horses. But, while the serjeant disclaimed all official knowledge of wind and weather, the troopers caught the requisite number of nags, and next morning the luckless wights were thrown, all drenched and splashed, into the general's *calabozo* or dungeon, to chew the cud, in hunger and thirst, on the contraband hospitalities of Bodega and Ross. So much for the freedom and equity of California republicanism.[3]

Early the next morning, against the tide, the party crossed to Sonoma Creek and up the tule-bordered channel to the "landing place" and a camp site.

A note by an Indian to the General brought a drove of horses in the morning. Choosing the best animals, the party rode up the flooded plain to the mission, past the many irrigated fields and ditches.

They were received by Salvador Vallejo, the General's brother; Mr. Leese, a brother-in-law, and the General in his chambers as the General was somewhat indisposed. After a late breakfast they mounted horses and started out to see the country from a high hill nearby.

They saw many deer, quite tame, but they were not hunted except for their finer tallow. Many other wild animals are found in the valley and surrounding hills: the wild goat, bears, panthers, wolves, foxes and rabbits. In the plains, the fields of grain had been damaged by the storm and some plowing had to be repeated. The plow, a pointed log shod with iron, with a handle and long pole yoked to the horns of the oxen, just about scratched the near virgin soil -- yet large returns were customary.[3]

During the day, we visited a village of General Vallego's Indians, about three hundred in number, who were the most miserable of the race I ever saw, excepting always the slaves of the savages of the northwest coast. Though many of them are well formed and well grown, yet every face bears the impress of poverty and wretchedness; and they are, moreover, a prey to several malignant diseases, among which an hereditary syphilis ranks as the predominant scourge alike of old and young. They are badly clothed, badly lodged, and badly fed. As to clothing, they are pretty nearly in a state of nature; as to lodging, their hovels are made of boughs wattled with bulrushes in the form of beehives, with a hole in the top for a chimney, and with two holes at the bottom, towards the northwest and the southeast, so as to enable the poor creatures, by closing them in turns, to exclude both the prevailing winds; and as to food, they eat the worst bullock's worst joints, with bread of acorns and chestnuts, which are most laboriously and carefully prepared by pounding and rinsing and grinding. Though not so recognized by law, yet they are thralls in all but the name; while, borne to the earth by the toils of civilization superadded to the privations of savage life, they vegetate rather than live, without the wish to enjoy their former pastimes or the skill to resume their former avocations.

This picture, which is a correct likeness not only of General Vallego's Indians, but of all civilized aborigines of California, is the only remaining monument of the zeal of the church and the munificence of the state........

Previously to dressing for dinner we took a closer survey of the buildings and premises. The general's plan seems to be to throw his principal edifices into the form of a square, or rather of three sides of a square. The center is already filled up with the general's own house, flanked on one side by a barrack, and on the other by Don Salvador's residence; but as yet the wings contain respectively only a billiard-room and Mr. Leese's dwelling, opposite to each other. On the outside of this square are many detached buildings, such as the *calabozo*, the church, etc. The *calabozo* is most probably a part of the original establishment, for every mission had its cage for refractory converts; but the church, which even now is large, has been built by Vallego to *replace a still larger one*, though no priest lives at Sonoma, and Father Quigas of San Rafael, after his experience of the dungeon, has but little stomach for officiating at headquarters.

All the buildings are of *adobes*, or unbaked bricks, which are cemented with mud instead of mortar; and in order to protect such perishable materials from the rain, besides keeping off the rays of the sun, the houses are very neatly finished with verandas and overhanging eaves. If tolerably protected for a time, the walls, which are generally four or five feet thick, become, in a measure, vitrified, and are nearly as durable as stone. To increase the expenditure of labor and materials, the partitions are nearly as thick as the outer walls, each room of any size having its own separate roof -- a circumstance which explained what at first surprised us, the great length and breadth of the apartments........

Our evening, however, passed over most amicably and agreeably, winding up, after several other songs, with "Auld Lang Syne," in which the Californians joined the foreigners very heartily; so that, as next day was Old Christmas, I could almost have fancied that I was welcoming "Auld Yule" in the North of Scotland.[3]

On the morning of the 6th, the party left the mission about 7 o'clock in the rain and, after breakfast at the landing place, dropped down to the Bay on the ebb tide. However, a strong head wind drove them back and they returned to the landing and camped there another night. In the morning, they sailed down to the Bay again and on west past the lands of Timothy Murphy to the *Cowlitz*, arriving by four in the afternoon.[3]

On his pueblo lot on *Calle Huerta*, opposite the southwest corner of the plaza, Jacob Leese was having his two-story adobe house built. It was to be used for his merchandise store as well as his dwelling.

Chief Solano had petitioned for a tract of land surrounding his native home, now called Rancho Suisun, and in 1842 received the grant of four square leagues. It was part of the original Mission Rancho St. Eulalia established by Fr. Altimira.

General Vallejo received a permanent commission of Lieutenant Colonel in the Mexican Army on May 2nd of 1842 and Victor Prudon was made a captain a couple of days later. The General had resigned his commission of General of the Army in favor of the new Governor Micheltorena. Later in the year the Governor appointed the General *Gefe de linea militar desde Sonoma hasta Sta Suez* -- or Commandant of the Northern Lines south to Santa Inez.[4]

On the plaza a watchtower, 12 *varas* square, was being built on the west end of the General's large adobe house *El Casa Grande*. It was three stories high with balconies around the floors so that the sentries on duty could see far out over the valley in all directions.

In the middle of October of the same year, 1842, the pueblo received a visit from the merchant and artist Edward Vischer. He had arrived in Monterey on the schooner *California*, John B.R. Cooper of Rancho Molino, captain, and had then traveled overland to Yerba Buena. While waiting for the ship *Clarita* to prepare for a voyage back to Germany via the southern California ports, Vischer took the opportunity to visit Sonoma pueblo. His report following, is very descriptive in its detail.

To complete the picture, I shall mention the other traveling companions on board the little vessel: an English sailor called Richardson, who served as pilot; a fat Franciscan monk, Padre Guijas, who, with his servants (consisting of three Indians with their families), was on his way to the mission across the bay; and finally my special companion, the Swiss, Jean Vioget. The latter had been my guest at Acapulco years ago, and to his graceful brush I owe several pretty sketches of California........

We rowed or sailed all night, and arrived the next morning at Sonoma. The Padre, remembering gratefully the hospitality he had enjoyed on board the *Clarita*, provided us all with horses, a whole drove of which had been brought in by Indians. We journeyed ashore, saddled the horses and, after a short gallop, arrived under the hospitable roof of our good host, who refreshed us with apples and grapes from the little mission garden, until the lunch table provided us with more substantial food.

Sonoma is a recent, that is, a ten or twelve-year-old, settlement. As a frontier point, it is provided against possible attacks with a garrison and several field pieces under the command of Colonel Don Mariano Guadalupe Vallejo, military commander of California. Since I had letters of introduction to him, he received me in full uniform and told me in a rambling conversation many true things, together with many others that sounded incredible. He showed me his establishment and the plan of the town, and treated me with grapes and wine of his own production. My Swiss friend took me to several other homes, mostly those of foreign settlers, who had acquired comparative wealth because of the unbelievably quick increase of stock. After our return to the Mission San Francisco Solano, the good Padre served us a modest but convivial supper and ordered horses and guides for our return trip the next morning. For several hours we enjoyed the jocular entertainment of our host, and then retired for the night.

We returned to the vessel overland in California fashion, in almost constant gallop, with a change of horses every three or four hours. We passed a camp of migratory heathen Indians. They were used to camping during certain seasons near frontier settlements to earn, by means of communal labor, a better living than is possible for them in the wilderness. When they thus come in contact with civilization and learn to know necessities of life which were foreign to them, it is easy to persuade them to become Christians and to be established definitely around the missions. Self-interest is, of course, the primary reason for approaching the Indians. The gradual infiltration of civilization remains very superficial, limited to certain religious formulas. Yet it is sufficient for the purposes of the landowners, who need the services of the Indians. In any case, it is a transition from the completely barbaric condition of the heathen savage to the benefits of human society. They lose their freedom, but their subsistence is assured, and the next generation is usually won for the settlement. As interesting as the visit to such an Indian *rancheria* was to me, I must confess that the impression was not at all cheering; the conditions are too beastly. I wish the romantic champions of primitive life and unfettered nature could throw a glance into the interior of these huts and holes, into the disgusting community life in a dark, smoky space, amidst dirt and vermin- I think he would forever be cured of his dreams. Only when the Indian is in his element, hunting or fighting, showing his muscular agility, can he temporarily arouse our admiration; when forced to inactivity in the circle of his home, he is below the level of an animal.

The *rancheria* consisted of about fifteen or twenty cone-shaped huts of straw. (Tolay *Rancheria*) There was only one opening through which one could crawl. Unless they were on duty with their white neighbors or on a fishing or hunting trip, old and young, male and female, lay inside around a fire. Knowledge of Spanish was of no use with these people; we had to resort to signs and gestures if we wanted a drink of water from their basket-work pitcher. Similar vessels were used for cooking utensils. They do not place them over a fire, for fear that the close basket-work may start to burn. Instead, they place heated rocks in them to make the contents boil.

The occupants of these huts show neither shyness nor readiness to oblige. Black and red tattoo-like stripes painted on their cheeks and chins and pitch-black hair falling loosely over their shoulders lend, particularly to the women, a strange appearance, which is intensified by the impressive restless cast of the savage's eye.

An acquaintance who had traveled the same route several times told me that one day, tired of riding, he had stretched out under a spreading tree to have an afternoon nap. When he awoke, he saw himself surrounded by several hundred of these wandering Indians, some of whom observed him with greatest curiosity and even touched his body. Distributing his tobacco, the only thing he could give them, earned him general gratitude, and after his first fright he could continue his trip without trouble. The inborn passive character of California's Indian tribes has made the task of the missionaries easier, whereas, on the other hand, their apathy and the mortality due to carelessness and uncleanliness among the tamed tribes have greatly retarded the extent of their advancement.

At a rancho where we changed horses to reach the

Mission ruins, 1846. Sketched by Wm. N. Boggs, son of Alcalde *Boggs. Courtesy California Department of Parks and Recreation.*

Mission of San Rafael on time, we saw the skin of a huge female bear that had been killed the previous day. Near the house there lay on the grass two cubs of the size of a mastiff, which had been clubbed to death by the people. Not infrequently one sees in these regions large herds of deer.

In San Rafael we met friends, among them Captain Henry D. Fitch, the same American with whom I had made my first trip to Lima ten years before. After a good lunch with ample dessert of grapes, we continued our journey together.

At sunset we again passed an inhabited place, when suddenly a German roundelay awakened me from a momentary dream. Germans so far distant from the homeland? They were sailors from a Bremen whaler who had used their leave for a pleasure and hunting trip. They told us that a large barque, rigged like a schooner, lay ready to sail down the narrows. We made use of this information and unharnessed, to make the last leg of our trip comfortably by water. After a trip of an hour and a half in soft moonlight, we were on board the *Clarita* in the bay of Sausalito.[5]

Over on the Pacific Ocean area all was quiet again as the Russians had moved their people from the settlements at Ross and *Puerto* Bodega to their Alaskan headquarters at Sitka. Captain Sutter of New Helvetia on the Rio Sacramento was in possession of their California properties and was transferring movables to his Sacramento fort and Rancho New Helvetia.

A critical situation developed in the pueblo near the holidays but was soon cleared up. Commander Thomas A. Catesby Jones, U.S.N., with two Naval vessels, on October 20, 1842, occupied the capital at Monterey in the name of the United States on the assumption that war had been declared with Mexico. Also, he had suspected that British warships were about to occupy the California ports.

However, after holding Monterey for a day and a half, Commander Jones decided that the reason for the occupation had been accomplished. He withdrew his men and returned the capital and fort to the Mexican commander. He then made friendly relations with the officials and townspeople and replaced the only powder burnt for salutes twofold.

Sailing from Monterey, Commodore Jones arrived at San Francisco on December 14. While there he wrote to Vallejo, expressing a desire to visit Sonoma with some members of his staff. Vallejo was flattered to receive so distinguished a guest and sent him directions for the trip. On the day of their arrival, Vallejo dispatched soldiers and servants with horses to the Sonoma Creek landing to convey his guests to the town, but the American arrived by a different route. Jones assured Vallejo that the change was entirely accidental, due to their unfamiliarity with the sloughs and inlets of the Bay, but Leese told him later he had heard that the Americans had changed their route in order to explore more of the country, as the United States might take the territory. Vallejo, however, preferred to believe what Jones told him.

Failing to recognize Sonoma Creek, Commodore Jones and his officers entered Huichica Creek, and landed near the Huichica hills about 5:00 p.m. As they were making their way toward Sonoma they were discovered by Lieutenant Ramon Carrillo and a picket of militia, who took them as prisoners to the Indian encampment at Huichica Ranch, where Salvador Vallejo and Chief Solano were stationed. These two ordered horses and, taking personal command of the guard, conveyed the prisoners to Sonoma, where they were locked in the garrison flagroom.

About midnight an orderly aroused Colonel Vallejo to report that Solano had arrived from Huichica with a number of prisoners in strange uniforms. Alarmed at the news, Vallejo dressed hurriedly, afraid that some land expedition had entered the country with hostile intent. He buckled on his best sword and followed by his aides, Lieutenant Colonel Prudon and Lieutenant Sabas Fernández, hastened to the barracks. There he discovered Commodore Jones, who asked if this was the reception he had prepared for his guests. Vallejo offered his hand and made profuse apologies. Taking the Commodore's arm, he escorted the party to his home, where a fine breakfast was set before them at 2:00 a.m. After they had eaten, they were shown to their rooms and slept until seven o'clock. At eight, Vallejo paraded his troops, hoisted the colors and fired a thirteen-gun salute in honor of the Commodore, which greatly pleased him. Jones jestingly said that if Micheltorena had been present he would have received a twenty-one gun salute, because, judging from the correspondence, the Governor considered him the ruler of the United States.

Vallejo and Jones discussed Micheltorena's character at some length. Don Guadalupe was convinced that the Commodore had judged the Governor's character aright, and said he could not help blushing when Jones referred to the Governor's pompous proclamation.

Vallejo took his guests to inspect that camp at Huichica where 1,400 Suisun Indians were assembled under his brother Salvador and Chief Solano for training in the use of hand-and-fire-arms. They arrived to find the army eating instead of drilling, and Jones was surprised to discover that there were more women than men present. Turning to Don Salvador, he asked whether the women also fought in the battles. Salvador, who was in a bad humor, replied: "Those women do not fight against the Satiyomis; but if it were a case of battling the Yankees, they would take part in the front rank, and would know how to give a good account of themselves."

Vallejo was indignant at his brother's rudeness and lost no time in giving him to understand that Commodore Jones was his friend and that he was to be treated as such.

While the Americans were conversing with Don Salvador, Ramón Carrillo approached. Jones recognized him, extended his hand pleasantly, congratulated him and then offered him a gold penknife in token of his gratitude for the manner in which he had been treated when a prisoner. Don Ramón, without understanding the words, recognized the meaning and accepted the present.

That evening, from the balcony of Vallejo's home, the American officers watched an Indian dance presented in the plaza. The following day Vallejo staged a rodeo, and another Indian dance in the evening. And the third day, Christmas, there were foot races between ten chosen Suisun and ten Cainamero Indians. To the winner Vallejo gave a beautiful hunting rifle, to which Commodore Jones added a ten-dollar gold coin. That day the guests departed, Vallejo escorting them to the boat landing.[6]

XVII

Mission Affairs — Father Quijas Retires
Ranchos, Rancheros, and the Pueblo

Early in 1843 Governor Micheltorena found his national treasury nearly empty and endeavored to borrow funds from the large rancheros. He sent several appeals to General Vallejo but the General responded showing his outlays to keep the northern post operating. He also offered his resignation as Comandante. The Governor answered praising Vallejo's past work and wishing him to continue in office. Also, to reimburse him for claims for military supplies furnished and salaries paid, amounting to 11,000 *pesos*, he granted the General on March 15, 1843, title to 11 square leagues -- *Nacional Rancho Suscol* covering the lower valleys of the Napas and Suisuns. In earlier years it was one of the mission ranchos. In return, General Vallejo sent the *California* south to San Pedro with a load of supplies and provisions for the Governor's army, as well as a sum of money -- both of which the Governor was in much need.[1]

In his travels around Alta California in 1843, Dr. G.M. Sandel, the "King's Orphan," a native of Finland, visited the pueblo. He was pleased with the location and what he saw there and noted that "a watermill for grinding (built by Thompson) was standing on the creek near the station (mission) but the ignorant Indian who had it in charge could not manage the machinery, simple as it was, and there was not a Yankee about who could attend to it, so the mill stood still and the people satisfied themselves with eating frijoles and meat, spending more time in one day beating corn for tortillas when they indulged in luxuries, than would have been necessary to have fixed the machinery of the mill...."[2]

In the upper valley of the Rio Napa, Jorge Conception Yount had settled on Caymus Rancho near the *rancheria* of the Caymus Indians in 1836. Nearby there was fine pasture and meadowland on one square league. Don Yount had been working around the mission and for the General since arriving in the area for trap-ping 10 years before. He was well known for his split shingles that many were now using for their roofs. Governor Micheltorena granted him the adjacent Rancho Jota on October 21, 1843, and he planned to erect a water powered grist and sawmill by the stream near his log cabin.

North from the settlement at Santa Rosa, in the far end of the valley and northeast of Don Fitch's Rancho Sotoyomi, José German Pina of Pueblo Sonoma requested land for his cattle and his family. In 1843, the Governor granted his request and he became the grantee of Rancho Tzabaco, 4 square leagues west of Rio Ruso and east of Arroyo Seco, or Dry Arroyo. Here he had built his adobe house near the west bank of Rio Ruso.

Farther west, at the old Russian settlement, Captain Stephen Smith of the Boston bark *George Henry* had arrived at Port Bodega with his steam powered sawmill -- the first steam powered mill on the Pacific Coast. He obtained the Russian improvements in the Bodega area from Captain Sutter and applied to the Mexican authorities for a land and timber grant in the area as per a previous agreement. He was installing the mill on a creek a league or so inland from Port Bodega at the edge of a large redwood forest.

In the pueblo, the presidial company consisted of from 40 to 50 men, with some at outside posts. Lieutenant José Antonio Pico was company commander and Captain Salvador Vallejo post commander. The military authority was to end this year of 1843 and the General recommended that a civil government be organized for the pueblo and also advised that his commission as director of colonization had expired.[3]

During June 1843, a meeting was held to provide support for the garrison and also to build a town hall, new jail, and cemetery. Thirty-one persons subscribed over $3,000, 155 *fanegas* of grain, 20 cattle, 1,100 feet of boards, 12,700 adobes, and labor force of 22.

At the mission, the buildings that were left were slowly showing the effects of the weather and lack of the maintenance so necessary with adobe construction. The large adobe church which Fr. Fortuny had built on the east end of the quadrangle was fast being dismantled as the valuable roof tiles and large timbers were being used for new adobe houses on the plaza. The doors and windows soon were taken, as well as usable adobe bricks, and the remaining walls were left to the mercy of the winter rains and weather.

On the 29th of March of this year 1843, Governor Micheltorena had issued his *Directo* restoring the temporal management of 12 missions to the padres -- and rules for their management and that of the neophytes. But Mission San Francisco Solano was not among these 12 favored ones as Mission San Jose was the one farthest north that was included.[4]

Fr. Quijas was appointed vice-commissary prefect on April 8, 1843, and so ended his long service at Mission San Francisco Solano. The mission was now cared for by Fr. Jesús María Vásquez del Mercado, a Zacatecan residing at Mission Santa Clara. Some visits were made by padres from the Monterey area to the three orphan missions in the north. Fr. Quijas left in April of 1844 from Monterey, returning to his old home in Mexico. He had served these most northerly missions for 11 years during the bitter secularizastion period. Seeing the prosperous mission establishments, that he and his fellow padres had so patiently developed, being dismantled, confiscated, wrecked, and abandoned, was his discouraging lot and one to try the soul of any strong man. He, personally, had the sorrowful duty of turning over each of the three northern missions to their destroyers.

For the support of the mission churches, the Bishop formerly had use of the income from the large Pious Fund of Mexico. But it was now taken by the government treasury and only donations and the *diezmos* or tithes of the Catholic members were available for support. In the past, the missions had been nearly self-supporting with their large ranchos and herds of animals, supplemented by annual payment from the central Pious Fund. Now those sources of income were ended, or nearly so, and it was a problem to convince the parishioners that they had to support the churches themselves. The Bishop appointed certain padres as collectors of the *diezmos* and their efforts often were causes of controversy. The only recourse the Church had was excommunication, a penalty seldom used.

Padre Mercado of Mission Santa Clara, who also had charge of Missions Dolores, San Rafael Arcangel and San Francisco Solano, was named collector for his district. He wrote to General Vallejo on March 18, 1843, regarding his non-payment of the *diezmos* and his position as a leader in the area. The General answered on the 19th, refused to pay and questioned the padre's right to request payment. He claimed that he kept up the church at Sonoma at his own expense but would not contribute further to the general fund of the Church -- and so the matter stood for quite a period.[5]

The pueblo was now, in 1844, under civil government and Jacob P. Leese was *alcalde* with Cayetano Juárez as second *alcalde*. And the plaza was the scene of a local fracas between two of the leading residents. Dr. Edward T. Bale, grantee of Rancho Carne Humane, and whose wife was Maria Sobranes (a niece of Salvador Vallejo), was living in the pueblo. He was accused of spreading rumors of the veracity of Don Salvador who heard about it and had him publicly flogged. Dr. Bale left the pueblo for some time but later returned with a number of American friends. He found Captain Salvador Vallejo on the plaza and shot him from behind, as well as his companion Cayetano Juárez. However, Salvador was only grazed on the neck and his companion slightly hurt on the jaw. Nearby citizens rushed in and Bale and his friends sought protection from *Alcalde* Leese. But Chief Solano, with his company of armed Indians, broke in and had Bale headed for the hanging tree. General Vallejo heard about it and rescued Dr. Bale, saying he must be tried.

A trial declared him guilty but, before any punishment was declared, Governor Micheltorena ordered that he be set free as they did not want any trouble with the British, Bale being still a British citizen. Captain Salvador Vallejo then was directed to take the doctor to the Napa Valley, which he did. On parting, Dr. Bale asked to be forgiven. It was accepted and they separated as friends.[6]

The plaza also was the scene of a fist fight between now Colonel Victor Prudon, secretary to the General, and *Alcalde* Jacob Leese. After about 30 minutes, the *alcalde* planted a blow on Prudon's chin that ended the fight. Later, Prudon offered to renew the argument with pistols but then both decided to make up and forget it. The net result was the dismissal of Jacob Leese as *alcalde* of the pueblo.[7]

Ranchos were still being granted in the old mission areas in 1844. General Vallejo applied for and received an addition to his Rancho Petaluma of 5 square leagues farther north in June, making this rancho 15 square leagues in all. The grant was in return for 2,000 *pesos* in gold loaned the government by Vallejo.

Mission San Francisco Solano with carretta and oxen. Courtesy Great Western Savings and Loan Association.

Over in the Santa Rosa area Joaquin Carrillo, son of Señora Carrillo, the mother-in-law of the General and grantee of Rancho Cabeza de Santa Rosa, applied for and received the adjacent Rancho Llano de Santa Rosa - 3 square leagues. It had been part of an original grant to Don Mark West which had been allowed to lapse. Don Carrillo built his adobe house beside the old Spanish trail from the Santa Rosa area to Port Bodega.

Over in the Port Bodega area, Captain Stephen Smith received his grant of Rancho Bodega - 8 square leagues - with its stand of timber for his steam sawmill. He also received the Rancho Blucher - 6 square leagues adjacent to and south of Rancho Bodega. The former Rancho Bodega had been claimed by Victor Prudon of Sonoma in 1841 but his title was not considered valid by Governor Micheltorena when he granted this rancho to Captain Smith on September 12, 1844.

In the area of the Petalumas, Rancho Cotati - 4 square leagues - which had been used by both Mission San Rafael Arcangel and San Francisco Solano, was granted to Juan Castaneda, a soldier of the Sonoma company. And next to

Rancho Cotati on the north, Rancho Yulupa - 3 square leagues - was granted to Miguel Alvarado, another soldier of the Sonoma garrison. Far up the Rio Ruso, north of Rancho Molino, Eng Montenegro applied for a grant of the mountain area to the east and received an 8 square league grant called Rancho Caslamayomi or Laguna de los Gentiles.

Not to be outdone by the others, Don Henry Fitch, grantee of Rancho Sotoyomi north of the Santa Rosa area, requested and received an addition of 8 square leagues to his rancho, now 11 square leagues in extent. And Don Mark West also received an addition to his 6 square league Rancho San Miguel on Arroyo Mark West, 2 leagues north of Santa Rosa Rancho area.

Back at the pueblo, a small vineyard had been started by Damaso Antonio Rodriguez, a former *alférez* in the Sonoma garrison, now an *inválido* and instructor *defensores*, half a league east of the plaza. He applied for a grant and received it for an area 1,000 *varas* square, called Lac. It was at the base of the eastern hills with a fine arroyo of water along its east side. And to the south, Jacob Leese, owner of Rancho Huichica (the former mission and *nacional* rancho of two square leagues), received an addition of 3½ square leagues from the Governor on July 6, 1844.

This last grant just about used up all the best land of the former ranchos of the Mission San Francisco Solano. The area for many leagues in all directions from the pueblo was now in the hands of private owners, with General Vallejo and his relatives in possession of most of these ranchos.

The mission still was without a resident padre and was used only on the occasional visits of padres from as far south as Mission Santa Clara. Fr. Jesús María Vásquez del Mercado of Mission Santa Clara still had the responsibility of caring for what was left of Missions Dolores, San Rafael Arcangel, and San Francisco Solano, as well as Mission Santa Clara.

He, with Fr. Muro of Mission San Jose, in 1844 attempted to collect cattle loaned out by the missions to rancheros. General Vallejo was contacted by Francisco Arce, who was acting for the padres, regarding the recovery of 6,000 sheep that belonged to the mission. The General answered on August 30, 1844 and denied that he had any sheep that belonged to the mission; that there were only 4,000 sheep and they were taken legally by him to aid the government.[8]

The work on the ranchos was done mostly by the former neophytes of the mission, often for their keep and clothing. Some ex-soldiers or their offspring were *vaqueros* but did little beside riding and caring for the range cattle. The women folk often worked for the ranchero's family as described by Manuel Torres, on a visit to the Vallejo home in Sonoma.

In 1844 I visited General Vallejo at his residence in Sonoma, (Manuel Torres tells us). I found the patio of his grand house full of servants of both sexes, but in the group the women predominated. Not accustomed to such a sight, I asked the General's wife with what so many Indians were occupied? She replied: "Each one of my children, boys and girls, has a servant who has no other duty than to care for him or her. I have two for my own personal service. Four or five grind the corn for the tortillas; for here we entertain so many guests that three could not furnish enough meal to feed them all. About six or seven are set apart for service in the kitchen. Five or six are continually occupied in washing the clothes of the children and of the rest employed in the house; and finally, nearly a dozen are charged to attend to the sewing and spinning; for you must know that, as a rule, Indian women are not much inclined to learn many things. For this reason she who is taught cooking will not hear of washing clothes, and, on the other hand, a good washwoman will regard herself insulted if she were to be compelled to sew or spin. All these servants whom we have in the house are very much attached. *No acostumbran pedirnos dinero ni tampoco tienen sueldo fijo.*

(They are not accustomed to ask us for money, nor do they have any fixed wages.) We give them all they need. When they are sick we care for them as though they belonged to the family. When their children are born, we act as godfathers and godmothers, and we take charge of the education of their children. When they want to go some great distance to see their relatives, we give them animals and guards for the journey. In a word, we treat the servants as friends rather than as servants."[9]

The only rancho granted during the next year (1845) was 4 square leagues in a long valley southwest of Rancho Cotati. It was called Roblar de la Miseria and was granted to Juan N. Padilla, Mexican captain, who was Lieutenant of *Defensores* at Yerba Buena and also resided at the Pueblo of Sonoma. Captain Padilla later moved to Southern California.

Practically all of the ranchos that the Mission San Francisco Solano had operated and claimed had now been granted and in the hands of private rancheros, and it was now the Ranchero period in the *Frontera del Norte Este* with the Pueblo de Sonoma as its busy center.

In April of 1845 the new Governor, Pío Pico, issued a *bando* (proclamation) per a resolution of the Junta suspending all granting of lands near the missions. These lands may be needed as *egidos* for new towns. He also suspended the granting of freedom papers to neophytes, and padres were not to sell any movable property. The missions were ordered to submit complete accounts of their debts and assets.[10]

On May 28, 1845, the new Department Assembly of four members passed:

"A Decree for the Renting of Some and converting of other Missions into Pueblos."

It consisted of eight articles of general instructions of which Article 2 read:

"The Missions of Carmelo, San Juan Bautista, San Juan Capistrano and San Francisco Solano shall be considered as Pueblos, which is the character they have at present; and the government after separating sufficient space for the curate's house, for churches and belongings, and courthouse, will proceed to sell the remaining premises at public auction in order to pay their respective debts; and the surplus, should there be any, shall remain for the benefit and preservations of Divine Worship....." (Article has further detail but none applies to Sonoma.)[11]

The following month on the 30th, Governor Pico appointed Andrés Pico and Juan Manso as commissioners to visit each mission and inventory the property there. The padres were advised through President Durán of their coming visits during July and August. The report of San Francisco Solano stated there was no inventory of value.[12] In October, regulations under which mission properties could be sold and dates of the sales were issued but as nothing saleable was left at Solano, no mention or date was made.

And still no padres were resident at the three northern missions in 1845. Padre José María Súarez del Real came up from his residence at Mission Santa Clara, during the year, to care for the parish duties while making his round trips to Missions San Rafel Arcangel and Dolores.

In the pueblo, the building of new houses was progressing. Salvador Vallejo was erecting a large adobe building on *Calle Huerta* on his pueblo lot opposite the northwest corner of the plaza. Elected *alcaldes* for the new term were José de la Rosa with Marcos Vega as second *alcalde*. They took over the offices in July.

General Castro, on a tour of the north in November to check on the foreign settlers, visited the pueblo. A rumor of possible war between Mexico and United States over the Texas situation had excited the authorities in California and the large number of American settlers in the northern areas were considered a menace should war break out. However, everything seemed to be quiet among the settlers in the Sonoma and New Helvetia areas.

The year 1846 brought a new padre to the northern missions, Fr. Jose Prudéncio Santillan, a young Mexican 24 years old, who had been ordained in January. He was placed in charge of Mission Dolores, as well as Missions San Rafael Arcangel and San Francisco Solano.

The old mission vineyard, 200 *varas* by 300 *varas*, east of the chapel and padres' house, was granted to José de los Santos Berreyessa on May 30th. He was the new *alcalde* of the pueblo for the year 1846.[13]

On June 6th, General Castro again visited the pueblo with Lieutenant Francisco Arce. He wanted necessary supplies for a proposed army action against Governor Pico. He received some supplies, guns and ammunition -- and also obtained 200 horses from Don Murphy at Mission San Rafael Arcangel. He dispatched these to Santa Clara via Sacramento Valley in charge of Lieutenant Arce.

Part of the padres' house that belonged to the Mission San Francisco Solano was granted on June 2, 1846, by General Castro to Victor Prudon, secretary to General Vallejo, although the grant was opposed by the padre and the *alcalde*.

Unclaimed ranchos were getting scarce early in 1846 and far out from the pueblo. The relatives of *Alcalde* Berreyessa were petitioning for ranchos far to the north and were finally granted them by Governor Pío Pico. José Ign. Berreyessa was granted his Rancho Chimiles, 4 square leagues in the area north of Rancho Suisun of Chief Solano, in May. His son, José Jesús Berreyessa was granted the large 8 square league Rancho Yucuy, in the vicinity of the large lake called Clear by the Americans, in the same year. Francisco Berreyessa, brother of the *alcalde* of the pueblo, received the grant of Rancho Rincon de Muscalon, 2 square leagues along Rio Ruso far to the north beyond the Rancho Tzabaco of José G. Pina.

PART IV

THE MISSION DOMAIN
AN AMERICAN PIONEER AREA

XVIII

Los Osos—The Bear Flaggers
The Stars and Stripes Over The Plaza

As dawn was breaking on Sunday, June 14, 1846, the little chapel of Mission San Francisco Solano on its corner opposite the plaza in the pueblo stood white and silent in the morning light. Quietly, 33 mounted men -- many dressed in deer skin and with coon skin hats, others with large slouch hats and boots and all with arms -- passed by and occupied the corner of the plaza and surrounded the *Casa Grande*, the home of General Vallejo.

On awakening, the General realized that the situation was tense and, donning his uniform, invited the leaders into the large hall. He asked what they wanted and who was their leader. Captain Ezekiel Merritt, a trapper, was the leader and explained that they had decided not to live under the Mexican government and had resolved to declare California independent; that they had no feeling against the General and his family but that it was necessary to take them prisoners. Lieutenant Colonel Salvador Vallejo and Captain Victor Prudon arrived and were also made prisoners. Jacob Leese was brought in to act as interpreter.

As time passed, the crowd of men became restless and wanted to begin looting but was restrained by one of the leaders, Dr. Robert Semple. A barrel of brandy helped quiet the men outside and ease the situation in the main hall. Articles of capitulation were suggested and agreed upon and were soon put down in writing. In the meantime, the leaders imbibed of the brandy and the crowd called for William B. Ide to take charge and report on the progress.

When the capitulation was completed by Jacob Leese and Dr. Semple, it was signed by General Vallejo, Victor Prudon and Salvador Vallejo and, for the Americans, by Ezekiel Merritt, Samuel Kelsey and William Fallon.

Capitulation Documents

No. 1. An exact copy, except that as the duplicates do not exactly agree in orthography and contractions, I have written each word correctly and in full.[1]
'Conste por la presente que, habiendo sido sor-prendido por una numerosa fuerza armada que me tomó prisionero y á los gefes y oficiales que estaban de guarnicion en esta plaza, de la que se apoderó la expresada fuerza, habiendo la encontrado absolutamente indefensa, tanto yo como los señores oficiales que suscriben comprometemos nuestra palabra de honor de que estando bajo las garantías de prisioneros de guerra no tomaremos ni á favor ni contra la repetida fuerza armada de quien hemos recibido la intimacion del momento y un escrito firmado que garantiza nuestras vidas familias é intereses y las de todo el vecindario de esta jurisdiccion mientras no hagamos oposicion. Sonoma, Junio 14 de 1846. M.G. Vallejo, Victor Prudon, Salvador Vallejo.' In English the document is as follows: 'Be it known by these presents, that, having been surprised by a numerous armed force which took me prisoner, with the chief and officers belonging to the garrison of this place that the said force took possession of, having found it absolutely defenceless, myself as well as the undersigned officers pledge our word of honor that, being under the guaranties of prisoners of war, we will not take up arms for or against the said armed force, from which we have received the present intimation, and a signed writing which guarantees our lives, families, and property, and those of all the residents of this jurisdiction, so long as we make no opposition.'

No. 2. 'We, the undersigned, members of the republican party in California, having taken Gen. M.G. Vallejo, Lieut.-col. Victor Prudon, and Capt. D. Salvidor Vallejo as prisoners pledge ourselves that in so doing, or in any other portion of our actions, we will not disturb private property, molest themselves, their families, or the citizens of the town of Zanoma or its vicinity, our object alone being to prevent their opposition in the progress of the end(s?) of the liberation'....(one or two words perhaps at the end, and the signatures, if there were any, are torn off.)

No. 3. 'We, the undersigned, having resolved to establish a government of on (upon?) republican principles, in connection with others of our fellow-citizens, and having taken up arms to support it, we have taken three Mexican officers as prisoners, Gen. M.G. Vallejo, Lieut-col. Victor Prudon, and Capt. D. Salvador Vallejo, having formed and published to the world no regular plan of government, feel it our duty to say that it is not our intention to take or

Original Bear Flag raised at Sonoma June 14, 1846. Destroyed in the San Francisco fire, April 18, 1906. Courtesy Society of California Pioneers.

injure any person who is not found in opposition to the cause, nor will we take or destroy the property of private individuals further than is necessary for our immediate support. Ezekiel Merritt, R. Semple, William Fallon, Samuel Kelsay.'[1]

On hearing the terms of the capitulation, the majority of the crowd was not satisfied and finally it was agreed to take the prisoners to New Helvetia or Fremont's camp near there. So, at 11 a.m., the General and Salvador Vallejo, Victor Prudon and Jacob Leese left Sonoma under guard of 10 California Republic men for New Helvetia. Camping for the night at Vaca's Rancho, the General was awakened by Juan Padilla, who had a strong force of Californians with him to rescue the party. But the General feared retaliation on their families at Sonoma and refused the aid.

On the afternoon of the 15th, they arrived at Fremont's camp on the American River and were turned over to the Colonel. He answered General Vallejo's question as to what they were to expect and said that he would consult his followers. They decided to execute the prisoners but Dr. Semple objected so strongly that they agreed to send them to New Helvetia to be confined by Captain Sutter. They were transferred to Fort Sutter that afternoon where Captain Sutter met them and locked them all up in a bare room together. Fremont sent his own men under command of Lieutenant Edward M. Kern to guard them.

At the pueblo, the General had been able to send out Don José de la Rosa his printer, unnoticed, to his friend Captain Montgomery of the U.S. Warship *Portsmouth* anchored at Sausalito, with the news and requesting that he do what he could to prevent violence at the pueblo. The Captain answered that he must stay neutral in any Mexican affairs but, later, sent Lieutenant John Misroon to Sonoma to see the *alcalde* and the leader of the insurgents and to impress upon them that the U.S. was interested in the protection of the people and families of the pueblo.[2] William Ide was in command at the pueblo with 25 men and seemed to have everything under control. There had been no looting or trouble with the local people and the Mexican garrison was non-existent.

On the plaza flagpole just across from the barracks and the mission, the Mexican flag had been replaced by the new California Republic flag with its red star, red bar -- CALIFORNIA REPUBLIC -- and grizzly bear on a white background. It was soon dubbed the "Bear Flag" and the entire engagement took on the name "Bear Flag Revolt." To the native Californians the Bear Flaggers were "Los Osos" (The Bears).[3] The flag was made by four men of the party, Granville Swift, Peter Storm, Henry L. Ford and William L. Todd -- two of whom were exsailmakers. The white cotton muslin was obtained at the house where they were staying and the red flannel strip from Mrs. John Sears of Sonoma. William Todd did the lettering and art work.[3]

The pueblo quieted down but the families of the prisoners were very upset as they did not have any information as to their whereabouts or treatment until later in the month. The *alcalde* and some citizens were under arrest though they were not confined. Though no padre was in residence, many were the prayers said and candles burned at the altar in the chapel of Mission San Francisco Solano during these trying times.

Commander Ide had issued a proclamation to the people explaining the reason for the revolt, plans for the new republic and giving the natives assurance their lives and property were not in danger and calling on residents to join the new government being formed. After the flag raising was completed, the men organized into a military company. Ide was elected Captain General; Henry L. Ford, 1st lieutenant; Samuel Kelsey, 2nd lieutenant; Granville P. Swift and Samuel Gibson, sergeants. Fifteen more men joined -- making the troop 40 men in all.[4]

Alcalde Berreyessa was discharged as Mexican *alcalde* and reinstalled as *alcalde* under the new government. On the 18th, the *alcalde* issued the following: "The 14th day of the present month this present commander took possession of the town of Sonoma, and up to this date there has not been the least disorder, there having been nothing taken but arms, ammunition, and horses; and for whatever else they may have required they have solicited it of individuals, under a promise of payment in full value the moment the government is properly installed in the Republic of California, which they are determined to do. José S. Berreyessa, 1st *alcalde* in Sonoma."[5]

On the 17th, Julio Carrillo was sent to New Helvetia with a letter from Señora Vallejo and, though he had a passport from U.S.N. Lieutenant Misroon, he was arrested and confined by Lieutenant Kern with the others.

Captain Montgomery sent Lieutenant Washington A. Bartlett, U.S.N. and Dr. Andrew J. Henderson to Sonoma to care for and relieve the fears of the people and families. Lieutenant Bartlett advised General Vallejo at New Helvetia that all were safe and in good health. On Tuesday, Lieutenant Misroon left Sonoma to return to Yerba Buena to report on the situation to Captain Montgomery.

On the 18th of June Captain Ide issued a new proclamation of more moderate tone with plans for the formation of the permanent government. On the day following, two men -- Fowler and Cowie -- left to obtain powder from the Fitch Rancho "Sotoyome" on the Russian River. Near Santa Rosa Rancho, they were captured by a roving band of Californians led by Juan Padillo and Ramon Carrillo and were executed.

Lieutenant Ford then sent four men who resisted an attack by a small party, and brought the powder and one captive. The action caused many families to move into Sonoma and the military company increased to about 100 men. Grigsby returned about the 21st from New Helvetia and assumed command of the rifle company.

Rumors that General Castro was planning to cross the Bay with his army were rife. Lieutenant Ford left with a small force to rescue prisoners held by Padilla and, on the 23rd, found the camp near Santa Rosa Rancho deserted. They followed the trail to Padilla's Rancho where they learned that Padilla was probably at Rancho Laguna de San Antonio. Next morning, the 24th, they charged the rancho but found only four men.

Continuing on towards San Rafael, they found Padilla's force eating breakfast at Rancho Olompali but, to their surprise, Padilla had been reinforced with men by the arrival of a division of 46 men under Joaquin de la Torre from General Castro at San Pablo. Ford's men made a charge on Padilla's men but when they saw Torre's men in addition, retired behind the trees in defense. The Californians made a charge and withdrew -- their *Alférez* Manuel Cantua dead and A. Ruiz badly wounded. Firing at a distance continued and Torre's and Padilla's men withdrew towards San Rafael. Lieutenant Ford's men took some horses from the rancho corral and returned victorious to Sonoma. And so ended the war action for the California Republic Army on the 24th day of June 1846.[6]

The prisoners were still kept at Sutter's Fort by Lieutenant Kern and were striving to obtain their release by sending word to the U.S. authorities in Yerba Buena and on the American ships, but nothing had been accomplished. Lieutenant Revere and Dr. Henderson of the *Portsmouth* had visited them and treated General Vallejo especially, who was ill as a result of the rough and poor treatment they were receiving.

About the 20th, Lieutenant Ford of the Sonoma California Republic garrison had sent a messenger to New Helvetia with the news that it was reported General Castro was crossing the Bay with the plan of attacking Sonoma. It arrived at the time two others from Marsh's Rancho near Monte Diablo came with the same information. Fremont, on hearing the

Bear Flag Monument as first dedicated June 14, 1914. Courtesy California State Library.

above, decided to act and prepared to move his troops to the pueblo. On the 23rd of June he left with approximately 90 men, arriving at Sonoma on the 25th. With more men from the pueblo, 130 in all, he proceeded on to San Rafael where Padilla and Torre were reported. But there were no Californians at the mission and Fremont and his men occupied it for a week.

The only casualties were three Californians who arrived by boat and, after landing, started to walk to San Rafael not knowing any Bear Flaggers or soldiers were near. They were the twin sons of De Haro, former *alcalde* of San Francisco, and José de los Reyes Berreyessa, father of the *alcalde* at the Sonoma pueblo, on his way to see the family at Sonoma. Without taking the men prisoners, the three were shot without warning on the *camino* by men sent by Fremont to intercept them. It caused a great deal of resentment among the native residents of the country, as it was considered a wanton killing.

A messenger was intercepted by Fremont's men on the 28th and his dispatches indicated that General Castro was ready to attack the Pueblo of Sonoma on the 29th. Fremont left San Rafael at once and, on a forced march with most of his men, arrived at the pueblo early the next morning.

The town was armed for defense and nearly opened fire on Fremont and his troops. But no attack by General Castro came about and Fremont realized the dispatches had been planted. He hurried back to San Rafael -- but too late -- Padilla and Torre had come in out of hiding in the back country and had ferried their troops across the Bay to San Pablo in the Contra Costa and were now on their way to join General Castro at Santa Clara.

While at San Rafael, Fremont visited Captain Phelps aboard the *Moscow* and, with his help and 20 of his own men, landed on July 1st below the Mexican *Castillo* of the Presidio de San Francisco. The presidio was deserted and they spiked the 10 cannon mounted at the

89

castillo and returned to San Rafael. The next day a party went over to Yerba Buena and arrested the only officer there, Captain of the Port Robert Ridley, and sent him to join the prisoners at New Helvetia.[7]

The 4th of July 1846 found Fremont and his men back at the Pueblo of Sonoma and celebrating the success of the campaign as well as the Glorious Fourth. Speeches, cannon, *fandangos* and parades filled the day. The next day a new declaration was issued by Fremont. The military force at Sonoma was reorganized: the California battalion, with about 250 men of the Bear Flaggers and Fremont's Explorers, was divided into three companies. John Grigsby, Henry L. Ford and Granville P. Swift were the captains; Fremont was acting major, and Lieutenant Archibald H. Gillespie was adjutant.

Now, Fremont was Commander of the *Frontera del Norte Este* in place of General Vallejo, who was still a prisoner confined at Fremont's mercy in New Helvetia. The Bear Flaggers had pulled his chestnuts out of the fire for him and now Major Fremont could take command and assume the glory with little danger of official disapproval. However, the command was to be of short duration. On the 6th, Fremont left with two companies for his camp on the American River, leaving Captain Grigsby and his command of 50 men, Company "C" California Battalion, at Sonoma.[8]

On Tuesday, July 4, 1846, the American flag was raised over the Custom House at the capital at Monterey as Commodore John D. Sloat, U.S.N. landed 250 men under Captain Mervine from his squadron in the harbor. The United States was at war with the Republic of Mexico and Commander Sloat was occupying California for the United States and was acting Military Governor.

The following Thursday, the Stars and Stripes were hoisted at Yerba Buena Custom House by Captain Montgomery. Lieutenant Joseph Warren Revere, U.S.N. of the *Cyane* was sent by ship's boat up to Sonoma and, on July 9th, as Lieutenant Revere stated: "Having caused the troops of the garrison (Bear Flaggers) and the inhabitants of the place to be summoned to the public square, I then read the proclamation of Commodore Sloat to them, and then hoisted the U.S. Flag upon the staff in front of the barracks, under a salute from the artillery of the garrison."

"I also caused the proclamation to be translated into Spanish and posted up in the plaza. A notice to the people of California was also sent the next day, to be forwarded to the country around, requesting the people to assemble at Sonoma on Saturday next, the 11th to hear the news confirmed of the country having been taken possession of by the United States........"
"I am happy to report that great satisfaction appeared to prevail in the community of Sonoma, of all classes, and among both foreigners and natives, as the country having been taken possession of by the United States and their flag hoisted; more particularly after the general feeling of insecurity of life and property caused by the recent events of the revolution in this part of California."[9]

Thus ended the California Republic at Sonoma -- a short though eventful life of 25 days -- June 14th to July 9th, 1846.

By the 29th of July 1846, Commodore Robert F. Stockton had assumed command of the Pacific Fleet and Military Governor of California, as Commodore Sloat was returning to the east. He sent Lieutenant Joseph Warren Revere back to Sonoma to take command of the forces at the pueblo, Company "C" under Captain Grigsby.

Lieutenant Revere was a descendant of the famous Paul Revere of the American Revolution days. It was a pleasant assignment for Lieutenant Revere with only one small expedition to the Point Reyes area of no matter. Also, an exploratory trip to Clear Lake via Napa Valley was made, returning by the Russian River area. Later, a rumor of a Walla Walla Indian invasion of the Sacramento Valley caused a trip to Sutter's Fort but the rumor was baseless. Lieutenant Misroon, in September, assumed command of the garrison from Lieutenant Revere.

On August 1st, General Vallejo and Julio Carrillo were released under orders of Captain Montgomery and returned to the pueblo. The General was very sick but soon recovered under the care of Dr. Henderson, who had been sent up by the Captain. The rest, including Salvador Vallejo, Victor Prudon, and Jacob Leese, were released a week later by Lieutenant Misroon. All signed parole papers.[10]

And so the little white chapel of San Francisco Solano quietly remained on its corner of the pueblo plaza while the two major events that changed the future of Alta California swirled around its whitewashed adobe walls.

XIX

Pueblo Activity
U.S. Military Post

The pueblo received a new *alcalde* in the fall of 1846, Manuel E. McIntosh assuming the position for a short period. John A. Nash was later elected and filled the office for the rest of the year.[1] After his arrival home, Captain Montgomery visited General Vallejo at Sonoma during early August. The General, still an officer in the Mexican Army, received promotion to Brevet Colonel in July and, later in September, was promoted to a full colonel by the Mexican government.[2] Chief Solano, who had been appalled at the recent changes, was very much disturbed and, when the General was made prisoner, disappeared and had not been heard from. It was supposed he had gone into the far northern area of the country in his grief.

The U.S. military occupation of the pueblo had become routine by fall and the residents settled down to their regular activities. The supplies required by the soldiers were drawn from the army and naval stores and food was bought from local sources with government receipts. Claims for past damages were being submitted and pueblo commerce increased two-fold.

A weekly event was the arrival of the military mail carrier by horseback from Sacramento. This service was commenced in October of 1846 with Adolph Bruheim the carrier. He left Sacramento on Tuesdays and met a Navy launch at the Sonoma embarcadero which carried the military mail to San Francisco. It was the first military mail route developed by the American forces in California. The pay was $10.00 per round trip, using government horses supplied by both the Sacramento and Sonoma units.[3]

Mission San Francisco Solano did its part for the newcomers as Fr. José Santillan made his trips up from Mission Dolores frequently to offer worship in the whitewashed chapel on the corner of the plaza. Some quarters were still habitable in the padres' house for his use.

Edwin Bryant, traveller, visited the pueblo during these stirring times as he relates in "What I Saw in California."

October 13. (1846) - This morning the United States frigate *Congress*, Commodore Stockton, and the merchant ship *Sterling*, employed to transport the volunteers under the command of Captain Fremont, (one hundred and eighty in number,) sailed for the south. The destination of these vessels was understood to be San Pedro or San Diego. While these vessels were leaving the harbor, accompanied by Mr. Jacob, I took passage for Sonoma in a cutter belonging to the sloop-of-war *Portsmouth*. Sonoma is situated on the northern side of the Bay of San Francisco, about 15 miles from the shore, and about 45 miles from the town of San Francisco. Sonoma creek is navigable for vessels of considerable burden to within four miles of the town.

Among the passengers in the boat, were Mr. Ide, who acted so conspicuous a part in what is called the "Bear Revolution," and Messrs. Nash and Grigsby, who were likewise prominent in this movement. The boat was manned by six sailors and a cockswain. We passed Yerba Buena, Bird, and several other small islands in the bay. Some of these are white, as if covered with snow, from the deposite upon them of bird-manure. Tens of thousands of wild geese, ducks, gulls, and other water-fowls were perched upon them, or sporting in the waters of the bay, making a prodigious cackling and clatter with their voices and wings. By the aid of oars and sails we reached the mouth of Sonoma creek about 9 o'clock at night, where we landed and encamped on the low marsh which borders the bay on this side. The marshes contiguous to the Bay of San Francisco are extensive, and with little trouble I believe they could be reclaimed and transformed into valuable and productive rice plantations. Having made our supper on raw salt-pork and bread generously furnished by the sailors, as soon as we landed, we spread our blankets on the damp and rank vegetation, and slept soundly until morning.

October 14. - Wind and tide being favorable, at daylight we proceeded up the serpentine creek, which winds through a flat and fertile plain, sometimes marshy, at others more elevated and dry, to the embarcadero, ten or twelve miles from the bay. We landed here between nine and ten o'clock, A.M. All the passengers, except ourselves, proceeded immediately to the town. By them we sent for a cart to transport our saddles, bridles, blankets, and other baggage, which we had brought with us. While some of the sailors were preparing breakfast, others, with their muskets, shot wild geese, with which the plain was covered. An excellent breakfast was prepared in a short time by the sailor companions, of which we partook with them. No benevolent old gentleman provides more bountifully for his servants than "Uncle Sam." These sailors from the regular rations served out to them from their ship, gave an excellent breakfast, of bread, butter, coffee, tea, fresh beef-steaks, fried salt-pork, cheese, pickles, and a variety of other delicacies, to which we had been unaccustomed for several months, and which cannot be obtained at present in this country. They all said that their rations were more than ample in quantity, and excellent in quality, and that no government was so generous in supplying its sailors as the government of the United States. They appeared to be happy, and contented with their condition and service; and animated with a patriotic pride for the honor of their country, and the flag under which they sailed. The open frankness, and honest patriotism of these single-hearted and weather-beaten tars, gave a spice and flavor to our entertainment which I shall not soon forget.

From the embarcadero we walked under the influence of the rays of an almost broiling sun, four miles to the town of Sonoma. The plain which lies between the landing and Sonoma, is timbered sparsely with evergeen oaks. The luxuriant grass is now brown and crisp. The hills surrounding this beautiful valley or plain, are gentle, sloping, highly picturesque, and covered to their tops with wild oats. Reaching Sonoma, we procured lodgings in a large and half-finished adobe house, erected by Don Salvador Vallejo, but now occupied by Mr. Griffith, an American emigrant, originally from North Carolina. Sonoma is one of the old mission establishments of California; but there is now scarcely a mission building standing, most of them having fallen into shapeless masses of mud; and a few years will prostrate the roofless walls which are now standing. The principal houses in the place are the residences of Gen. Don Mariano Guadaloupe Vallejo, his brother-in-law, Mr. J.P. Leese, an American, and his brother Don Salvador Vallejo. The *quartel*, a barn-like adobe house, faces the public square. The town presents a most dull and ruinous appearance; but the country surrounding it is exuberantly fertile, and romantically picturesque, and Sonoma, under American authority, and with an American population, will very soon become a secondary commercial point, and a delightful residence. Most of the buildings are erected around a plaza, about two hundred yards square. The only ornaments in this square are numerous skulls and dislocated skeletons of slaughtered beeves, with which hideous remains the ground is strewn. Cold and warm springs gush from the hills near the town, and supply, at all seasons, a sufficiency of water to irrigate any required extent of ground on the plain below. I noticed outside of the square several groves of peach, and other fruit-trees, and vineyards, which were planted here by the padres; but the walls and fences that once surrounded them are now fallen, or have been consumed for fuel; and they are exposed to the mercies of the immense herds of cattle which roam over and graze upon the plain.

October 15. - I do not like to trouble the reader with a frequent reference to the myriads of fleas and other vermin which infest the *rancherías* and old mission establishments in California; but if any sinning soul ever suffered the punishments of purgatory before leaving its tenement of clay, those torments were endured by myself last night. When I rose from my blankets this morning, after a sleepless night, I do not think there was an inch-square of my body that did not exhibit the inflammation consequent upon a puncture by a flea, or some other equally rabid and poisonous insect. Smallpox, erysipelas, measles, and scarlet-fever combined, could not have imparted to my skin a more inflamed and sanguineous appearance. The multitudes of these insects, however, have been generated by Indian filthiness. They do not disturb the inmates of those *casas* where cleanliness prevails.

Having letters of introduction to General Vallejo and Mr. Leese, I delivered them this morning. General Vallejo is a native Californian, and a gentleman of intelligence and taste far superior to most of his countrymen......... This evening Thomas O. Larkin, Esq., late United States Consul for California, arrived here, having left San Francisco on the same morning that we did, travelling by land.

October 17. - The last two mornings have been cloudy and cool. The rainy season, it is thought by the weather-wise in this climate, will set in earlier this year than usual. The periodical rains ordinarily commence about the middle of November. It is now a month earlier, and the meteorological phenomena portend "falling weather." The rains during the winter, in California, are not continuous, as is generally supposed. It sometimes rains during an entire day, without cessation; but most generally the weather is showery, with intervals of bright sunshine and a delightful temperature. The first rains of the year fall usually in November, and the last about the middle of May. As soon as the ground becomes moistened, the grass, and other hardy vegetation, springs up, and by the middle of December the landscape is arrayed in a robe of fresh verdure. The grasses grow through the entire winter, and most of them mature by the first of May. The season for sowing wheat commences as soon as the ground is sufficiently softened by moisture to admit of plowing, and continues until March or April.

We had made preparations this morning to visit a rancho belonging to General Vallejo, in company with the general and Mr. Larkin. This rancho contains about eleven leagues of land, bordering upon a portion of the Bay of San Francisco, twenty-five or thirty miles distant from Sonoma. Just as we were about mounting our horses, however, a courier arrived from San Francisco with dispatches from Captain Montgomery, addressed to Lieutenant Revere, the military commandant of this post, giving such intelligence in regard to the insurrection at the

Mission San Francisco Solano in the 1850's [founded July 4, 1823]. Courtesy Missions and Missionaries, Engelhardt.

south, that we determined to return to San Francisco forthwith. Procuring horses, and accompanied by Mr. Larkin, we left Sonoma about two o'clock in the afternoon, riding at the usual California speed. After leaving Sonoma plain we crossed a ridge of hills, and entered the fertile and picturesque valley of Petaluma creek, which empties into the bay. General Vallejo has an extensive rancho in this valley, upon which he has recently erected, at great expense, a very large house. Architecture, however, in this country is in its infancy. The money expended in erecting this house, which presents to the eye no tasteful architectural attractions, would in the United States have raised a palace of symmetrical proportions, and adorned it with every requisite ornament. Large herds of cattle were grazing in this valley.[4]

In November 1846, Lieutenant Colonel Fremont was assembling his command in the Monterey area in preparation for a march to Southern California where a revolt of the Californians had broken out. So the company at Sonoma, now designated Company "E" under Captain Grigsby, and with only about 30 men, moved out and joined the regiment at Monterey on the 12th. Thus the pueblo at Sonoma was without military troops for a short period -- until April of the next year.

The Governor's seat in the new territory was changing with military command changes. On January 18, 1847, Lieutenant Colonel Fremont was made Military Governor after Stockton's departure and issued his proclamation and plans; but, on March 1st, General Stephen W.

Kearny took over the position along with his military duties. He carried on with another proclamation and lasted until May 31st.

Colonel Richard B. Mason, of the 1st Dragoons, had arrived in Yerba Buena from Washington on February 12th with instructions for the General that the senior officer of the land forces was to be civil governor. Also, he reported that Fremont should return to the east and that Colonel Mason was to command in the absence of General Kearny, who was permitted to retire when things were peaceful and a temporary civil government was organized. On receiving these instructions, General Kearny assumed the seat of Governor.

May 31st, Colonel Mason became Governor, on General Kearny's retirement, and it required his full attention. Monterey was still considered the capital. The war with Mexico came to an end as far as California was concerned on January 13, 1847, when Lieutenant Colonel Fremont and Andres Pico signed the Cahuenga Treaty at Rancho Cahuenga, west of the Pueblo of Los Angeles.

At the sister town of Yerba Buena, *Alcalde* Lieutenant Washington A. Bartlett, on January 31, 1847, issued a proclamation that, hereafter, the town would be known as San Francisco.

In the Pueblo of Sonoma, new buildings were going up and the plaza was taking the shape of its planned square. Of the mission buildings, one-half of the padres' house had been granted

Catholic Church by S. Borregessa agent — Issued Fer. same day
vs } Ejectment
Victor Prudon

The Writ returned served by the Sheriff on the 18th day of January the parties appeared H. A. Green for plff. and deft. appeared in person whereupon the deft entered a motion to dismiss the suit on account of the illegality of the agency and the cause was continued until the 19th inst. the said motion being argued it was continued until the 20th inst. the parties appeared and the motion overruled whereupon an issue being formed the parties proceeded to trial on its merits The titles to the property in issue being carefully examined and the testimony connected therewith and arguments heard, it is ordered by the court in view of all the premises, that the plff recover the property in issue and that an order issue to the Sheriff putting the plff in possession of said property, and that the said plff recover of and from the said deft four hundred and twenty dollars for his damages and costs about this suit in this behalf expended, and execution issue therefor

Writ issued on [redacted] Botelho Ex. 1847

Clerk's fees	— —	$5.40
Sheriff's "	— —	6.6
Witnesses	—	1.5
		$13.5

John H. Nash J. P.

Rec'd the amount on the costs in this case March 4th 1847
John H. Nash J. P.

Court decision favoring church in the case of Catholic Church vs. Victor Prudon over Padre House Grant. Sonoma County Records.

to Victor Prudon by General Castro in 1846. The padres had objected to the grant and now, with a new government, they brought it up in the local county court January 16, 1847. The plaintiff, the Catholic Church, S. Berreyessa, Agent, against Victor Prudon was a suit of ejectment. Judge Nash agreed to a continuance until the 19th. On that date the motion was argued; the Judge denied the motion, and the hearing opened. The court found for the plaintiff, putting the sheriff in possession of the property, and assessed V. Prudon $420 damages and $13.50 court costs. The record shows the costs paid. It was taken for granted that the damages were also paid.[5] This decision was later reversed by Governor Mason.

On a lot on *Calle Cuartel*, a block south of the plaza, H.A. Green built his adobe house in 1847. *Alcalde* John Nash was his boarder. A block east of the mission chapel, on the southeast corner, a large two-story adobe house was erected for John G. Ray. Both men were members of the town council in 1847. General Mariano Vallejo, now fully recovered, was appointed sub Indian Agent of the Sonoma-Napa section in April 1847.

April found the area near the mission chapel filled with soldiers again. Company "C" of Stevenson's New York Volunteer Regiment, with Captain John Ely Brackett in command, had been assigned to the Sonoma area and occupied the barracks. The officers established their quarters and mess at the new Ray adobe, a block to the east. Their tour of duty was a pleasant one of peacetime routine in a quiet area. The soldiers' only complaint was that the poor condition of the local jail, or near lack of one, made it necessary for them to continually guard the local prisoners.

In April of 1847, General Kearney appointed Lilburn W. Boggs *alcalde* for the Sonoma pueblo to take the place of John A. Nash. Boggs had arrived some time before with his family via the overland route. His wife was a granddaughter of Daniel Boone. But Nash refused to give up the position or records and quite a controversy arose. It ended in July when Lieutenant William T. Sherman arrived and took Nash prisoner at his lodgings at the Green adobe and escorted him to Monterey. There, the Governor reprimanded him and gave him his release. On his return to the pueblo, the post and records were turned over to the new *Alcalde* Boggs.[6]

A visitor in September was Major William Rich, U.S.A. paymaster, and his clerk, William R. Hutton. They left San Francisco by boat and, after a night on the water, reached the Sonoma embarcadero at noon on the 29th. Walking on to the pueblo, they remained overnight, paid the troops and returned to the embarcadero the next day at 3; another night on the Bay via Rancho Corte Madera and back to San Francisco on October 1st.

In the pueblo, there were now over 200 citizens and 45 houses as per the new estimate for 1847. And theatrical performances were offered in a large building owned by the General. The actors were members of the garrison and others. It was probably the first theater in California and a number of different plays were programmed as was reported in the *San Jose Pioneer* of September 15, 1847.[7]

The embarcadero was the entrance to the north Bay section in this period, and schooners were frequent arrivals. Much excitement was created when the first steamer arrived on November 25, 1847. It was the *Sitka* owned by Liedesdorff of San Francisco -- a side wheeler 9' by 37' with 18" draft -- and that called for a big celebration.[8]

In the pueblo, *Alcalde* Boggs employed Jasper O'Farrell to survey the balance of the pueblo grant into town and out-lots of small square units. They were to be sold to those who had built on them at $5 per acre. The unsold balance was to be sold to the highest bidder. And that was about the end of the former lands of Mission San Francisco Solano.[9]

Captain Brackett of "C" Company received orders from H.W. Halleck, Lieutenant of Engineers, U.S.A., Secretary of State, Territory of California, on Sept. 18, 1847, to procure the records of Mission San Francisco Solano and forward them to his office in Monterey for safekeeping. He was sending similar orders to all the other northern missions.[10]

At Mission San Francisco Solano, Fr. Prudencio Santillan made his occasional visits from his residence at Mission Dolores and cared for the spiritual wants of the pueblo residents and the soldiers stationed at the barracks. Funds of the mission were low, as few paid the required tithes, even though Fr. Santillan had been appointed administrator of tithes for his district.[10a]

Early in 1848, Charles E. Pickett, a freelance newsman and traveller, shipped some fine sheep to Sonoma and received some land from General Vallejo. He was one of the few guards at Sutter's Fort when the General was confined there, and had been kind and considerate to the General. He moved to Sonoma and remained for six months, planting an orchard and berry patch. He relates a Sunday morning spent with the General:

In the spring of 1848, being then a resident of Sonoma, Cal., I had written Governor Douglas of the Hudson Bay Company at Vancouver, in Oregon, filling to send with it, a box of grape vine cuttings......

Just before dispatching them, General Vallejo

95

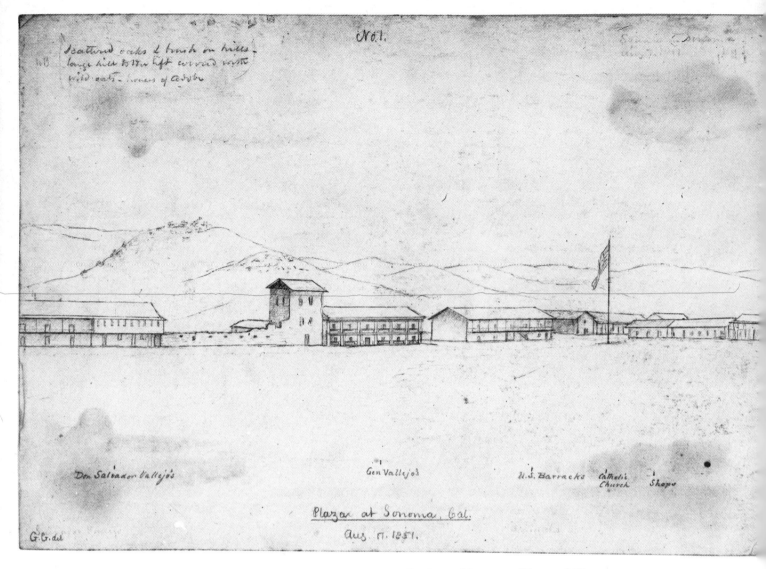

Plaza at Sonoma, August 17, 1851. Courtesy Peabody Museum, Harvard University.

and myself had been playing billiards one Sunday morning at the Beasley & Cooper Hotel at that little burg, situated opposite the old mission buildings. On coming out we heard some one preaching in the church. This being an unusual occurrence, I asked the General what it meant, suggesting that we go in for curiosity.

"Diablo," he responded, "it is that little Indian rascal, Santillan, and I would sooner call the dogs and run him out of town."

I stepped to the door and looked in, when there was the little padre preaching away to one solitary listener - old Berryessa - and he (see Note 11) so drunk as to lean against the wall for support, it not being the custom then to have seats in these old churches.[11]

Pickett was a man about town for the time but when the gold rush started, he left with the others and soon had general merchandise stores in Sacramento and at "Colloma Saw-mill."

Governor Mason announced that "the Government fully recognizes and will sustain the rights of the priests at the missions and to all mission property, against all who cannot in due course of law show a just and sound legal title." This stopped sales of immediate church areas at Mission San Francisco Solano and for the present acknowledged the church titles to them. On May 17th, 1848, Governor Mason wrote to the *alcalde* denying the right of council or any other authority to dispute title given by General Vallejo to Juan Castañeda before the U.S. Flag was raised at the pueblo.[12]

The first home built of sawn boards in Sonoma was erected by Samuel Kelsey in 1848, using no nails. And down on the waterfront at the embarcadero, the sloop *Stockton*, Briggs captain, started making scheduled tri-weekly trips from Sonoma to San Francisco.

XX

Gold—Gold—Gold— The Days of '49 Mission —A Church of New Parish

Then, near the end of January 1848, on the 24th, James A. Marshall, sawmill foreman for Captain Sutter, picked up a few small shining pebbles out of the new millrace they were building on the south fork of the American River. They proved it to be pure gold -- GOLD -- it was there by the panful.

It was another event that changed the destiny of California and all its inhabitants, especially those of the northern half. Soon the news leaked out and a confidential letter to General Vallejo from Captain Sutter confirmed it. When the country realized how rich "the diggins" were, every able-bodied man headed for the gold fields.

Alcalde Boggs of the pueblo made a trip early to the diggings to check up on the reports and returned, confirming the news and with samples of gold to show. That convinced the male population of the pueblo and quickly there were only old men, women, and children left to carry on. Many of the soldiers took off, reducing the Company by more than half.

In May, preparations were made to move Company "C" out, but people objected to being without troop protection and they remained until August. Then there were only 23 men left out of the regular 60 because of desertions to the "diggins." They moved to San Francisco and were mustered out on August 15, 1848. Company "H", Captain John B. Frisbie commanding officer, of the same N. Y. Volunteer Regiment, took their place on August 5th and remained until the 24th of the same month. Then they too were moved to San Francisco and mustered out on the 25th - and the pueblo was without a detachment of soldiers again.[1]

The "days of '49" found the Mission San Francisco Solano quietly holding its position on the corner of the busy pueblo plaza. The gold excitement had turned into a gold rush with thousands going to and coming from the "diggins," many by water direct from San Francisco

to Stockton and Sacramento.

However, many travelled overland and the pueblo had become a lively center of miners' supplies and transportation. Pack trains and teamsters' wagons were using the roads from the pueblo and its embarcadero through the Napa and Suisun Valleys to reach New Helvetia, now Sacramento City, and the "diggins" to the east and northeast. New stores were opened in the old adobes and new buildings and houses of sawn lumber were being erected around the plaza and on adjacent streets.

Many of the citizens of the pueblo had returned from the mines -- some had found wealth -- some had returned discouraged and resumed their old activities. Many newcomers, especially from the Bear Flaggers and Volunteers of Stevenson's Regiment had settled in the pueblo or had bought small ranches in the area. Some had found open land and had filed for homesteads while others had "squatted" on likely land that they hoped they could hold on to.

The San Francisco *Californian* correspondent "Franklin" reports in "Alta California" March 12, 1848:

The old mission church is near ruin and the old Mexican Padre's visits have become few and far between.

A well kept hotel and restruant on the French plan has been opened in an apartment of the old mission building and a store for general commodities in another. And now the very "Sanctum sanctorum" where the Priest formerly performed his sacendoral rites and administered Latin prayers and holy water to the poor "Digger," (Indian) is used as a dispensatory for not only the good edibles of this world, but sutch spiritual things as aquadiente and annisette, punch and porter, mint juleps and brown Havanas.[2]

Mission San Francisco Solano, early in the year, was one of three missions cared for by Fr. Paulino Romani, O.F.M., an Italian who had recently arrived in California. He took over the duties of Fr. Santillan at Mission Dolores May 30, 1849, and for Mission San Rafael Arcangel as well as at San Francisco Solano. However, it soon appeared that Fr. Romani was not capable of handling the assignment and it was not long before Fr. Santillan was sent back to Mission Dolores to assume charge again. Fr. Romani departed for other fields. Fr. J.B.A. Brouillet, recently from Washington, assisted Fr. Santillan on a few occasions during the year. He resided at the new St. Francis Church in San Francisco.

But, by the end of the year 1849, a new padre was assigned to Mission San Francisco Solano to care for the increased population of the Pueblo of Sonoma. He was a recently arrived padre from the Sandwich Islands, Rev. Stanislaus LeBret, C.SS,C.C. He established residence in the padres' house, or that part which was still usable, and held divine services in the chapel on the corner. Padre LeBret soon restored some of the mission's furnishings in the padres' quarters, making them more livable. And, with his residence, the mission began to assume its rightful position in the fast growing community.

The big adobe church, east of the padres' house, had become a ruin with its roof and walls partly torn down and used in other pueblo constructions. The walls left were gradually melting down as the rains returned the adobe bricks to their original soil. The other buildings of the quadrangle had long since suffered the same fate and the quadrangle area was littered with refuse dumped there, as in an empty lot, by the neighbors.

On May 3, 1849, Company "C" of the 1st U.S. Dragoons, Captain Andrew J. Smith commanding, arrived and was stationed in the pueblo. The Ray adobe on Spain Street, east of the mission, was again used for quarters and mess by the officers.

During the following month, the headquarters of the Pacific Division of the U.S. Army was moved to Sonoma by its commander, Brigadier General Persifer F. Smith. He and his staff occupied the Jacob Leese adobe house on the west side of the plaza. Colonel Joseph Hooker was a member of the staff and later lived in an adobe house on pueblo lot number 50 -- on the next corner to the south.[3] This lot was sold by the *alcalde* to Samuel Kelsey in November of 1849 for the price of $9.25 and was 109 *varas* square, more or less.[4]

The large adobe built by Salvador Vallejo opposite the northwest corner of the plaza was now used as a hotel, being operated by Isaac N. Randolph and George Pearce. Across from the padres' house at the mission, the adobe house owned by Antonio Ortega on lot number 35 was sold and deeded to James Cooper and Thomas Spriggs. The lot was 50 *varas* on Spain Street and 40 *varas* deep. The new owners had established a fine new hotel and saloon in the building -- The Sonoma House -- in 1849.[5]

James Cooper had previously been a partner in the Beasley and Cooper Hotel and bar, Sonoma's first hotel opened a few years earlier in the corner adobe Casa del Billar.[6]

On the corner, in the old *El Biliar* adobe, Lilburn William Boggs opened the new U.S. Post Office, established on November 8, 1849. East of the mission on *Calle* Vallejo, now called Spain Street, Lewis Adler had opened a store; and beyond it, on the northwest corner, was another store operated by A.C. McDonald. Earlier, a store was operated on the west side of the plaza by Captain John Frisbie, in connection with General Vallejo, at the Jacob Leese adobe which had been purchased from Leese. When General Smith arrived, they leased the adobe to him to be used for the Army headquarters.

Down on the Arroyo Sonoma at the old mission embarcadero, new wharves were caring for the cargoes that were coming and going to and from the valley. Lewis Adler, formerly employed by San Francisco merchant William H. Davis, had his warehouse there. He bought and sold cargoes and gold dust, and was a general shipping agent in addition to owning his Spain Street store.

In September, the General had left for Monterey as he was selected as a delegate to the convention to draft the constitution for the new State of California. The other Sonoma delegates were *Alcalde* Boggs and Joel P. Walker.

Subsequently, in the general election for State offices in November, the General was elected first State Senator for the Sonoma area. He was also concerned with his large ranchos at this time, especially the Rancho Petaluma where the headquarters adobe on the west side of the hills was the center of activity. Many settlers were coming into the northern area and much land was being sold to them. Squatter trouble was beginning but, as yet, had not become too serious.

The year 1850 was a turning point for the Pueblo of Sonoma. The new County of Sonoma was incorporated on February 18th and the new City of Sonoma, also incorporated on April 4th, was made the Seat of Justice or County Seat. John Cameron was the first mayor of the new city. The large adobe on the south side of the plaza, on the east corner of Petaluma and *Calle*, or now called Napa Street and Broadway owned by Judge Green -- was the County Courthouse. The county bought the adobe building of two stories with wide verandas for

$5,000 on long term notes.

General Vallejo and his family were still living in the *Casa Grande* on Spain Street but he had recently purchased a section of Rancho Agua Caliente next to the pueblo north boundary. A fine spring of cold water came out of the base of the mountain, as well as some warm springs. It was beside his vineyard and other property in that area. Here, on the old Indian *rancheria* ground "Chiucuyom," he was building his new home, a victorian type house of the period with a storehouse nearby that he had ordered brought "around the Horn" in pieces -- to be put together with pins and fitted joints. He named the new home "Lachryma Montis," Latin for the many springs weeping from the mountain.

In the new city, Salvador Vallejo built a large adobe on Spain Street adjoining his old house built in 1836. It was for his new wife, María de la Luz Carrillo.

Out on East Napa Street, in a log cabin, the first Protestant church north of San Francisco was organized in February 1850. Isaac Owen was the first presiding elder of the new Methodist congregation and led the services.

September 9, 1850, was a big date in the new State as it was on that day that California became the thirty-first state of the United States and a celebration was in order when the news arrived in Sonoma.

In the spring, a party of men passed through Sonoma returning to San Francisco from their exploration trip to find Humboldt Bay. They had left the Trinity Mines the previous November, eight strong, and after undergoing untold hardships in the rugged Trinity and Coast Range mountains, had found the elusive bay. On returning, they had lost their leader, Gregg; had divided, and the men were in pretty poor shape. L.K. Wood, one of the party, had been badly mauled by two grizzly bears. He had been brought out and cared for by Mrs. Mark West on her rancho on Mark West Creek. After six weeks, though still on crutches, he stopped in Sonoma April 2nd.

Opposite the mission padres' house, the tavern, or Sonoma House, was being enlarged with a wing to care for the increased trade it was receiving. It was now 95' long, 35' deep, with two stories, a front porch and rear balcony. It had the reputation for being the best stopping place north of the Bay.

On December 6, 1850, Bishop Joseph Sadoc Alemany arrived in California in charge of the entire state for the Church, and he soon began to build up the badly neglected mission units. Mission San Francisco Solano was made a full parish church and, as such, received new fittings, repairs and a full set of seats were installed. Fr. LeBret was in residence and was holding regular services for the parish.

So, from a strictly Indian mission viewpoint, San Francisco Solano's eventful period came to the end after 27 years. The mission Indian neophytes were gone except a few working for the rancheros and as domestics in the town. The parishioners, who recently were nearly all Californianos, now included many Yankees and soldiers, new settlers and townspeople. And so ended another period in the story of Mission San Francisco Solano.

Sonoma Plaza, as shown in an old engraving. Courtesy Robert Lynch.

Early photo of northeast corner of Sonoma Plaza. Courtesy California Department of Parks and Recreation.

PART V

THE MISSION DOMAIN

TOWNS — TOWNSHIPS — RANCHES

XXI

Rival Towns Spring Up
Mission Land Grant Approved

The old Pueblo of Sonoma had changed into a bustling center of activity by the year 1851. Schooners brought their cargoes to the embarcadero and took the valley produce to the big city, San Francisco. Wagon trains left for the "diggins" and north and east to the ranches. The stores supplied the wants of a large area and mail was distributed both east and west. The county seat created a lot of activity and the county officials and employees added to the town's population. The Army headquarters gave the town a lot of prestige and many officers, as well as soldiers, were on duty. In July, Companies "A" and "E" arrived on station at Sonoma, commanding officer Brevet Major Phillip H. Kearny, Jr. Indian troubles caused the troops to leave occasionally and, in 1851, they were sent to Oregon to put down an uprising of the Indians there -- but they returned in December.[1]

In August of 1851, Redick McKee, the new Indian commissioner for the northern section of California, arrived in Sonoma to prepare for his first trip to the northwest and Humboldt Bay area. The Interior Department in Washington had taken over jurisdiction of Indian affairs from the War Department in 1849 and three commissioners had been assigned to California. McKee took over from General Vallejo who had been handling the Indians north of the Bay for the Army. With a unit of 36 U.S. Dragoons, under Major W.W. Wessels from Benicia, he left for the north on August 11, 1851. George Gibbs was along as interpreter. A unit of California militia accompanied them as far as the Clear Lake area, bringing 300 head of cattle for use of the Indians. The trip lasted four months, during which reservations were laid out and treaties made with the tribes up to the Oregon border. Later, these treaties were approved and signed by President Millard Fillmore but were rejected by the Senate, due to pressure from anti-Indian sentiment of the

California Legislature and senators.[1]

But October found the female population of Sonoma quite sad as General Smith moved the Army headquarters, with all the attractive staff officers, to the new Army arsenal at Benicia on Carquinez Strait. And, with the companies on their Oregon expedition, the town was sort of empty of gaiety. But the year-end holidays were gay as the troops returned in December, though only for a short stay as they left again in January -- not to return. It was the end of the military occupation; however, quite a few officers and men returned later and became citizens, marrying many of the local girls.[2]

Mission San Francisco Solano, at the corner of the plaza, was holding its own with its new seats and improvements and, on June 20, 1851, received a new padre, Rev. Leo Chemin -- replacing Rev. LeBret who had returned to Mission Dolores. Earlier in the year, Padre John Mary A. Delmas from the new Saint Francis Church in San Francisco held services and baptized children at the mission chapel. Rev. Antoine Langlois did the same. Don José de la Rosa, the local printer, was church clerk during this period. Bishop Joseph Alemany visited on his inspection tour and baptized while in Sonoma.

With the officers and soldiers leaving in January of 1852, Sonoma reverted to a typical country county seat and business center of the area again. A new stage line, Peter Peterson proprietor, ran weekly on Saturdays, from Sonoma to Bodega via the Petaluma Valley. A steamer, the *Georgiana*, Captain Hoenshield, sailed three times weekly between the embarcadero and San Francisco.

The Sonoma Bulletin, a weekly newspaper, started publication on June 12, 1852. A.J. Cox, ex-Stevenson Regiment, was the owner and editor. The office was opposite the southeast corner of the plaza.

And a Methodist Church of frame construction had been built out on Napa Street by the congregation established in 1850. Rev. E.B. Lockley was now the pastor. This made two churches for the townsfolk to worship in. M. Nathanson purchased the surplus lumber from the builders of the new Methodist Church and used it to build a store on the lot which he had purchased on Spain Street. It was the empty space between the *Casa Grande* and the barracks.[3]

Over the hills to the west, on the wide slough Arroyo Petaluma that led north from the Bay past the Petaluma Rancho, a landing had been established by A. M. Bradley. It was called Lakeville, as it was just beyond the large Lake Tolay and its old Indian *rancheria*. Grain and produce from the lower valley of the Petalumas began to be shipped from there, saving the longer haul to the old Sonoma embarcadero. For some time a few game hunters had been living on lands of Rancho Arroyo de San Antonio, granted in 1840 to Antonio Ortega of Sonoma, alongside Arroyo Petaluma at the old Indian crossing and head of tidewater, Chocuali. They shipped their game to the San Francisco market. In January of 1852, a Mr. Keller obtained a tract of land and the town called Petaluma was surveyed by Mr. Brewster. A warehouse and wharf were soon built on the deeper water for the schooners to load their cargoes from the Petaluma Valley, the Santa Rosa area, and nearby Bodega. The first steamer arrived in November.[4]

To the east, in the Valley of the Napas, the town of Napa had been laid out on the northeast part of Rancho Entre Napa -- the land granted in 1836 to Nicolas Higuera. The courthouse, a two-story frame building, had been built in 1850 as it was now the county seat of Napa County, one of the original 27 counties created in 1850. The Napa River had been used by some smaller schooners and now was being deepened for better water transportation to the Bay area.

In the next Valley of the Suisuns, east of the old Rancho St. Eulalia of the early mission days, Captain Josiah Wing had been using an island at the head of the Suisun Slough for landing cargoes. In 1852, a warehouse with wharf was built and products of that area began to move through that embarcadero to the San Francisco market and Bay area. A townsite was planned at this point also -- to be laid out two years hence -- and called Suisun.[5]

Down at the southern end of Solano County, also one of the original 27 California counties and named after Chief Solano, the town of Benicia was the county seat. The location of Benicia, originally in 1847 called Francisca -- both names of General Vallejo's wife -- was on Car-

quinez Strait. It was the location of the U.S. Army arsenal, established in 1852, and now the headquarters of the Pacific Division of the U.S. Army, formerly at Sonoma. The General had donated the land for the town. The post office, established November 8, 1849 with Charles W. Hayden, postmaster, received the mail for the north area by boat from San Francisco weekly. From Benicia, the mail route by horseback now extended west to Sonoma, Petaluma, Santa Rosa and San Rafael.

Another town, at the west end of the Carquinez Strait and across the mouth of the Napa River from an island called Mare Island, was started and named Vallejo. It was proposed as a new state capital and the State Legislature moved up from San Jose on January 5, 1852. However, accommodations were not ample so the legislature moved up to Sacramento on January 12th. They were flooded out of Sacramento and moved back to Vallejo for the January 3, 1853 session. But they stayed only a few days and moved over to nearby Benicia February 4, 1853 for a stay of 14 months before returning again to Sacramento.

In this same year of 1852, Padre Leo Chemin still cared for Mission San Francisco Solano, signing himself *Pastor en liteo Sonoma* (in residence).

In the area around the old Carrillo adobe on Rancho Cabeza de Santa Rosa, a lot of activity had developed by 1853. Across the arroyo to the northwest, where the trails of *caminos* from the Russian River and the north met the east-west trail from Bodega and the Coast, a town, "Franklin Town," had been laid out by J. W. Ball. A few buildings had been erected and the pack trains were busy moving supplies and produce in and out. In 1853, a townsite a short two miles to the west on land of the same rancho was laid out by a rough survey. The post office established at the Carrillo adobe by Alonzo Meacham in 1852, called Santa Rosa, was transferred to the new townsite which made a slow beginning. The lots sold for $25 each. However, it soon outgrew the Franklin Town, whose merchants eventually moved to the new town of Santa Rosa, buildings and all. Mail arrived weekly to and from Benicia via Napa, Sonoma, to Santa Rosa, Petaluma, and on to San Rafael and Sausalito.[6]

Bishop Alemany was declared Archbishop of the new Archdiocese of San Francisco, which included all churches of the San Jose area and north. A new Bishop, Rt. Rev. Thaddeus Amat, C.M. was appointed to the Monterey diocese, which included everything from Mission San Juan Bautista on south.

Archbishop Alemany, still legally custodian of all the missions, began taking testimony for

View looking west on Spain Street from Mission Corner in the late 1860's.

Looking south on First Street East from Mission Corner. Both photos courtesy Sonoma State Historic Park.

his presentation of a petition to the United States Land Commission which was passing on the Mexican titles to the ranchos. He had lawyers working on the documents for each mission and surveyors mapping the areas to be requested. Mission San Francisco Solano, now the parish church, was to be included with the padres' house, the area of the ruined buildings around the quadrangle, and also the mission vineyard to the east.

In December of 1853, Sheriff Brockman ordered the adobe house built by Salvador Vallejo on the southwest corner of West First Street (old *Calle Huerta*) and Spain Street sold at auction to satisfy a judgment of $2,683.36 against George Pearce and Isaac N. Randolph, the owners. On the 31st, the property was bought by the Cumberland Presbytery for use as a college.

At the same time, the *Sonoma Bulletin* published a notice of an auction for a large lot of personal belongings of Salvador Vallejo.[7]

Fr. Leo Chemin, Pastor *en liteo* Sonoma, 1853, continued his duties at the mission. Though the parish was large in extent, the population of *gente de razón* (non-Indians) was small. The Archbishop inspected at Sonoma in August.

In 1854, the grand jury meeting in the courthouse on the plaza was very much dissatisfied with their building, condemning it as unfit for a cattle shed. It was partly roofless and badly run down. A stage line was now running from Sonoma to the new settlement of Petaluma, operated by Robertson and Parsons.

General Vallejo moved out of the *Casa Grande* to his new palatial home, "Lachryma

Montis," next to the eastern hills just north of the town, where he was laying out his extensive gardens and vineyards. His old building, the *Casa Grande* on the plaza, was leased to Dr. John L. Vermehr, the Episcopalian Minister who had come to Sonoma the year before and started a girls' school. He called his seminary St. Mary's Hall and had quite a large attendance from the northern area.

And the *Sonoma Bulletin*, A. J. Cox, editor, kept the town informed of the local news each week -- along with reports from the national scene as they came to the San Francisco press.

Padre Chemin's hopes for the mission's future were revived when G. Black, a civil engineer employed by Archbishop Alemany, arrived and made a survey of the mission area including the mission chapel, padres' house, and the quadrangle surrounded with the ruins that were left from the adobe church, *monjerio*, shops, storerooms and adobe walls -- 0.57 acres in extent. The mission vineyard, 953 feet east fronting on Spain Street, that had been granted to *Alcalde* Berryessa in 1846, was also surveyed -- 2.03 acres -- and included in the mission lands that were claimed by the Archbishop in his petition to the U.S. Land Commission. The adobe wall around the vineyard had melted down when the protecting topping tiles were taken away. The rock wall section was still partly intact.

Fr. Leo Chemin was holding services until the middle of the year 1854 when he left for other duties. No padre replaced him but the Archbishop baptized the needy in September and Padre Joanne Ingoldsby of Mission Dolores came up later in the year and cared for the services.

In September 1854, on the 6th, an election was held throughout the county to choose a new county seat. Sonoma lost out as the newcomers around Santa Rosa had put on a strong campaign and barbecue and won the election -- 716 votes against Sonoma's 563. On the 18th, the Supervisors met and declared Santa Rosa the new county seat. However, Sonoma did not give up the county records and supplies, so a group from Santa Rosa slipped into Sonoma on Friday, September 22nd, with a wagon and team, loaded the records and took them to Santa Rosa where they still are to be found.[6]

This was the third blow to the pueblo and its hopes of continuing to be the principal town of the northern area. The Petaluma Valley now had the two fast growing towns of Petaluma and Santa Rosa with increasing river traffic from San Francisco to the center of Petaluma. To the east, just over the hills, the town of Napa was a fast growing center of that valley, with boats running up and down Napa Slough to the center of town, giving the shippers of Napa Valley direct service to San Francisco Bay markets. And farther east, the towns of Benicia and Vallejo were on deep water of Carquinez Strait. The Army headquarters and troops had moved to Benicia and left an empty space in the social and business activity of Sonoma and now the county officials and employees moved out to Santa Rosa.

The *Sonoma Bulletin* gave up the ghost with its last issue on September 9, 1855. Editor Cox could not carry on financially as the local support was at a low ebb. However, over in the town of Petaluma, a new weekly, *The Sonoma County Journal*, had started on August 18th and some copies found their way to Sonoma each week. Cox published the "obituary" of the *Bulletin* in the *Journal*.[8]

And the town of Sonoma settled down to caring for the people and business of their own valley -- and remained so for many years -- more pueblo and early Californian than its surrounding "modern towns."

An orphanage, St. Vincent's (a gift of Timothy Murphy) had been established by the Catholic Church over in Marin county north of San Rafael Arcangel Mission and padres assigned to it were given the additional duty of conducting the services in the surrounding area. Padre Louis A. Anges was in charge. In February of 1855, Archbishop Alemany visited Mission San Francisco Solano and baptized the young. The next month Fr. Louis A. Anges of St. Vincent's Orphanage began his many trips to Sonoma and his duties at Mission San Francisco Solano. The Archbishop repeated his visit in September. Fr. Robertus A. N. Maurice, on a visit in November, administered baptisms and returned early in 1856 for the same service. Padre Anges also continued his services during 1856 at the Mission Solano chapel for the families of the valley and what few Indians of the old mission neophyte colony were still in the vicinity.

At the end of the year, the good news arrived that the U.S. Land Commission had made a favorable decision in favor of Archbishop Alemany in his Land Case No. 609: "Mission Church Edifices, Cemeteries, and Priests' Houses, with the Curtilages and Appurtenances at the Several Missions and certain gardens and vineyards at or near the same." This included the area around Mission San Francisco Solano quadrangle as well as the large vineyard to the east. In 1856, the appeal by the U.S. Attorney was dismissed and orders were issued for the U.S. Surveyor General to survey the property and prepare a plat, to enable the Archbishop to apply for a patent to the areas requested.

XXII

Colonel Haraszthy— Commercial Vintage
President Lincoln— Mission Land Grant

Mission San Francisco Solano in 1857 was still filling its obligations to the parishioners even though the building was not being well maintained and the padres' house was in worse condition. Yet, Padre Louis Anges did what he could under the trying circumstances as the entire town was feeling the letdown in its prosperity. In November, the padre had the help of his assistant, Padre James J. Largan. They also had the new church in Petaluma, St. Vincent de Paul, on their circuit now.

Count De Mokesa Agoston Haraszthy, a Hungarian nobleman who had been a vineyardist in his native country, visited Sonoma as a guest of General Vallejo during 1856. He was in business in San Francisco but was interested in obtaining land for his proposed vineyard and winery project. He had planted, in 1852, a vineyard in the Crystal Spring Valley region south of San Francisco but the climate was not favorable and the vineyard had been abandoned. The successful growing of excellent grapes in the Sonoma area convinced him that here was the location he desired and, in 1857, he purchased a large acreage east of the town, including part of Rancho Lac where an Indian had first commenced with a wide variety of wine grapes. His son Arpad, who had arrived in California with his father in 1849, had been sent to school in the east and was returning to help with the vineyard and winery next year. In a shady glen on a branch of Arroyo Seco, two miles east of the plaza, Colonel Haraszthy started building his winery and cellars. The cellars were being dug into the limestone rock walls where temperatures could be controlled for the fine wines he planned to produce. The name "Buena Vista" was given to his new estate. The vineyard at Buna Vista was enlarged with the planting of over 85,000 grape vines. Many were of foreign varieties, besides the older mission types that had been used in California up to this time. It was hoped that similar wines to

those produced in sections of Europe could be produced in the Sonoma Valley where soil and climate were similar to some of the European wine growing areas.

The barracks was used by General Vallejo for a winery now, as no soldiers were on duty in Sonoma. The heavy adobe walls kept the temperature down and provided ample space for the large casks and barrels in the storage rooms.

In 1858, Padre Anges was still the pastor responsible for San Francisco Solano and its parishioners, as he had been for the last three years. Fr. James Largan, his assistant at St. Vincent's Orphanage, also administered some baptisms.

On January 15, 1859, an auction sale was held in Sonoma by the receivers for the estate in the case of Maria Bruner vs. Christian Bruner. The parcel of property to which they claimed title was "the Eastern moiety or half of town or city Lot No. 24, being part of the Roman Catholic Church lot and premises....." Archbishop Joseph S. Alemany was the high bidder and received the deed executed by the receivers, Harold L. Kamp and Israel Brockman on January 30, 1858.[1]

The adobe chapel had a new roof of modern split shingles now, replacing the original construction which was badly in need of repair. A cupola or belfry was added to the front peak to mount one of the church bells and a small cornice rose above its roof. A burnt brick facing over the *fachada* (outside front wall) was part of the chapel "modernization."

U.S. Deputy Surveyor, C. C. Tracy, had completed his survey of the mission quadrangle area and the mission vineyard. In August of 1859 they were forwarded to the U.S. Land Office in San Francisco. The quadrangle area was 2.6 acres and the vineyard 12.14 acres. On October 11, 1859, the U.S. Surveyor's Office in San Francisco issued its confirmation of the Mission San Francisco Solano land grant to

Now Know Ye

That the United States of America in ———————— in consideration of the premises and pursuant to the provisions of the act of Congress aforesaid of 3rd March 1851 Have Given and Granted and by these presents do Give and Grant unto the said Joseph S Alemany Bishop of Monterey and to his successors in trust for the religious purposes and uses to which the same have been respectively appropriated the tracts of land embraced and described in the foregoing Survey but with the stipulation that in Virtue of the 15th Section of the said act the confirmation of this said claim and this patent shall not affect the interests of Third persons: To have and To Hold the said tracts of land with the appurtenances and with the stipulation aforesaid unto the said Joseph S Alemany Bishop of Monterey and to his successors in trust for the uses and purposes aforsaid

In testimony whereof I Abraham Lincoln President of the United States have Caused These letters to be made patent and the Seal of the General Land Office to be hereunto affixed Given under my hand at the City of Washington this thirty first day of May in the year of our Lord One Thousand eight hundred and sixty two and of the Independence of the United States the eighty sixth

By the President Abraham Lincoln

By W.O. Stoddard

N Granger Recorder of the General Land Office

Recorded Vol. 3 Pages 362 to 367 inclusive

Recorded at request of J. S Alemany Sept 29th A.D. 1880 at 11 oclock A. M.

Ben. S. Wood. County Recorder.

Last page of a land gra giving Bishop Joseph Alemany title to land [. surveyor's map, page 107] " the religious purposes and u. to which the same have be respectively appropriated Signed for President Linco May 31, 1862, by W. Stoddard of the General La Office. Sonoma Coun Records.

Archbishop Alemany and sent the data on to their head office in Washington. The Archbishop then applied for the patent on the mission property, as surveyed, to be issued by the U.S. Government.[2]

In the summer of 1859, the padre of the new Napa church assumed the duties at San Francisco Solano Mission. On August 22nd, Padre Peter Deyaert of St. John the Baptist Church in Napa administered his first baptism at the mission, the first of many services that he was to perform during the next decade.

In 1859 a reporter for the *San Francisco Bulletin* described the condition of the mission

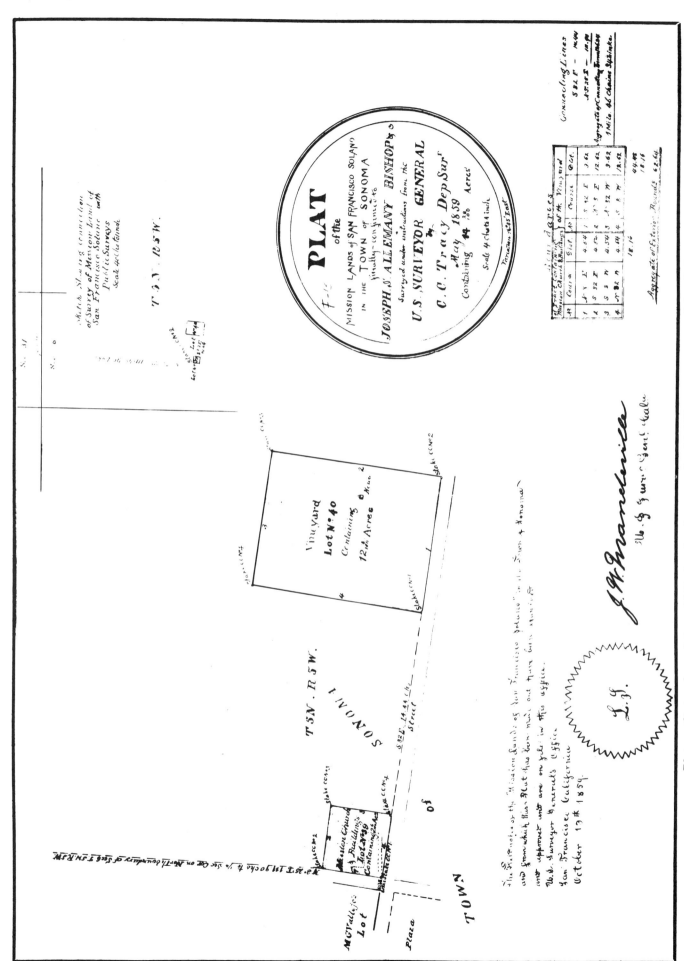

Plat outlining boundries of Mission lands, a total of 14.20 acres, surveyed by C.C. Tracy, May, 1859. Sonoma County Records.

in their November 5th edition:

This square is now mainly in ruin, and is said to have been the scene of contest between Gen. Vallejo and its original occupants, at the time of his entrance into the valley. This square is about 225 feet front, on the street forming the line of the north side of the plaza, on the opposite side of the street, and east of the plaza - and running back 210 feet. The southwest corner is now occupied with a building used as the present Catholic church, a structure measuring about 20 feet wide, inside the walls, and running back between 80 and 100 feet, and is 18 feet high. It has but little finish to it, such as people of the present age would admire - the naked joist above, and through them - the roof above forming the ceiling. A few plain wooden benches form the pews, and the house is lighted by some three small, square windows. Extending eastward from this, is a range of one-story adobes, to the Cathedral, which occupies the southeast corner of the square, fronting on the same street. This was unquestionably the most prominent feature of the ancient town. It exists now only in ruined fragments. The walls were nearly four feet thick. It was about 30 feet wide clear of the walls inside, about 150 feet long, and over 30 feet high - a regular fortress in itself. The front wall is entirely demolished, and so are the side walls for some distance - the east one for some 40 feet. The entire walls are fast crumbling, in places peeling off, and others the whole thickness has given way, and the debris lying at the base. In this way a number of points in the walls are left standing at their original height, while between them are immense gaps extending down midway, giving it a saw-tooth appearance."[3]

The mission records at the end of 1859 showed a total since founding in 1823 of -

    1,906 baptisms
      375 marriages
      896 burials (to 1840 included)

In 1860 the chapel was refurnished inside by Archbishop Alemany. New seats, cushions, and carpets were installed. The lights were changed over to the new gas illumination which was now available. An orchestra was organized and supplied with fine musical instruments. Padre Peter Deyaert of Napa was now able to take better care of his increasing flock and offer a more modern church atmosphere. The usual services were held, often every two weeks, and the padre also cared for the baptisms and weddings of the parish. The burials in the *campo santo* or cemetery on Napa Road went on as usual.

Over on the plaza, the Cumberland Presbyterian Church, which had bought the Salvador Vallejo adobe opposite the northwest corner and opened its Cumberland College in 1858, now had a large student body from the leading families of the valley and northern California. There were both boy and girl students, some boarders and some day pupils. Presbyterian Church service was held on Sundays.

Travel to and from San Francisco, which often had been slow and infrequent from the embarcadero, was now improved with an additional route. A steamer, owned by Charles Minturn, in 1860 began regular daily trips from San Francisco to Lakeville Landing. Stages connected to Petaluma and another stage company began service to and from Lakeville Landing and Sonoma. This gave the residents the most convenient and fastest service between the old pueblo and San Francisco.[4] A Lakeville Post Office was established January 31, 1859.

In the Valley of the Sonomans, as well as in the Valleys of the Petalumas and Napas, most rancheros had obtained the early land grants to the mission lands while General Vallejo was *Comisionado* of the mission and Director of Colonization of the *Frontera del Norte Este*. Now in the last few years they had been busy applying to the U.S. Land Commission for confirmation of their titles. Many had sold their lands or parts of them. Some heirs claimed others. They had to take their cases through the courts as well and the Yankee lawyers made a killing. Many rancheros spent their all and borrowed; and some lost their land to pay the heavy expenses, fees and lawyers' high charges.

A final patent was issued which usually cleared the titles -- but after much delay. And, in many cases, the squatters had come in and, taking a chance that the title would not be granted and the rancho be declared public land, squatted the best land and dared the owners to evict them.

One example was the Rancho Petaluma. The title was finally granted to General Vallejo, or subsequent purchasers of parts, and squatters removed or compromised. But on the Rancho Suscol, over in the Benicia-Vallejo area, the U.S. Supreme Court finally disapproved the grant and declared it public lands and the squatters who had taken over filed for their respective homesteads, though the government allowed the cities their areas.[5]

Mission San Francisco Solano was securely in the hands of the Catholic Church now, or at least what was left of the original mission lands and buildings. Archbishop Alemany received the United States Patent, dated May 31, 1862 - issued by President Abraham Lincoln and signed for him by his secretary, W. O. Stoddard.

It granted to him the mission church and padres' house area -- 2.06 acres, and the mission vineyard out Spain Street to the east -- 12.14 acres, with a clear title. Both areas were as surveyed by G. Black in 1854 and the U.S. Surveyor, C. C. Tracy in May 1859.[6]

XXIII

Doña Benicia Vallejo, Daughters, and the General Modernize Mission Chapel

Colonel Agoston Haraszthy returned from his collecting trip to Europe where he had been sent by the State of California to make a study of the grape growing and wine industry of Europe. He brought back many cuttings of European varieties of grapes as well as other fruits. Most of these were planted in his experimental vineyard at Buena Vista.

In the summer of 1863, on June 1st, the grand double wedding of the pueblo took place at Lachryma Montis. Here, Padre L. Deyaert who cared for Mission San Francisco Solano, united two young ladies of the Vallejo family, Natalia and Julio, to two young sons of the Haraszthy clan, Arpad and Attila, in wedlock. There was a large list of prominent guests and the merry-making lasted long into the night with the General and his wife being the genial host and hostess.

The town or pueblo of Sonoma slept through the decade of the 60's with little change. The valley was taking on an agricultural status with the grape vine becoming more important as the new settlers found that the valley climate and soil favored the vine. In 1866, a few days before Christmas, a Mexican by the name of Tiburcio Vásquez was arrested in Petaluma for burglarizing a store and sent to San Quentin for four years by the judge. Later, he was to become California's famous bandit.

The *Casa Grande* on Spain Street, General Vallejo's original home in Sonoma, burned on April 13, 1867. It was completely gutted, as well as the tower, and the adobe walls were the only thing that saved the adjoining building, a store between it and the barracks. The local bucket brigade also helped. On October 21, 1868, the heavy earthquake that shook Northern California caused some damage to the mission, though no major buildings were destroyed.

During the decade, Fr. L. Deyaert of St. John the Baptist Church in Napa was visiting pastor at the mission. The record shows that at the end of 1869 there had been:

Baptisms during the decade - 79

Marriages during the decade - no complete record available.

Burials during the decade - no complete record available.

Over in Petaluma Valley a new railroad, the San Francisco and North Pacific Railroad, was opening up its initial section. On October 31, 1870, the first train ran from Petaluma to Santa Rosa amid a great celebration. By the end of the year, the line was extended south to the boat landing at Donahue, just below the Lakeville Landing on Petaluma Creek. The steamers *Sacramento* and *Wilson G. Hunt* ran from the landing to San Francisco. The new service began January 1, 1871. An up-to-date two-story hotel, "The Sonoma," had been built at the landing as well as warehouses, shops, and roundhouses. It was owned by the Donahue interests of the Union Iron Works of San Francisco. Now the people of Sonoma had faster service with their stages meeting the trains at Lakeville and Donahue Landing and on to San Francisco by fast steamer; or, if they desired, by train to Petaluma or Santa Rosa.

Services at the mission were cared for in the year of 1871 and the following year by Rev. John P. Harrington, Pastor of St. Vincent de Paul Church in Petaluma. He also served at the orphanage but was the first padre in residence in Petaluma. In January of 1873, Archbishop J. Alemany made his usual visit to Mission Solano and baptized the young.

Solomon Schocken opened a small store in Sonoma in the fall of 1873, moving over from Napa County where he had started a mercantile business in 1868 at the village of Monticello.

Letter From Archbishop Jose Alemany
To Señora Benicia Vallejo

Mrs. Felipa Benicia de Vallejo, as they assure and we believe has been named, President of the Church's Altar Society of San Francisco Solano in Sonoma and wishing to obtain funds for the ornaments on the Altar we ask the congregation that they will help her in this task. At the same time we ask our Lady to see if she can find an honest person who would like to rent the vacant lot of the Church, so we will, if convenient, arrange the rental documents for the benefit of the Church.

San Francisco May 16, 1874
José S. Alemany Archbishop of
San Francisco

When the mission chapel was badly in need of additional repair, the padre appointed a subcommittee to raise funds for the needed work. As described by Henry Cerruti (it was at a later date than the construction period of 1840-41) the story follows:

After Mr. Haste's departure I paid a visit to the Catholic Church of Sonoma, a small edifice built of adobes in the times of the good father missionaries. That church in the early days of California was quite a large building, about four times its present size; but, the Catholic population having decreased considerably, when the old building went to ruin the inhabitants were not able to muster funds sufficient for the construction of a large building and resolved to replace the ancient edifice with a good-size chapel. After the walls and roof had been completed, the managing committee found itself reduced to a very low ebb, for upwards of three thousand dollars were needed for the completion of the edifice, for the purchase of benches, pictures, priestly ornaments, etc., and not a dollar had they to their credit.

In this emergency the priest appointed a subcommittee composed of Madame General Vallejo and her three daughters who, having accepted the honor (sic) conferred on them, set about collecting the needed dollars. A few days after the appointment of the subcommittee a gentleman from San Francisco who happened to have business to transact with General Vallejo called at his house. The "subcommittee" engaged him in conversation and by hook or crook induced him to contribute twenty dollars towards the repairs of the church - though the town of Sonoma possesses only a chapel, the inhabitants of that place insist on calling their place of worship a church. When the visitor had taken his departure, the General called his daughters to his presence, requested them to give him the keys of the church, expressed his displeasure at having been a witness to the begging scene which had been enacted in his presence, and warned them against accepting offices of that class.

No sooner had General Vallejo got possession of the keys of the embryo chapel than he sent for plasterers and carpenters, gave them instructions as to the manner in which he desired the work to be done, and agreed to pay for it. The next thing he did was to send to San Francisco every worn-out saint and picture, with orders to have them truly renovated. As he forwarded funds at the same time, the whole work was soon finished in good style. The General spent twenty-seven hundred dollars. The chapel was completed in a genteel manner, and the priests who a few months prior to this event were loud in denouncing M. G. Vallejo as a heathen were afterwards very loud in his praises. As soon as the house of God had been truly renovated, General Vallejo gave back the key of the chapel to his daughters, who felt delighted on hearing the good news and faithfully promised to abstain in the future from accepting offices at the hands of priests.[1]

Further "renovation" of the mission was the rebuilding of the door and window frames with arched tops, similar to the churches of the period. The entire building was given a new coat of white plaster, inside and out. The padres' house beside it was not included in the exterior renovation. At the chapel end, the passageway 10 feet wide, was left open for an entrance into the quadrangle, with a front wall containing a large gateway and heavy wooden gate.

Services had been held during 1873 every other Sunday by padres from St. Vincent's Orphanage in Marin County -- usually Rev. S. Scanlon or, later in the year, Rev. Jacobus Cleary. The congregation was composed of residents and ranch owner families of Sonoma Valley and had become quite large for the small chapel.

Edward Vischer, the artist and trader who had visited the pueblo in 1842, came to Sonoma and took time in June 1874 to paint a picture of the partly-ruined padres' house and the newly renovated mission chapel in its new coat of white plaster. He also made a sketch of the large adobe church and the east end of the padres' house, as described to him by General Vallejo.[2]

The new Schocken store on the plaza soon aroused the ire of the old-time Sonoma merchants with its cut rates, etc. and they retaliated, as noted by Henry Cerruti -

Another anecdote worth recording is the following. Six months before I took it into my head to visit Sonoma, (in 1874) a little Jew called Shocken opened a store in that town. Being a sharp businessman, he soon obtained the greater part of the trade of Sonoma, greatly to the discomfort of the other merchants, who with an envious eye watched the growing popularity of the diminutive Jew and of his coquettish wife. On several occasions they tried to undersell him, but to no purpose - Shocken always held his ground. Finding at last that they could not compete with him in a business way, they unearthed the law which requires stores to be kept closed on Sunday. Some person of mean disposition swore out the complaint, and Mr. Shocken was arrested and brought before the Justice of the Peace, who fined the delinquent to the tune of ten dollars. The fine was paid, and the victim allowed to return to his

Ruins of Mission San Francisco Solano, showing renovated chapel at left. Painted by Edward Vischer. Courtesy Bancroft Library.

store.

On the following week, the victim of religious fanaticism who had been made to serve private views, in accordance with the rites of the Jewish faith, kept his store closed on Saturday and opened it on Sunday. He believed himself to be on the safe side and never dreamed that on the following Monday he would again be made to stand face to face with stern justice. About two o'clock on Monday Shocken was again arrested for having sold goods on Sunday. He pleaded as an excuse that he kept the Sabbath by observing the Saturday, as prescribed by his religion. Those words had hardly been uttered when the Justice of the Peace howled, "Damn you do you wish to transplant Jerusalem to Sonoma? Mr. Clerk, please collect a fine of twenty-five dollars from the prisoner, and if he be ever again brought before me on a charge of this kind he shall be sent to prison." Shocken departed crestfallen and fully convinced that Jerusalem could not be conveniently transplanted to Sonoma.[3]

Henry Cerruti, a member of Hubert Bancroft's History collecting organization had visited Sonoma at the invitation of General Vallejo. He spent quite a bit of time in Sonoma during 1874 interviewing the General and others of the older inhabitants. And, later he was successful in having the General turn over his many early California documents and his *Historia*, which he had written, to Mr. Bancroft.

One of his visits to the mission chapel is described:

When I entered the church I perceived some eighty or ninety persons engaged in praying for the salvation of their souls. I bent my knees and did likewise; at least I made a bold attempt at prayer, but failed most signally, for my mind became too excitable. Fortune has so often frowned upon me that I have lost faith in a benign Providence, and whenever I sit down to pray the wrongs I have suffered at the hands of a cruel and heartless world come back to my mind, stir up a tempest within my bosom, and prevent me from communing with my Creator.

Perceiving that I was doing no good in church I took my departure, but I was not allowed to depart in peace, for while I was in the act of putting on my hat, an elderly gentleman came towards me and in a courteous and polite manner notified me that I was expected to contribute a few dollars towards purchasing a carriage and a pair of horses for the use of the priest who every other Sunday came to Sonoma to attend to the welfare of the immortal souls of the Catholics. I told my interlocutor that I would cheerfully comply with his request and gave him an invitation to step into my office. He did so, and I handed him one dollar. Oh, what a face he made when he felt convinced that my bump of generosity had not been fully developed. I shall remember it to my dying hour. Perceiving that he refused to receive the dollar, I was going to replace it in my pocket when he broke the silence that for upward of two minutes had reigned supreme and said, "Do you know that Mr. Smith has given twenty-five dollars for this noble object? Are you aware that Major Rufus has

111

Letter from Bishop José Alemany to Mrs. Vallejo, dated May 16, 1874. He requested that she, in her capacity as President of the Church's Altar Society of San Francisco Solano, solicit funds from the congregation for altar ornaments and to "find an honest person who would like to rent the vacant lot of the church." Courtesy Sonoma State Historic Park.

promised to give thirty dollars? How would you like to have your name placed between these two gentlemen and have the people know that you, a general, had given only one dollar while a simple major had contributed twenty-five?

I could not help laughing heartily, and to tell the truth I almost felt inclined to drive the beggar from my presence. However, after a second thought I replied to him in these words, "Now listen, my friend, if you are willing to take ten cents I will allow you to publish my name and title, but if you take the whole dollar I will sign N.N." (No name). He cast a furtive glance at me and perceived that I was not to be swayed by his entreaties, so he pocketed the dollar and went after some new victim.[4]

Later, on a trip to San Francisco with the General and family, via Lakeville -

There we took the cars to Donahue, and then we went on board the *Antelope*, which brought us safely to San Francisco.

At the wharf Squire H.. Bancroft received the whole family. He had two coaches in readiness, and in one of them rode Squire Bancroft, the Misses Val-lejo, and Mr. Napoleon Vallejo. In the other General Vallejo and I took our places. The party in charge of Mr. Bancroft drove straight for Bancroft's villa, while my companion and I went to a store where hardware is sold. There General Vallejo purchased a handsome bell which he ordered to be sent to Sonoma as a present to the chapel that was greatly in need of it. General Vallejo is not a very staunch Catholic and never goes to church except under peculiar circumstances, namely when asked to take part in some political function. He, however, contributes greatly to the support of the Sonoma chapel and does it for the sake of his wife, Doña Benicia Francisca de Vallejo, and his favorite son, Doctor Platon Vallejo, a young gentleman with sound religious tendencies:[5]

Padre Jacobus Cleary from St. Vincent de Paul Church in Petaluma was making the trips up to the mission chapel as usual, in 1874 and 1875, though sometimes his assistants, Rev. John Cassidy or Rev. Emaneul Estraque, came in his place.

XXIV

Mission San Francisco Solano Sold
New Parish Church— St. Francis Solano

Railroads were the fashion of the times and a town without one was out of style and doomed to isolation. Sonoma citizens were all excited over the prospect of a railroad from the town to deep water on the Bay front where the steamers could land passengers and freight. In 1876, down in the tules two miles east of the old mission embarcadero, a railroad was being built with local capital from a new landing named Norfolk. It was of a new design, using a single supporting rail with sloping side supports upon which guide wheels also ran.

After three miles were built, the Sonoma Valley Prismoidal Railway ran a special train and boat excursion from San Francisco and people were really surprised at the smooth and pleasant ride over the single track. The three miles ended on solid ground, on the land of T. L. Schell, at the first road crossing and, as there had been no solution found for crossing the country roads, that was the extent of the line. The road was soon shut down and the people still took the stage to Lakeville for the trip by steamer to San Francisco and Bay points.

Throughout these years, 1875-77, Mission San Francisco Solano struggled along with the help each second week, when possible, of Fr. Jacobus Cleary, Pastor at St. Vincent de Paul Church of Petaluma, and his assistants Rev. Patrick Ward and, later, Rev. John McCarthy. The adobe chapel needed repairs and maintenance but the parish was poor and expenses of the caretaker and bell ringer just about depleted the resources.

In 1877, the steamer *Clinton* now ran from the embarcadero to San Francisco. At the old townsite St. Louis, at the embarcadero, new town lots were for sale and the latest real estate speculation in the valley was on its usual way. Money borrowed brought high interest and when the "town" failed to prosper, some valley people had learned an expensive lesson.

The new *Sonoma Tribune* was an 1878 addition to Sonoma, giving the weekly news locally and from San Francisco sources. However, its life was short.

The *Index* arrived on the streets April 17, 1879, with Ben Frank, editor. It was four pages of six columns each. At the end of the year, August L. Drahms was editor and publisher. In the next four years, the editors were Frank K. Merritt, C. Merlin Jones, and E. J. Livernash, who called the paper the *Index-Tribune*.[1]

The Sonoma Valley Prismoidal Railway Co., that had ended its three-mile track through the tules at the crossroad south of town, only operated a few months after its initial run in November of 1876. Now in 1878, the company was reorganized as the Sonoma Valley Railroad. The roadbed was reworked and 36-inch narrow gauge tracks laid and new rolling stock purchased. By the end of the year, the roadbed was extended over the lands of T. L. Schell on its way north to the town center.[2]

The town plaza was now entirely surrounded with buildings, mostly one-story, some two-story adobes and numerous frame buildings with high false fronts; some with stores or saloons on the ground floors and living quarters on the second floor. Across Spain Street, the old barracks building that used to house the soldiers of the Mexican and then the U.S. Army, now had a new owner. Merchant Solomon Schocken, on June 15, 1878, bought it for his store and warehouse, a house of many items and uses. The streets were wide, unpaved, and dusty in the summer and muddy in the winter. The plaza was bare of trees and criss-crossed with paths. Its only adornment was the tall Bear party flagpole.

And opposite the northeast corner stood the lone mission chapel with its plastered walls showing the ravages of time and weather. Yet the usual semi-monthly services were held when Padre Cleary or his assistants, Rev. J. Ryan or Rev. J. Donnelly, came over from the

Railroad Saloon on Mission Corner, built between 1897 and 1903.

Hay stored in unused Mission chapel sanctuary, about 1900. Note plaster and gaslight fixture on ceiling. Both photos courtesy Sonoma State Historic Park.

Winery at left and chapel on east side, circa 1889. Sketch by author from San Francisco Call.

Petaluma church.

The new railroad tracks were headed towards Sonoma but coming very slowly as the finances were not ample for the project. Peter Donahue of San Francisco, who had built the San Francisco and North Pacific Railroad over in the Petaluma Valley, solved the problem by obtaining control and finishing the line to the pueblo plaza. The route was from Norfolk on the lower Sonoma Creek, north through Schell's land to a point one mile and a third east of the plaza, then west to and down Spain Street. The rails were laid in front of the mission buildings and entered the north side of the plaza. Here were erected the station, turntable, freight house, car barns, and other buildings -- all on city land. In December of 1879, the first train came down the track amid a grand celebration and Sonoma now had a railroad from town to tidewater, replacing the stages and freight teams to the old embarcadero. The Donahue steamer made its trip from Norfolk to San Francisco, connecting with the daily train.[2] The Donahue interests planned to extend the Sonoma Valley Railroad to the Bay shore east of the mouth of Petaluma Creek. Here, a pier was planned out to where the water was a depth of 14 feet so that Bay steamers of deep draft could land at the new dock at all times.[3]

As the months passed, the new train service was accepted by the Sonoma people and merchants as a big step forward. But, to the members of the mission congregation it was not accepted with favor. The noise of the train passing the front door, with its rattling and pounding, upset the quiet of the services and the smoke and dust and frightened horses made the area around the corner very disagreeable. And the shaking set up by the heavy trains was not good for the adobe construction of the buildings. Also, the church was now in the center of the business area surrounded by stores, wine cellars and saloons, which were all open on Sundays as well.

During the years of 1879 and 1880, Rev. Donnelly from St. Vincent's in Petaluma attended to the wants of the congregation of Mission San Francisco Solano.

A store in the barracks was leased in August 1880 by its owner, Solomon Schocken, to Frederic Clewe. The rent was $50 in gold coin per month, and he was allowed to use it for general merchandise but not lumber or feed. Schocken agreed to refrain from selling general merchandise during the one-year term of the lease.[4]

The year of 1881 was well on its way when the news was confirmed in Sonoma that the old mission was being sold. Archbishop Joseph Alemany had decided that a new church building was needed by the growing parish and a permanent priest was necessary. Another location was also desirable. Rev. Hubert Esser was appointed resident priest in charge of the parish. Land was purchased half a mile west of the mission on Napa Street, which was the road to the upper valley and the county seat in Santa Rosa. The old mission chapel, the padres' house beside it, and the land in the rear, granted to the Archbishop by the United States Government Patent in 1862 -- 2.06 acres in all -- was sold to Solomon Schocken, the Jewish merchant who owned the barracks just across the street. The price was $3,000 in gold coin. A down payment of $500 was made on May 19, 1881, and the balance received when the deed was delivered July 11, 1881. The old mission vineyard, two and three blocks to the east, was not included.[5]

The new wooden frame church on Napa Street was started, and, by the end of the year, Father Esser held the first service on Christmas Day in the still incomplete building. The new church did not carry on the old name but was named "Saint Francis Solano" instead. The parishioners had been kept busy moving the church vestments, furnishings, and records over from the old mission. The new building was of a modern style with a tall steeple and was declared very artistic. It was dedicated by Archbishop Alemany on June 4, 1882. Rev. Hubert Esser was the pastor. While the new church was being built, services were held in the old mission chapel. And then the great bell that had hung on the sturdy beam and had rung out the daily Angelus over the years was stilled and, in its sorrow, mysteriously disappeared.

And, thus, the old leather bound books containing the history of Mission San Francisco Solano as a place of worship over the last 58 years in the Valley of the Sonomans were closed forever. They recorded a history of achievement that occupies a high place in the annals of the early California Missions.

First wood Catholic Church Saint Francis Solano, built in 1881 at Third and Napa Streets, was destroyed by fire in 1896. Courtesy Sonoma Valley Historical Society.

XXV

The Ex-Mission's Disgraceful Years

The ex-mission chapel was now, in 1882, a bare tall building and was soon put to use by its new owner, Solomon Schocken, as a warehouse for his general merchandise store across the street in the old barracks. Often hay was piled high in its interior, as well as other bulk merchandise and supplies. The ex-padres' house was put in reasonable shape and used for various purposes. Some parts were rented out to tenants who conducted different commercial activities there. The rear quadrangle, or patio, was opened to the street and used for teams and wagons. It was a convenient place to pile the stocks of heavy hardware, and part of it became a common trash dump.

The Sonoma Valley Railroad, in 1882, extended its tracks and service up the valley along the west side of Rancho Agua Caliente to the settlement of Glen Ellen. The contemplated extension from Norfolk south to Sears Point over a drawbridge and on to a deep water pier, Sonoma Landing, had been built also. Through trains now ran from Glen Ellen to deep water past the ex-mission door.

The next year the town of Sonoma was reincorporated as there had been a great deal of controversy over the northern boundary (one hill or another), as "City of Sonoma, 6th Class." The new town was a small square, leaving out the former "out lots" and the "out lotters" could fight it out among themselves. The town had been without a newspaper for some time and the defunct *Index-Tribune* was purchased by H. H. Granice -- lately of the *San Francisco Bulletin*. He was an experienced newsman and soon had the paper on its feet and running again in December of 1884. It was the weekly of the Valley.

The title to the Catholic Cemetery on the Napa road, four blocks east of the plaza, was transferred to the new Archbishop Patrick W. Riordan by Archbishop Alemany on May 9, 1885. The Archbishop stated that the lot now and for many years past had been used as a Catholic Cemetery. In 1832 it had replaced the old *campo santo* that was east of the now demolished large adobe church. This cemetery was in the center of the old pueblo Out Lot No. 510, originally granted in 1850 to Rubin Davis by Alcalde William A. Fuller, and had been the subject of various ownership claims since that date.[1]

Archbishop Joseph Sadoc Alemany resigned in December 1884 after 35 years of strenuous work in California. He wished to return to his native Spain. Coadjutor Rev. Patrick William Riordan assumed the position of Archbishop on his retirement. During the next months until he left in May of 1885, Archbishop Alemany turned over to Archbishop Riordan all the Church property and contracts, throughout the State that were in his name as trustee for the Church. The one concerning items in Sonoma County included the Catholic Cemetery (as noted above) on Napa Street, the new lands of St. Francis Solano Church, and title to the Mission Solano property remaining and, in the general paragraph, the old mission vineyard on Spain Street east.[2]

In a vineyard on Agua Caliente Creek in 1886, the grape vines began dying of a mysterious disease which spread out from dying vines. Finally, a powdery covering on the roots was noted which proved to be minute insects which destroyed the root. They spread to other vines through the gravelly soil -- killing the vines in circles. It was identified as *phylloxera vestatrix*, a pest from the vineyards in France. There was no known cure or preventative and, in the ensuing years, the wine grape vineyards were practically wiped out, both here and in other valleys. Fortunately a few varieties appeared resistant, especially the California wild grape. New plantings and graftings solved the problem and the vineyards were flourishing again after the new vines matured four or five years

Hudson House, Jim Martin's blacksmith shop, circa 1880. The building previously served as the Cooper and Beasley Hotel in 1848, and as Sonoma's first Post Office in 1849. The padre house of the ex-mission is shown at left. Courtesy Sonoma Valley Historical Society.

Sonoma Plaza N.E., July 4, 1887. Courtesy Sonoma State Historic Park.

later.

In this year 1886, the map of Sonoma showed the mission chapel intact. The padres' house was "very dilapidated" and was used as storage for wine and empty casks. Both corridors, front and rear, were still intact. In front of the padres' house, facing the street, was a small building used as a cooper's shop. To the east, about where the great adobe church had been, two houses were built by Solomon Schocken and rented out. First Street, between the chapel and the old barracks (now a merchandise store) was not cut through and three buildings occupied the frontage: a saloon with bowling alley in the rear, a passageway or alley, a store and tinware shop, and a dwelling close to the chapel building.

William Pickett, who had purchased pueblo Out Lot No. 510 in 1878, brought suit against Fr. Esser of the Catholic Church in 1886 claiming ownership of the Catholic cemetery which was in the southern center of that lot. The suit was tried in the County Superior Court in Santa Rosa, Case No. 1025, October 8, 1886. The findings of the court were that the cemetery plot had been given to Mission San Francisco Solano in 1835 by Lieutenant Vallejo for a Catholic burial ground; had been fenced, consecrated, cared for and so used since and, to date, by the Catholic Church. Therefore, the court declared in favor of the defendant the Catholic Church as rightful owner; the plaintiff, William Pickett to pay the costs.

Steel rails were being laid all over the Sonoma Valley by 1886. The Sonoma Valley Railroad Co. was connected by the Donahue interests with their lines in Marin County at Ignacio. This allowed the passengers to go through from Sonoma to the ferry at Tiburon with a change at Ignacio, and the passenger service to Sonoma Landing was discontinued. Then the Southern Pacific Railroad interests brought a line into the valley from Napa junction to Schellville and, by-passing the town of Sonoma to the west, continued up the valley towards Glen Ellen and eventually on to Santa Rosa. A new station west of Sonoma, El Verano, cared for the Sonoma patrons. Sonoma town fathers had decided support of one railroad was sufficient and did not offer the usual free land and right-of-way inducements. By the year 1890, all the Sonoma Valley Railroad from Glen Ellen south to Sonoma and over to Ignacio was broad gauge track, and competing with the Southern Pacific for the Valley freight and passenger business.

About this time, the populace of the town was objecting to the railroad using their plaza for their coal dusted buildings, and the merchants and their customers were objecting to the noise, smoke and street congestion along Spain Street. The railroad was forced to abandon its plaza terminal and opened its new station one block to the north. The new rails were laid north of Spain Street up through the old mission vineyard area before turning west to the new station.

The mission vineyard out on Spain Street was the last piece of the vast holdings of San Francisco Solano in the possession of the Church. A right-of-way for the Sonoma Valley Railroad through the vineyard area was sold by Archbishop Patrick Riordan to care for their move from Spain Street. Later, on September 13, 1894, the Archbishop sold the balance of the vineyard area to Thomas Brown of Sonoma.[3] This closed the book on the original mission properties in the Pueblo of Sonoma and in the Contra Costa del Norte Este.

In 1896 a future resident of Sonoma came to the area. He had arrived in 1893 from Italy. Now, 17 years old, he soon had a wagon and team hauling the basalt blocks down from the Sonoma quarries to the railroads. There were many Italians employed in the quarries and they provided a good market for a red wine. So, Sam Sebastiani soon had a small vineyard and little winery to care for his countrymen. Later, he bought part of the original mission vineyard acreage which had been granted to Archbishop Alemany and sold to Thomas Brown in 1894.

On June 25th of 1896, Fr. White of St. Francis Solano Church was burning off dry grass beside the frame church on West Napa Street. The grass fire ignited leaves against the wooden church building and soon it was in flames, burning to the ground. Inside were the ancient church vestments, books, records, and furniture from the old Mission San Francisco Solano. Few were saved. On the same site, a new edifice was built of frame construction. It opened with the Christmas Mass of the same year. Archbishop Riordan officiated at the formal dedication.

During the late years of the 1890's, the mission chapel was filled each year with bales of fragrant hay and grain -- storage for the general merchandise store of its owner across the street. At least the roof was kept in repair to protect the contents.

The cooper's shop had been moved away from in front of the padres' house, which now bore the title "Old Sonoma Winery." It had a "dirt floor" as, no doubt, the mission floor tiles had been taken out and used elsewhere, or sold. The frame buildings, including the saloon, still filled First Street but the bowling alley had been taken down. East of the padres' house, a third house had been built in the area of the

Ex-Mission San Francisco Solano being used as warehouse and winery, circa 1902. Courtesy Sonoma State Historic Park.

former mission *campo santo*. Its shape was the same as the previous two beside it.

An addition to the numerous saloons around the plaza was added across the front of the ex-mission chapel in the late 1890's. It was a frame building with the porch extending out over the sidewalk and the usual hitching posts. The corner was recessed with the swinging doors and decorated with a pair of Grace Bros. lager beer signs -- named "The Railroad Saloon." Over the top of the new shingles could be seen the peak of the old chapel and the belfry, still holding its own in defiance. Next to the saloon was the old padres' house half covered with its original tiles and the far end with sheets of tin. The picket fence was intact and enclosed its front yard.

During the turn of the century, the ex-mission, owned by merchant Solomon Schocken, was used for various commercial purposes. The chapel building, with the saloon in front of its *fachada*, was a store room; the vestibule was used for liquors for the saloon and the nave for bulk merchandise -- feed and hay for the store in the barracks. The ex-padres' house had Schocken's winery in part of it, an eating house rented other parts and, during the years, miscellaneous tenants had occupied the many rooms still usable.

A vivid description of the mission chapel and padres' house in the Fall of 1902 was published in the *San Francisco Chronicle* as follows:

On a corner of the plaza close to the old barracks there is a structure so crazy in appearance, so jumbled in architectural style, that one has to walk clear around it and view it from all sides before he can see its reason for being. Viewed directly from the front, it appears to be a saloon, with a ruined bell tower rising from somewhere behind it, and with a tiled shed extending out along the street. Not until it is viewed from the rear does one appreciate that he is looking at one of the California Missions. It is in truth San Francisco de Solano Mission, last holy place built by the heroic fathers in their campaign for the salvation of the California Indians, almost the first to be allowed to fall into ruin.

It is not so much the fact that it is ruined, either, that shocks the sensibilities of the student of California History, as the manner of the ruin. For a search through the strange old structure shows that the church proper is being employed as a storehouse for straw and partly as an overflow room for the liquors and empty bottles of the saloon building that has been erected against its front wall, while the tiled cloister, where the friars lived, is a chicken house at one end a and a wagon shed at the other.

The church itself is in pretty good condition. The roof holds tight; hence the straw. Founded later than the other missions, and at a time when pastoral California was learning some of the arts of life, it was made to be finished in lath and plaster, and the plaster still holds. It was not the architectural beauty of some of the more pretentious southern missions, for San Francisco de Solano was a comparatively poor mission, but it has a simple charm and beauty of its own. At the back there is a tiny gallery with a beautiful old window, this end forming a little nook of quaint and alluring charm -- charm which is not entirely spoiled by the fact that the gallery now holds beer cases. The opposite wall, where the high altar stood in the old days, is perfectly plain except for a niche at either side, and is piled high with straw.

It is the cloister which is in most need of attention and repair. Its uses have been mentioned. At the end which serves as a wagon shed a part of the roof has fallen in, spilling the tiles to the ground. It is one proof of the loneliness of old Sonoma that these tiles lie as they fell, untouched by relic hunters. The interior woodwork has long since disappeared, to be replaced by the perches and boxes of the hens. A little doorway through which the Franciscans crept to mass in the early dawn now lets the feathered flock out and in. The bell was taken down with the cross when the place was abandoned for Christian worship, and the ruin of its tower still surmounts that strange structure - a deserted church, a saloon, a barn and a henhouse, all in one.[4]

Second Catholic Church Saint Francis Solano [wood], built 1896 and destroyed by fire in 1922. Courtesy Sonoma Valley Historical Society.

St. Francis Solano, 1973. Photo by author.

XXVI

Mission San Francisco Solano Honored
Landmarks League— Sonoma State Historic Park

At the beginning of the century the Sonoma Valley Woman's Club took an active interest in the Mission San Francisco Solano ruins, and their preservation and eventual restoration of the mission. The owner, Schocken, was willing to sell and a purchasing fund-raising started. Permission to protect the two remaining buildings from further deterioration was received and some repairs were made.

The California Historic Landmarks League, with the Honorable Joseph R. Knowland, president and Laura Bride Powers, secretary, became interested in the project and took an active part in raising the needed funds. The Native Sons and Daughters of the Golden West joined in the drive and William Randolph Hearst led the drive with a donation of $500 with his *San Francisco Examiner* handling the publicity.

The combined effort was very successful and soon the fund totaled $13,000 with Mr. Hearst acting as trustee for the Landmarks League.

They bought the chapel and the padres' house with its immediate acreage. Solomon Schocken was paid $3,000 cash for it and he deeded the 150' x 166' piece to William Randolph Hearst, trustee, on July 1, 1903.[1]

And Mission San Francisco Solano was resurrected from the disgraceful condition that had been its lot under the merchant Schocken.

Work was begun at once, the saloon at the front was moved away and the chapel *fachada* exposed again. The turreted top of the cupola was removed and its roof rebuilt on simple lines. The padres' house was cleared up and the roof repaired. Reconstruction continued during the next few years on a small scale as finances were available.

But the goal for complete restoration was to have the State of California take over the property and include it in the State Parks system. On March 23, 1906, that was accomplished with William Randolph Hearst, trustee, deed-

ing the mission area he had received from Solomon Schocken in 1903 to the State of California unit, the Board of Sutter's Fort Trustees.[2]

And then came the earthquake of April 18, 1906 -- 26 days later.

Miraculously, although the 1906 earthquake shook up the mission, it apparently did little damage. There was a crack between the burnt brick veneer front and the adobe wall of the *fachada* and a few bricks fell from the southwest corner. The padres' house was weakened.

However, later, the brick veneer began to bulge out in places. In 1908, the roof of the padres' house gave way in some sections and the top of the walls fell in with the roof sections. Then, on February 12, 1909, the front half and southwest corner of the chapel wall fell in a pile in front of the church, leaving the choir loft and vestibule open to the elements. Temporary repairs were soon made and the mission buildings were surveyed for future plans and construction. The State-employed caretaker, who lived in the padres' house, kept the mission buildings in repair as best he could, even though they were not open to the public.

It took four or five years for sufficient money to be appropriated by the State and other interested parties for a major restoration. It was accomplished during the years 1911 to 1913, after the California Legislature appropriated $5,000 for the purpose.[3] The chapel was reroofed with attractive tiles, and the belfry was removed. The arched windows and doorframes were changed back to the original horizontal timber beam construction. The broken plaster on the front of the padres' house was removed and the burnt brick facing of the chapel *fachada* was not added in the reconstruction, exposing the adobe bricks of both.

The padres' house was reconstructed with its wide corridor along the front. However, only the front half -- one room wide of this long building -- was rebuilt, with a forward sloping

Sonoma Mission Chapel before 1906 earthquake. Courtesy Sonoma State Historic Park.

Sonoma Mission Chapel and padre house, circa 1900. Courtesy Sonoma State Historic Park.

Mission Chapel showing 1906 quake damage at lower left corner. Courtesy Sonoma State Historic Park.

Southwest corner of chapel, weakened by 1906 quake, collapsed in a heap on February 12, 1909. Courtesy California State Library.

tile roof which continued over the corridor. In place of the original 27 rooms, the reconstructed building now had two large and two small rooms in line, with an open passageway at the east end to the walled patio. The breezeway at the west end was closed and the space added to the end room with a door into the chapel vestibule.

And the great bell, which had hung on the beam in front of the mission since the early years, and which disappeared when the mission was sold, was found by members of the Woman's Club resting in the Sutro Baths Museum in San Francisco. It was soon recovered and took its proud and rightful place, hanging again from the heavy beam near the front of the chapel door.

The chapel of San Francisco Solano was now in shape and was opened to the public, with a curator in charge, on June 14, 1914. The nave was filled with items of local historic interest, making a museum with its exhibits and ar-

View of chapel and padre house after collapse in 1909. Courtesy Bancroft Library.

After the collapse, the padre house was cleared for reconstruction. The padre house walls were the only remaining part of the original mission. Courtesy Sonoma State Historic Park.

tifacts. The padres' house was closed but plans were in order for its rehabilitation and opening later on.

In all, the Mission San Francisco Solano was arising out of its past disgrace and wreckage. The tall adobe chapel on the corner was still holding her head high now, with the large wooden cross on the peak as in the days of the padres.

Fire, that relentless destroyer, again visited St. Francis Solano on Napa Street. The second wooden frame church, while it was being renovated and painted, on September 28, 1922, burned to the ground despite efforts of the local

fire brigade. The Union Hall was used for Mass until a new church could be built. This new third St. Francis Solano Church was built of reinforced concrete with a tile roof -- on the same Napa Street site. Fr. J. F. Byrne, the pastor, welcomed Archbishop Edward J. Hanna to dedicate it on September 9, 1923. It has been a leading church of the community ever since; presently (1974) under the guidance of genial Rt. Rev. Msgr. John P. Farrell, pastor, and his able assistant Fr. Patrick Moriarty.

In 1926, Mission San Francisco Solano was honored by being designated "California Historical Monument No. 3" -- along with the Mon-

Unveiling of bell at El Camino Real, 1910. Courtesy Sonoma Valley Historic Park.

Initial reconstruction partly completed. Note that doors and windows have been rebuilt with the original horizontal-beam construction instead of arches. Courtesy William Getchey.

Art and relic exhibit in reconstructed chapel, September, 1912. Courtesy California State Parks and Recreation.

Northeast Sonoma Plaza, circa 1930. Courtesy California State Parks and Recreation.

terey Custom House (No. 1) and Gaspar Portola's Journey's End Site at Palo Alto (No. 2). The Native Sons of the Golden West placed a tablet on the front wall of the chapel, giving a few of the historic dates of its past life. The following year, 1927, the State Parks Commission (recently organized) assumed responsibility for the mission property and its maintenance.[3]

Many persons visited Sonoma, as tourists, school children, and California residents came to see the Bear Flag monument and the old-time plaza and, across the street, the mission the last of the California Mission chain -- became a favorite attraction.

Miss Marie T. Walsh, the eminent authority on mission bells, visited Sonoma in 1934 searching out the bells that had been used at Mission San Francisco Solano. The only bell at the mission was the one cast in 1829 -- the second large bell which was lost after the mission was sold in 1881 and found by the Woman's Club 25 years later. No trace was found of the original bell brought to the mission in 1825 by Captain Richardson.

One of the smaller mission bells was found in the belfry of the small Catholic Church in Nicasio, Marin County. It is a Sheffield bell -- 1858 -- cast in England. Another Sheffield bell, cast in 1853, found its way to the St. Vincent's School in Vallejo. These English bells, no doubt, were purchased by General Vallejo for the mission after the chapel was built. A small handbell, also of Sheffield make, found its way

from the mission to the possession of the San Francisco Native Sons Parlor and, after some damage in the 1906 fire, reposes in their cabinet.

Since the large 1829 bell was recovered, it has hung in silence from its heavy beam in front of the padres' house and chapel.[4]

Solomon Schocken died on May 27, 1932, at the age of 89 years, five months. He was buried in the Jewish Cemetery in San Francisco. His wife, living in San Francisco, survived him. His estate was handled by executor Bernard Baer. On March 19, 1935, Emilio and Zaini Tomasini bought two lots with houses, a total of 82.28 feet fronting on Spain Street next to the mission, from the estate of Solomon Schocken. The area was 44-100 acre, and was formerly the site of the end of the padres' house, the large adobe church, and part of the *campo santo*, or cemetery.[5] Two square houses with four sided roofs coming to a decorated peak in the center were on these lots, as well as a similar house on the adjacent lot to the east, the site of the balance of the *campo santo*. This latter lot, with the house, was sold to Annibale and Rosie Ricci on October 26, 1934, by the executor Bernard Baer. It had a frontage on Spain Street of 53.15 feet and contained 27-100 acres.[6]

The same year, Walter L. Murphy, editor and publisher of the *Sonoma Index-Tribune*, bought the old barracks across East First Street from the Schocken estate and began renovating it, especially the second floor where he and his wife, Mrs. Celeste Granice Murphy, planned to

Permanent exhibit at the padre house. Daisy E. Barbour, Curator, 1944-55. Courtesy California Department of Parks and Recreation.

make their home. The Schocken store on the first floor had been closed and was rented out for offices and other uses. In June of 1936, Mr. Murphy was appointed Postmaster of Sonoma.

The State of California bought a portion of the original grant sold to Solomon Schocken lying directly north of the Landmark purchase. On April 12, 1939, Raoul R. and Julia T. Emparan, who had come into possession of the 74' x 168', 0.28 acre strip, signed the deed of sale to the State.[7] This brought back the area of the original quadrangle but still left outside part of the site of the *monjerio* and all of the site of the large adobe church and cemetery.

The mission blossomed out in 1943 and '44 with a coat of plaster, inside and out, over the chapel and padres' house walls. This brought it back to its original appearance though, no doubt, the present plastering done by experienced workmen obtained a smoother and whiter looking surface than that made by the native Indians. Floors were tiled in the padres' house.

In the chapel, new furnishings were installed with many ecclesiastical items donated by interested parties, some from the original church. Stations of the cross were placed on the newly plastered walls and an altar was erected and furnished. The interior walls were decorated with simulated fresco painting as found on a few remaining sections and on other mission church walls done by the early Indian painters. Mission style chandeliers were made and installed in both the chapel and padres' house.

The museum pieces were moved into the restored rooms of the padres' house and it was made part of the exhibit open to the public. The original quadrangle was enclosed with a tile topped adobe wall and the center leveled. A large clump of ancient cactus fills most of the north side, about the site of the *monjerio*. Restrooms occupy the northeast corner. An added attraction is the Blue Wing Hotel, the old adobe opposite the padres' house (formerly Sonoma House, Cooper & Spriggs) which was well restored in 1946 by its owner.

Throughout the next ten years, Mission San Francisco Solano was host to many people who came to Sonoma to see the old adobe buildings and relish the historic background of the area: the mission, the barracks, the many old adobes, the Bear Flag monument and State's birthplace, and the Vallejo home "Lachryma Montis."

Further acreage was purchased bordering the north side of the property and obtaining the balance of original land grant to the north, plus some vacant land beyond. Walter L. Murphy, editor of the *Sonoma Index-Tribune*, signed the deed on March 12, 1957, for 0.91 acres -- 131' x 300' in size -- giving the State possession. The State of California now had title to all the Mission San Francisco Solano area, 2.06 acres, except the three small lots to the east of the padres' house on the site of the large adobe church and *campo santo* -- the Tomasini and Ricci house lots. The State bought the barracks from Mr. & Mrs. Murphy in 1958 -- the Murphys remaining there until their recent deaths.

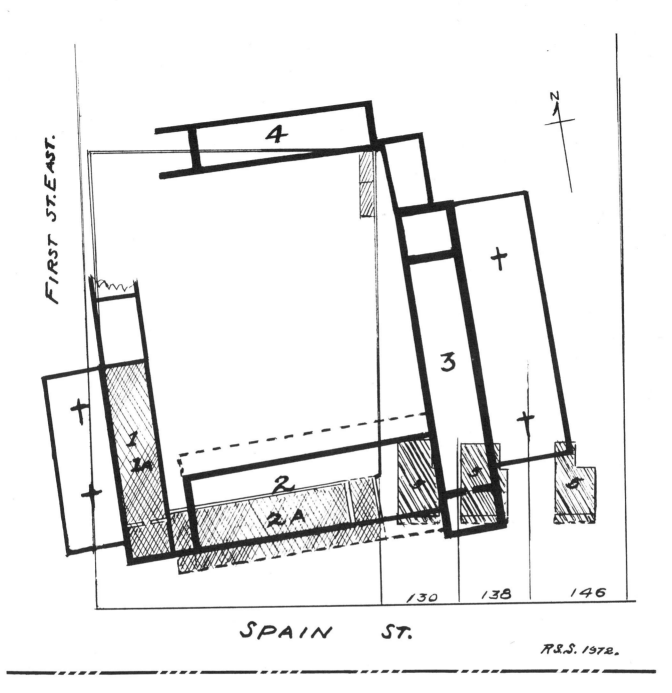

MAIN BUILDINGS - 1832-34

(1) Original church, wood, 1824
(2) Padre house
(3) Adobe church
(4) Monjerio

PRESENT BUILDINGS - RESTORED

(1a) Chapel, 1841-42 (on original church site)
(2a) Padre house (part)

PRIVATE HOUSES

(5) In original area

Mission San Francisco Solano - 1832 plan on 1972 area.

129

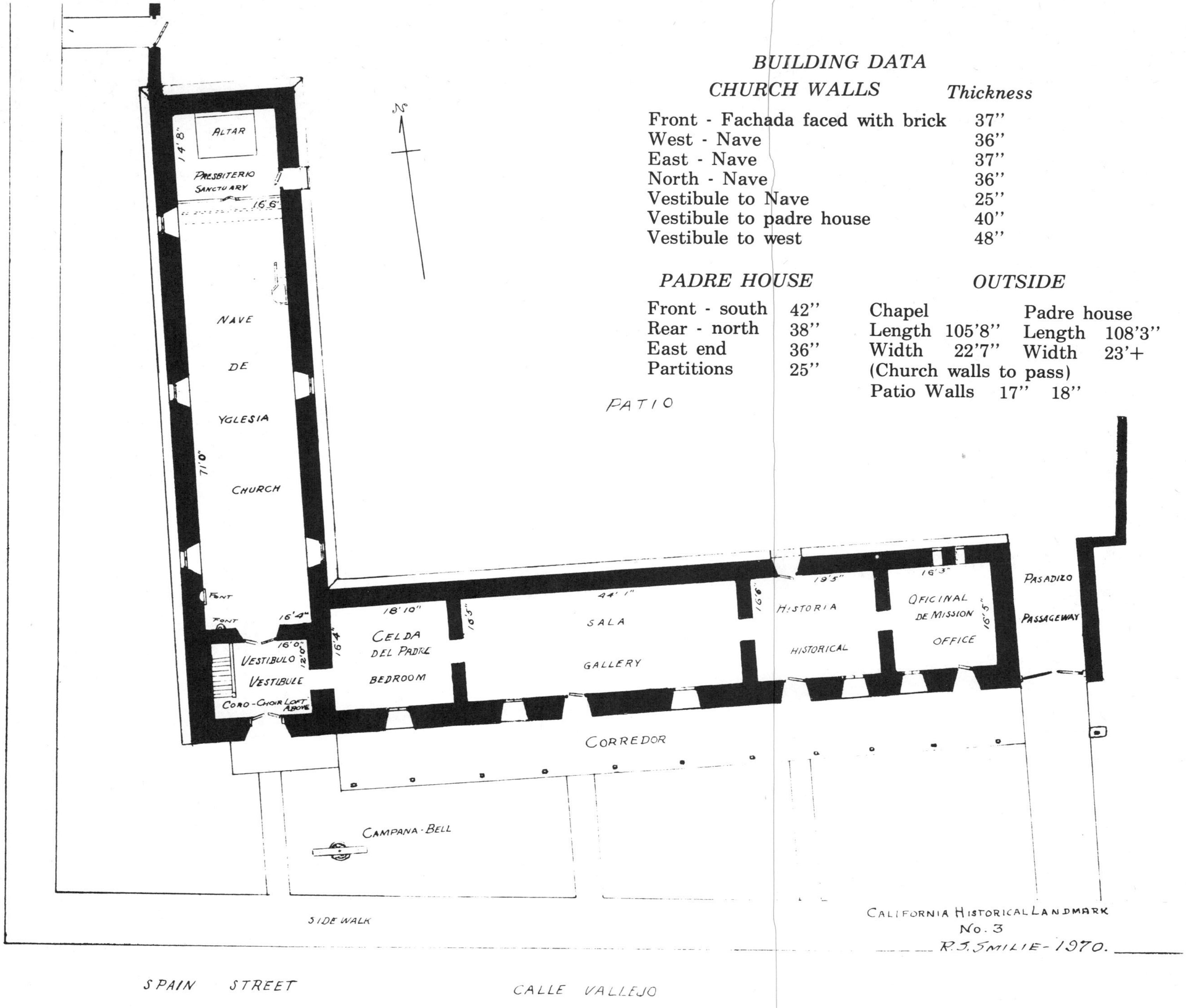

BUILDING DATA

CHURCH WALLS   *Thickness*

Front - Fachada faced with brick   37"
West - Nave   36"
East - Nave   37"
North - Nave   36"
Vestibule to Nave   25"
Vestibule to padre house   40"
Vestibule to west   48"

PADRE HOUSE
Front - south   42"
Rear - north   38"
East end   36"
Partitions   25"

OUTSIDE

Chapel   Padre house
Length 105'8"   Length 108'3"
Width 22'7"   Width 23'+
(Church walls to pass)
Patio Walls 17" 18"

PATIO

N

PASADIZO

PASSAGEWAY

OFICINA DE MISSION
OFFICE   16'5"
16'3"

HISTORIA
HISTORICAL   19'5"

16'6"

SALA
GALLERY   44'1"

16'5"

CORREDOR

CELDA DEL PADRE
BEDROOM   18'10"
16'6"

CAMPANA - BELL

SIDE WALK

ALTAR
PRESBITERIO SANCTUARY   14'8"   15'6"

NAVE
DE
YGLESIA
CHURCH   71'0"

16'4"

16'0"

FONT

VESTIBULO
VESTIBULE

CORO-CHOIR LOFT ABOVE

FIRST STREET EAST

CALLE CUARTO

SPAIN STREET   CALLE VALLEJO

California Historical Landmark No. 3

R.J.Smillie - 1970.

Mission San Francisco Solano, chapel and padre house as restored.

130

Mission San Francisco Solano, 1973. Photo by author.

Sonoma State Historic Park was formed as a unit of the State Division of Beaches and Parks, and grouped the Barracks, Mission San Francisco Solano, old Toscani Hotel, Lachryma Montis, and the *Casa Grande* site under one unit.

In 1953, archaeological research was made in the quadrangle area by University of California Survey Team -- James A. Bennyhoff and Albert B. Elsasser; and, later in 1954, by Dr. Adan E. Treganza. They uncovered foundations of the extensive original padres' house and the *monjerio* on the north side of the quadrangle. What had been considered the east wall of the padres' house and location of the adobe church was found to be a thick partition with four or more additional room foundations beyond. This agrees with the "Fabricas" report of "including the church rooms." The researchers also uncovered the small room or sacristy that was on the patio side of the chapel, or first wooden church, as well as walks and corridors in the patio.

During the subsequent years, the Parks Department has improved the mission area and interior of the buildings. Floor tiles were replaced where needed and the corridor in front of the padres' house was made very attractive and restful. Lawns were planted and kept up and the area of the quadrangle landscaped.

The chapel now presents a fine picture of an earlier Indian Mission Church, complete with sanctuary appointments, authentic Spanish paintings and Stations of the Cross, mainly of 18th Century origin. Harry Downie of Carmel, the Dean of California Mission Restoration, donated the items on the following list, in 1966, to accomplish this result as well as offering valuable advice on the decorations to Cliff Bisbee of the Sonoma Mission State Park staff and, later, Richard Douglas of the same staff:

List of Harry Downie's Donations

Oil Paintings -
Saint Francis Solano, Framed, Late 18th Century - 24" x 36"
Ecce House, Framed, Early 18th Century - 41" x 62"
Christ Nailed to the Cross, Framed, Early 18th Century - 36" x 47"
Annunciation, Framed, Early 19th Century - 18" x 24"
Saint Joseph, Framed, Early 18th Century - 15" x 21"
San Salvador, Framed, Early 18th Century - 32" x 56"
14 Stations of the Cross w/14 simple wooden crosses, Early 18th Century

Corridor of the padre house, 1973, the only remaining original building.

Sanctuary of Mission San Francisco Solano. Both photos by author.

Embellished, arched door from the chapel sanctuary to the quadrangle.

Baptismal corner of the chapel. Both photos by author.

Also -

1 Altar, complete w/gold tabernacle door, Italian copy, 1850 and '56.

1 Altar cloth

1 Structure, carved figure in relief for top of Altar

1 Crucifix, authentic 18th Century for top of above structure

Statues, frame body, 4' high, w/vestments - Mary and Joseph

Sacristy Lamp, Candle, Hanging

Also loaned -

Authentic wooden candle sticks so carpenter could make copies, and a pattern for altar railing.

At present, the large exhibit room in the padres' house contains a fine collection of 62 water colors of the California Missions by the noted artist Chris Jorgensen. It is very well arranged. Other rooms contain many cases of exhibits of local Indian lore and items, which are being added to as additional artifacts are received. Also, a collection of items, photos and drawings of the early history of the mission is on exhibit.

The padres' house is open and the exhibits are being added to. The padres' living quarters are restored with typical early mission style furniture and fittings. It is hoped that, in later years, more of the original buildings can be rebuilt on the old foundations around the former large quadrangle.

The Sonoma State Historic Park, of which Mission San Francisco Solano de Sonoma is a part, is a unit of the Department of Parks and Recreation which, in turn, is one of eight departments of the California Resources Agency. This agency is one of the four that compose the executive branch of the State under the Governor. Norman B. Livermore is Secretary of the California Resources Agency and William Penn Mott is Director of the Department of Parks and Recreation -- both offices in Sacramento.

The Park rangers of the Sonoma unit are on duty in the office and information section at the east end of the mission corridor at all open hours.

Today, after 150 years, Mission San Francisco Solano holds up her position as the northern end of the great chain of early California Missions with proud dignity -- on her corner opposite the historic Sonoma Pueblo Plaza. While only a small part of the original mission of the pre-secularization period remains, the size and simple design gives one an idea of the extent of the mission establishment when the padres and their neophytes were the only residents. The chapel has been restored to signify that period, with its long open nave void of pews, with tiled floor, and with the Stations of the Cross on the simply decorated walls.

Mission San Francisco Solano de Sonoma celebrated its sesquicentennial year in 1973, taking its rightful and important place as one of the "Beginnings of Alta California."

VALE

(Farewell)

133

S. Franciscus Solanus

Appendix A

St. Francis Solano

The patron saint of Mission San Francisco Solano, St. Francis Solano, came from Andalusia, Spain, where he was born March, 1549 in Montilla, Province of Cordoba of important and moderately wealthy parents.

He grew up in the city and entered the local Jesuit college. He, no doubt, was well advised on the Peruvian history early in life as Garcilaso Inca, the Peruvian writer, resided in Montilla after 1561 and often served Mass in the local church.

Solano entered the Franciscan Order locally and was ordained in 1570. He served in parts of Spain for 19 years. Here, he was novice, master, teacher, and Superior. He was also a preacher — with compassion for the sinner and the sick, especially among the plague-stricken. A splendid violinist, he assisted the choirs and church music development.

In 1589 Solano joined a band of missionaries being sent to missions in South America. Landing in Lima, Peru, he traveled overland to Santiago del Estero on foot to the Indians of Socotonio and La Magdalena. A year later he moved on to Tucuman and Paraguay as custos and, in 1598, back to Peru as Superior in Lima and Trujillo.

Francis Solano followed in the footsteps of his ideal, St. Francis of Assisi, and he never spared himself. A man of prayer; a student of St. Bonaventura; he also had advanced medical knowledge, as shown by his work during the plagues of the times.

His death occurred in Lima, Peru, on July 14, 1610 age 61 years, and his body rests in the Franciscan Church in Lima. Pope Clement X beatified him in 1675 and Pope Benedict XIII canonized him in 1726 — St. Francis Solano, the Apostle of South America.

Appendix B

List of Resident and Part Time Fathers
1823 - 1881
Mission San Francisco Solano de Sonoma

1823	7/4	Fr. José Altimira	Resident &	1854	9/22	Archbishop J. S. Alemany	
1826	8/3	---	Founder		9/24	Fr. Joannes Ingoldsby	(Dolores)
1826	9/	Fr. Buneaventura Fortuni	Resident	1855	2/	Archbishop J. S. Alemany	
1833	3/15	---			9/	---	
					3/	Fr. L. A. Angez	(St. Vincent's Orphanage)
1833	3/1	Fr. José de Jesus María Gutiérrez	Resident				
1834	2/24	---			11/	Fr. Robertus A. N. Maurice	?
1834	3/29	Fr. José Lorenzo de la Concepción Quijas	Resident				
1835	6/	---	Moved Residence to San Rafael	1856	7/17	Fr. L. A. Angez	(St. Vincent's Orphanage)
1843	6/4	---	From San Rafael	1858	6/21	------	
				1858	11/28	Fr. I. I. Largan	(St. Vincent's Orphanage)
1841	10/20	Fr. José María Suárez del Real	(Santa Clara)	1859	3/19	---	---
1843	3/18	Fr. Jesús María Vásquez del Mercado	(Santa	1859	8/22	Fr. P. Deyaert	(St. John the Baptist, Napa)
1844	10/	---	Clara)	1870		---	---
1845	5/5	Fr. José María Suárez del Real	(Santa Clara)	1863	4/12	Archbishop J. S. Alemany	
1845	10/	---					
				1870		Fr. I. F. Harrington	(St. Vincent de Paul,
1846	2/1	Fr. Prudencio Santillan	(Dolores)	1872	9/8	---	Petaluma)
1850	2/3	---					
				1872	1/28	Archbishop J. S. Alemany	
1849	4/28	Fr. J. B. A. Brouillet	(Dolores)		7/28	---	
1849	5/30	Fr. Paulino Romani	(Dolores)	1873	4/12	Fr. S. Scanlon	(St. Vincent de Paul,
					7/13	---	Petaluma)
1850	1/25	Fr. Stanislaus Le Bret	Resident				
1851	2/4	---		1873	8/10	Fr. Jacobus Cleary	(St. Vincent de Paul,
				1877		---	Petaluma)
1850	11/5	Fr. Anaclet Lastrade	Resident			w/ assistant Fr. Patrick Ward	---
1851	3/6	Fr. John Mary A. Delmas	(St. Francis, S.F.)	1878	10/13	Fr. J. Donnelly, assistant to Fr. Cleary	---
	4/3	---		1881	5/1	---	
	3/28	Fr. Antonio Langlois, Vicar General					
	6/1	Archbishop J. S. Alemany		1881	5/19	Fr. Hubert Esser	Resident — Pastor
	6/1	Fr. Joannes Shanahan	Pastor		5/19	Mission sold to Solomon Schocken	
	6/14-22	---				Chapel used for services until	
1851	6/20	Fr. Leo Chemin	Pastor	1882	6/4	New St. Francis Solano Church, Napa Street	
1854	6/8	---		dedicated.			

NOTE:
The dates, when shown, indicate the first and last time the Father officiated. He may have arrived earlier or departed later, however. Archbishops officiated on inspection tours.

Appendix C

C (1) SPIRITUAL RESULTS   MISSION S. F. SOLANO

YEAR	BAPTISMS				MARRIAGES			BURIALS			INDIAN POPULATION		
	Adults	Children	Gente de razon	Total	Indians	Gente de razon	Total	Indians	Gente de razon	Total	Men	Women	Total
A.1823	0	0	0	0	1	0	1	1	0	1	-	-	482
24	70	24	0	95	17	1	18	40	1	41	384	308	692
A.25	48	52	0	195	24	0	42	30	0	71	338	296	634
F.25				181			37			70	-	-	-
26	42	65	0	288	25	0	62	61	0	131	326	315	641
										Error 5			
27	62	28	0	378	41	0	103	64	0	200	340	327	667
28	73	54	0	505	35	0	138	88	1	289	372	332	704
29	74	45	0	624	36	0	174	51	0	340	394	378	772
30	6	19	0	649	20	0	194	37	0	377	393	367	760
31	106	126	0	881	35	0	229	53	0	430	495	444	939
32	86	41	0	1008	34	0	263	70	0	500	509	487	996
G.33	-	22	-	?1030	14	1	278	118?	0	604	-	-	750
Q.34	-	-	-	-	10	-	288	-	-	-	-	-	650
35				1315	21		309						550
36					11		320						
37					17		337						
38					8	1	347						
39				1518	3		350			876			
40	10	30	5	1563	8	1	359	19	1	896	89	45	134
													? 144
													Informe

A.   Fr. Altimira Informe   G.   Fr. Gutiérrez Informe
F.   Fr. Fortuny Informe   Q.   Fr. Quijas Informe

C (2)   MATERIAL RESULTS   MISSION S. F. SOLANO

Year	Cattle	Sheep	Horses	Mares	Oxen	Pigs	Goats	Mules	TOTAL
A.1823	180	1100	46	-	-	-	-	15	1341
24	1100	4000	130	300	(70)	-	-	16	4546
25	800	2000	100	400	(40)	-	-	15	3315
F.26	582	1439	100	400	(50)	80?B/C	-	11	2540
27	120?	3500	140	400	(50)	8	-	10	5258
28	1400	4000	125	400	(60)	-	-	6	5931
29	1500	5000	125	400	(60)	5	-	4	7034
30	2000	4000	125	600	(60)	60	-	4	6789
31	2500	5000	125	600	(60)	50	-	4	8279
32	3500	6000	200	700	(60)	50	-	13	10463
G.33	1849	7114	232	803	(60)	-	-	18B	12016

A.   Fr. Altimira Informe
F.   Fr. Fortuny Informe
G.   Fr. Gutiérrez Informe

C (3) MATERIAL RESULTS   MISSION S. F. SOLANO

Year	Wheat Pla.	Wheat Hrv.	Barley Pla.	Barley Hrv.	Peas Pla.	Peas Hrv.	Corn Pla.	Corn Hrv.	Kidney Beans Pla.	Kidney Beans Hrv.	Beans Pla.	Beans Hrv.	Lentils Pla.	Lentils Hrv.	Chick Peas Pla.	Chick Peas Hrv.	Total Planted	Total Harvested
1823	-	-	-	-	-	-		-	-	-	-	-	-	-	-	-		
A.24	180	500	-	-	-	-	2	200	¼	6	-	-	¼	2½	¼	2	180.7	710¼
25	40	758	18	280	1	25	2	142	1	16	0.6	6	-	-	-	-	62.6	1227
F.26	79.9	1741.6	14.2	663.9	1	87.6	2.3	87	1.3	13.6	2.6	34.6	-	-	.3	5.6	100.11	2627.9
27	100	1151	13.2	200	2.2	75	3	250	2	9.6	1.6	48	-	-	.3	2	122.8	1739
28	121	514	41	208	2.6	9	3.6	25	1.3	2	3	10	-	-	.6	.6	172.8	770
29	58	19	0	0	1	2	3	300	2	200	0.6	2	-	-	.6a	6a	65.2	523.6
30	87	1190	19	140	2	3	4	300	3	24 6a	2	12	-	-	.2a	10.2	117.6	1669.6
31	113	1171	22	211	2	19	2.9	200	5 1a	24	2	5.7	-	-	.2	2	147.2	1640.9
32	90	800	51.2	1025	1.2	52	4	300	4	32	1	3	-	-	1a.	20a.	151.4	2214
G.33	86	931	46	500	2	24	3	90	7	15	2	9	-	-			146.1	1569plus

A.   Fr. Altimira Informe
F.   Fr. Fortuny Informe
G.   Fr. Gutierrez Informe

Pla. - Planted
Hrv. - Harvested
a   - almud

Fanega - 110#
Bushel - 60#
Bushel Barley - 50#

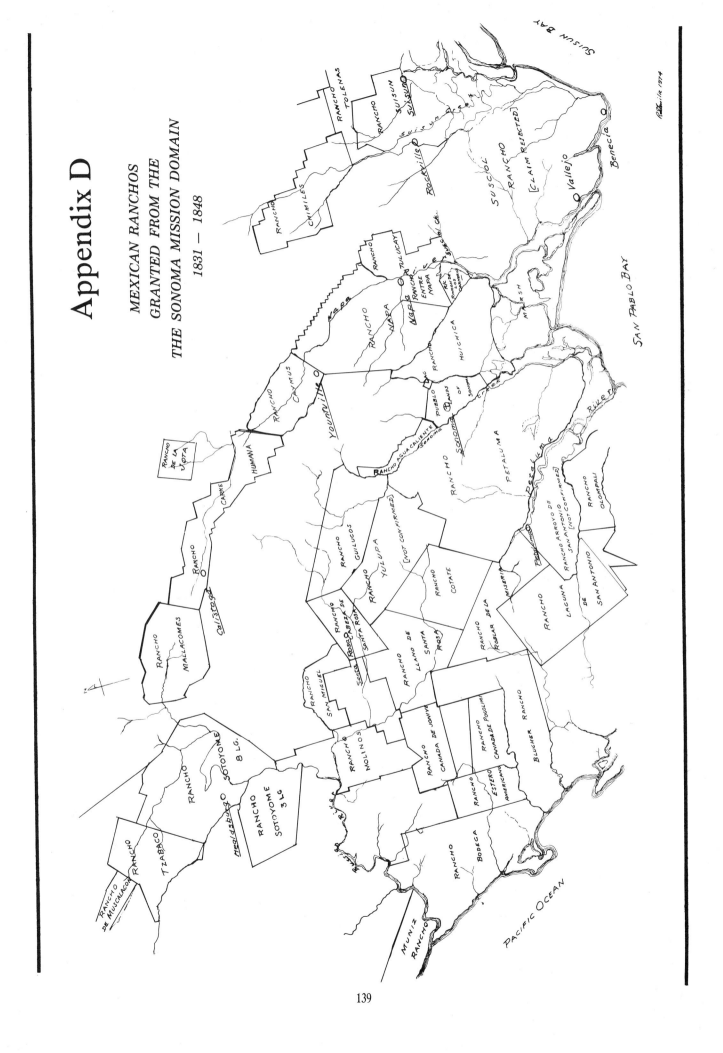

Appendix D

MEXICAN RANCHOS
GRANTED FROM THE
THE SONOMA MISSION DOMAIN
1831 – 1848

Appendix E

Signature illustrations courtesy Missions and Missionaries, Engelhardt.

Signatures of four padres who served during the mission period:

Fr. José Altimira, O.F.M.

Fr. Buenaventura Fortuny, O.F.M.

Fr. José Gutiérrez, O.F.M.

Fr. José Lorenzo Quijas, O.F.M.

Signatures of four important church officials during the Sonoma Mission period:

Fr. José Señan, O.F.M.

Fr. Mariano Payeras, O.F.M., Commissary Prefect.

Fr. Vicente Francisco de Sarría, O.F.M., Commissary Prefect.

Fr. José Alemany, O.P., Archbishop of San Francisco.

Notes

Chapter I

1. Eldridge, *The Beginnings of San Francisco,* I, 45.
2. Engelhardt, *Missions and Missionaries,* II, 228. (Hereinafter cited as Engelhardt, *M and M.*)
3. Chapman, *History of California, The Spanish Period,* 425.
4. *Ibid.,* 425; also Prov. State Papers Arch. Calif. XIX, 276-80.
5. Engelhardt, *San Francisco or Mission Dolores,* 407.
6. Engelhardt, *M and M,* III, 26-7.
7. *Ibid.,* 145-7.
8. Finley, *History of Sonoma County,* 41.
9. *Ibid.,* 210. Some records state 1819.
10. Tays, "Mariano Guadalupe Vallejo and Sonoma," *California Historical Society Quarterly,* XVI, No. 2, 110. (Hereinafter cited as Tays, *CHSQ.*)
11. Engelhardt, *M and M,* III, 154-7.
12. Tays, *CHSQ,* XVI, No. 2, 111.

Chapter II

1. Engelhardt, *Mission San Buenaventura,* 124-5.
2. Engelhardt, *M and M,* III, 176; also Bancroft, *History of California,* II, 497. (Hereinafter cited as B/C); also Tays, *CHSQ,* XVI, No. 2, 111.
3. Translation by R. S. Smilie, 1971, of original documents in Bancroft Library, co-ordinated with and added to from article (translation) Taylor, *Hutching's California Magazine,* V. Taylor, no doubt, had other documents or copies with extra sentences, etc., including Archbishop's Archive, S. F. copy.
4. Route of exploration, by author.
5. Engelhardt, *M and M,* III, 175.
6. Tays, *CHSQ,* XVI, No. 2, 114.
7. Kroeber, *Handbook of Indians of California,* Bureau of American Ethnology, Bulletin 78, Fig. 23, Plates 27-34.
8. Tays, *CHSQ,* XVI, No. 2, 115.
9. Finley, *History of Sonoma County,* 46; also letter Altimira to Arguello, 8/31/23, SBMA. Rancho San Pablo, north of Berkeley, was a cattle ranch of Mission Dolores.
10. The present site of Mission San Francisco Solano by the plaza. On returning to Sonoma Valley in August 1823, Fr. Altimira no doubt found the weeks of hot summer weather and the strong daily west winds had dried up most creeks on the Valley's west side and its higher sloping pastures.

    On the east side of the Valley, opposite the Embarcadero, was a large level area bounded by Agua Caliente, Arroyo Seco and Sonoma Creeks — crossed by some year round spring fed streams. The soil was good, land level and open, winds moderate, many large spreading oaks, good land, easily developed and irrigated for row crops. A large central spring was ample for domestic supply.

    Fr. Altimira stated in his August 31st, 1823 letter: "and the 25th (Aug.) we arrived and *selected this site* and began to build." and "all persons endorse *the site which we have discovered.*"

    The Rancheria Pul Pula site, where the first founding cross was raised and first mass celebrated, was abandoned in favor of this newly "discovered" location.

Chapter III

1. Engelhardt, *M and M,* III, 182-3.
2. *Ibid.,* 178-9.
3. *Ibid.,* 179-80.
4. *Ibid.,* 181-2.
5. *Ibid.,* 182-3.
6. B/C, II, 503-4, Sarría to Arguello.
7. Geiger, (Trans.) Extract letter, Sarría to Altimira, Santa Barbara Mission Archives. (Hereinafter cited as SBMA.)

Chapter IV

1. B/C, II, 504, Altimira to Arguello, 10/4/1824.
2. Taylor, *S.F. Bulletin,* 10/15/1860.
3. *Informe,* Mission S.F. Solano 1824, SBMA. (Hereinafter cited as Informe S.F. Solano, SBMA.)
4. Walsh, *Mission Bells of California,* 147.
5. Engelhardt, *Mission San Buenaventura,* 125.
6. *Informe,* S.F. Solano 1825, SBMA.
7. B/C, II, 504, Note 40.
8. Tays, *CHSQ,* XVI, No. 2, 118.
9. It appears that the story of the raid and fires at Mission San Francisco Solano grew with each historian's telling until it became a major attack and all had to flee for their lives with the mission a complete ruin. However, basic facts and the *Informe* at the end of the year 1825, a few months later, reported a normal year; nothing about an uprising or major destruction. This is also the conclusion of a study by Cassidy, 1889, as noted in Finley, *History of Sonoma County,* 46: "We find also, an accredited rumor that the Mission, S.F. Solano, was destroyed by the Indians a few years after it was founded. This story must be founded on uncertain tradition, for we have found no authentic record of such an occurrence." Lewis Publishing Co., *History of Sonoma County,* Chicago 1889. Cassidy of the *Petaluma Argus,* reported as a very thorough researcher, was considered local editor for the above publication.

Chapter V

1. Geiger, *Franciscan Missionaries in Hispanic California,* 89-90. (Reprinted with the permission of the Henry E. Huntington Library and Art Gallery, San Marino, California.)
2. *Informe,* S.F. Solano, 1826, SBMA.
3. *Informe,* S.F. Solano, 1827, SBMA. Some historians seemingly have read a 50 *vara* as a 30 *vara* length. The 50 *varas* is confirmed in Note 7 - 50 *varas* of tile.
4. *Inventario incompleto,* no date, Fabricas, SBMA.
5. Carter (tr.), "Duhaut-Cilly's Account of California in the Years 1827-1828," *CHSQ,* VIII, No. 3, 239-43.
6. *Informe,* S.F. Solano, 1827, SBMA.
7. *Informe,* S.F. Solano, 1828, SBMA.

Chapter VI

1. Engelhardt, *M and M,* II, 274-5.
2. *Informe,* S.F. Solano, 1829, SBMA.
3. ¼ mile below Cooper Bridge. Another ford was the same distance above the bridge, a short league above the embarcadero.
4. B/C, II, 506.

5. *Informe,* S.F. Solano, 1830, SBMA.
6. B/C, III, 719 - note.
7. *Informe,* S.F. Solano, 1831, SBMA.
8. Wilbur (tr.), *Duflot de Mofras' Travels on the Pacific Coast,* II, 202-3.

Chapter VII

1. *Informe,* S.F. Solano, 1832, SBMA; also *S. F. Bulletin,* 11/5/1859.
2. Painting, Oriana Day, 1882-83; also U. S. Land Grant 609, 20; also Sketch, Vischer, Bancroft Library, no date, probably 1870's, (Mission before 1832.) (Bancroft Library hereinafter cited as B/L.)

   Painting by above Oriana Day and E. Vischer both indicate the adobe church extending out beyond the padres' house and corridor, though both were painted from memory years later. However, a painting "Sonoma in 1840" by Victor Prudon, Vallejo's early secretary, and a sketch by W.M. Boggs, son of *Alcalde* Lilburn Boggs, dated 1846, who had the corner store across the street, confirm the position of the front of the church.

   The 1859 *San Francisco Bulletin* report (Chapter XXII, Note 3) states the front wall "was entirely demolished and the side walls for some distance, the east one for some 40 feet." As the front of the church was close to the street, it was the logical part to dismantle first and haul away — for use of the timbers, adobe bricks, etc. to construct other plaza buildings after the new chapel on the corner was built in 1841. As adobe mortar was used, the adobe bricks could easily be reclaimed.

   With the front portion of the church obliterated by 1854, it is assumed that G. Black, surveying the area for Archbishop Alemany, would run an extension of the front of the padres' house east across the empty space before taking a sight along what remained of the east wall of the adobe church. U.S. Surveyor C.C. Tracy apparently followed Surveyor Black in 1859 as all his distances and bearings are the same.

   Considering the above, and also that Fr. Fortuni had built a large adobe church of similar size and simple design at his former Mission San Jose station, with its *fachada* out beyond the corridor and padres' house, the author is convinced that the Mission San Francisco Solano Church was erected in the same manner.
3. The sacristy, no doubt, was in the rear as it would be in front of and close to the end of the *monjerio* if on the patio side and would block the tiled walk to the *monjerio.* Also, G. Black, 8/1854, Surveyor, shows adobe church ruins over 63 *varas* long with no indication of a sacristy on the patio side.
4. *U.S. Land Grant* 609, Map No. 21.
5. Treganza, *University of California Archaeological Survey.* (Hereinafter cited Treganza, *U.C. Survey.*)
6. *Informe,* S.F. Solano, 1832. No record is extant as to the date of finishing and dedication of the new adobe church, most likely late in 1833 or early 1834. The original wooden *palizada* church, west of the padres' house, appears to be still standing at that time. No mention of its being dismantled or burned down has been found in any mission record so far. Also, it must have been used for services until the adobe church was ready. Notes with *U.S. Land Grant* No. 609 Mission S.F. Solano refer to Map No. 21, 1832, showing east side a partly erected church, center curate's house, western part marked church. Later, it no doubt was used as an additional badly needed stores building until 1841 when it was replaced with the new and present chapel. It was

reportedly used by M. Vallejo as a small store prior to 1841.

   Local legend, as passed down through the years, relates that the mission churches, two were burned down before the present chapel was built. Yet the period before secularization was only of 12 years duration and six until '41. There were two fires recorded during this time. The first in the fall of '26, when Fr. Altimira left, and another in October '31 when some Indian huts burned in the neophyte village. No important buildings were destroyed either time as no mention was made in either annual *Informe.*

   However, two churches, the first and second wooden frame churches of St. Francis Solano on Napa Street in 1896 and 1922, burned down before the present concrete church building was erected. These were *not* mission churches.

Chapter VIII

1. Geiger, (Tr.) Letter Fr. Fortuny, Jan. 2, 1831, SBMA.
2. Engelhardt, *Mission San Buenaventura,* 131.
3. Bancroft, *California Pastoral,* 218.
4. See following Chapt. IX.
5. Engelhardt, Letter, *M and M,* III, 457-9.

Chapter IX

1. Thompson, *The Russian Settlement,* 3-5.
2. Tays, *CHSQ,* XVI, No. 3, 232.
3. Lothrop, "The Indian Campaigns of General M.G. Vallejo," *Quarterly Society of California Pioneers,* IX, No. 3, 171-2. (Quarterly hereinafter cited as QSC Pioneers.)
4. Tays, *CHSQ,* XVI, No. 3, 232-3.

   An alleged earlier undated exploration trip by Lt. Vallejo with 25 soldiers to the *Frontera del Norte* about 1828, while he was still stationed at the Presidio of Monterey, has been related in the *S. F. Bulletin,* January 27, 1914 - page 7 - "Memoirs of the Vallejos." The described route was north from Monterey, by-passing Pueblo San Jose to the east, through locations of later East Bay cities to Berkeley, San Pablo and a Pinole camp; across Carquinez Strait, west through Napa Valley, Sonoma Valley and Mission, up Sonoma Valley, down to Mission San Rafael to the Golden Gate; then a return trip over the same route to Monterey. However, no historical or documentary record, other than the above, has been found to verify this story. (The author.)
5. *Ibid.,* 235.
6. *Ibid.,* 235.
7. *Informe,* S.F. Solano, 1833, B/L.

Chapter X

1. Bancroft, *California Pastoral,* 219-20.
2. B/C, III, 318-9.
3. Chapman, *History of California, The Spanish Period,* 446-70.
4. B/C, III, 327-8.
5. *Ibid.,* 335-6.
6. *Ibid.,* 342-4.
7. Petaluma Land Grant, Patented Nov. 19, 1874.
8. B/C, III, 256-7; H. Mizner Land - 2 miles E. of Fulton - 4½ miles N. of Santa Rosa.
9. Tays, *CHSQ,* XVI, No. 3, 236-40.
10. *Inventario-Incompleto* - ms. de Solano, SBMA.

Chapter XI

1. B/C, III, 267-8.
2. *Ibid.,* 347-8, Note 11, last para.
3. *Ibid.,* 347-8, Note 11.
4. *Ibid.,* 347-8, Note 11.
5. Tays, *CHSQ,* XVI, No. 3, 242.
6. Gregory, *History Sonoma County,* 36-7; also B/C III, 294.
7. "Ortega - a rough, boisterous, loud-talking man; a man capable of doing any bad attack. At that time Vallejo, if he had had any such evil inclination, could have gotten him to kill a man for a trifle, for he was a tool of Vallejo to the last day of his life." Charles Brown, "Early Events," *QSC Pioneers,* VII, No. 1, 39.
8. B/C, III, 719, note; also Vallejo Doc. ms. III, 11-12.
9. Tays, *CHSQ,* XVI, No. 3, 238-9.
10. *U.S. Land Grants,* Sonoma Pueblo, March 31, 1880; also *U.S. Land Grants,* Sonoma City Lot, April 30, 1866.
11. Tays, *CHSQ,* XVI, No. 3, 243-4.
12. Bennyhoff and Elsasser, *University of California Archaeological Survey* No. 27, 1954, 46, Note 5, Ref. *Historia,* (Vallejo, n.d.) III, 19.
13. Civil Case No. 1025 Superior Court Sonoma County, Oct. 8, 1886, Wm. Pickett vs. H. Esser, et al, (Catholic Church). Plot was later included in Out Lot No. 510 of O'Farrell survey; also Alley, Bowen & Co., *History of Marin County,* 162.

Chapter XII

1. Letter, Fr. Quijas to Fr. Prefecto G. Diego, Trans. Engelhardt, *M and M,* III, 581-9. Fr. Perez, a Mexican priest, secretary to Fr. Commissary Prefect Garcia Diego y Moreno, residing at Mission Santa Clara, assisted Fr. Quijas on a visit to Mission San Francisco Solano. Also Cal. Mission Documents #1273, SBMA.
2. Letter, Vallejo to Gov. B/C III, 719-20, Note.
3. B/C, III, 720, Note.

Chapter XIII

1. B/C, IV, 71-2.
2. Tays, *CHSQ,* XVI, No. 4, 350.
3. An earlier larger foundation exists next to and west of the Santa Rosa Carrillo adobe, probably an early mission (swine) rancho building site.
4. Tays, *op. cit.,* 351.
5. *Ibid.,* 350-1, 355.
6. *Ibid.,* 355, Note 20.

Chapter XIV

1. Tays, *CHSQ,* XVI, No. 4, 360.
2. *Ibid.,* 362-3.
3. *Ibid.,* 360-1.
4. Thompson, *Historical Atlas of Sonoma County,* 20. Town of Petaluma area - a very controversial duplicate grant to Ortega and also Juan Miranda, later decided by U.S. Supreme Court.
5. Tays, *op. cit.* 369-70.
6. B/C, III, 723, note.
7. B/C, IV, 56 note, 57.
8. B/C, III, 719-20, note; also Tays, *CHSQ,* XVI, No. 4, 368-9.
9. Dakin, *The Lives of William Hartnell,* 235-6.
10. Dana, *Sutter of California,* 62-74.
11. B/C, V, 757; also B/C, III, 722 - Note 1839.
12. *Informe,* S.F. Solano, 1840 SBMA.
13. Davis, *60 Years in California,* 109-10.

Chapter XV

1. Engelhardt, *M and M,* III, 217.
2. Dana, *op. cit.,* 63.
3. California Historical Landmarks, No. 17, Blue Wing Inn. This building was probably newly built as all pictures, even though considered not too accurate, show mission structures (major-domo, etc.) at right angles (N & S) to the padres' house; also, the original mission plaza was, no doubt, larger than Spain St. in width.
4. B/C, IV, 59-61.
5. *Ibid.,* IV, 61-62.
6. *Informe,* S.F. Solano, 1840, SBMA.
7. B/C, IV, 165-81.
8. Insurance Map 1897; also Bennyhoff and Elsasser, *op. cit.,* 39; also the present (1972) chapel measures 105'9" x 22'8" overall or 38½ *varas* x 8¼ *varas.*

Chapter XVI

1. Wilkes, "Narrative of the United States Exploring Expedition, 1838-42," *QSC Pioneers,* IX, 180.
2. Wilbur (tr.), *Duflot de Mofras' Travels on the Pacific Coast,* I, 237.
   Error: Fr. Amoros was padre at Mission San Rafael Arcangel. Fr. Altimira was founder of Mission San Francisco Solano. August 25, 1823, date of *second* location.
3. Simpson, *An Overland Journey Round the World — During the Years 1841 and 1842,* 171-81.
4. B/C, IV, 285.
5. Gudde (tr.), "Edward Vischer's First Visit to California," *CHSQ,* XIX, No. 3, Reprint 6-8.
6. Tays, *CHSQ,* XVII, No. 2, 147-8.

Chapter XVII

1. B/C, IV, 351-2.
2. *Ibid.,* 346; also Murphy, *People of the Pueblo,* 82; also *QSC Pioneers,* III, No. 2, 78.
3. Finley, *op. cit.,* 83.
4. Chapman, *op. cit.,* 472.
5. Engelhardt, *M and M,* IV, 249.
6. Tays, *CHSQ,* XVII, No. 2, 155-6.
7. B/C, IV, 445 - note.
8. *Ibid.,* 423 - note.
9. Engelhardt, *M and M,* IV, 136.
10. B/C, IV, 548.
11. *Ibid.,* 549.
12. *Ibid.,* 550-1.
13. Bowman, "Adobes of 9 Counties," ms., B/L.
14. B/C, V, 561 - note 8.

Chapter XVIII

1. B/C, V, 113-4 - notes. Kelsay, written otherwise Kelsey.
2. *Ibid.,* 129-30.
3. *Ibid.,* 146-8 - note (Todd letter, June 16, 1872); also Forbes, *California Missions and Landmarks,* 244-5. There are other claimants to help making the Bear Flag: namely, Ben Dewell, Thos. Cowie - with cloth from Mrs. W.B. Elliot as well as from Mrs. Kelsey, etc. etc.
4. B/C, *op. cit.,* 151-3 - note.
5. *Ibid.,* 159 - Note.
6. *Ibid.,* 165-8.
7. *Ibid.,* 169-78.
8. *Ibid.,* 184-5.
9. *Ibid.,* 231, 238, 242.
10. *Ibid.,* 298-9.

Chapter XIX

1. Finley, *op. cit.,* 156.
2. B/C, V, 758.
3. *CHSQ,* X, No. 4, 353-4.
4. Bryant, *What I Saw in California,* 333-8.
5. Sonoma County Records, Justice Court Book, Item No. 52, 1847.
6. Finley, *op. cit.,* 156. For further details of the Vallejo-Nash-Boggs period in Sonoma, recommend *Pioneer Sonoma* by Robert D. Parmelee, Sonoma, 1972.
7. B/C, V, 667.
8. B/C, V, 575.
9. Alley, Bowen, *History Sonoma County,* 467.
10. Engelhardt, *Mission Dolores,* 316.
10a. *Ibid.,* 299.
11. "A Pioneer Reminiscential," *S. F. Bulletin* 1882, California Historical Library Archives. Note: "He," and the lack of seats, indicates other than Padre Santillan as no padre sits down while preaching - author.
12. Juan Castañeda house, middle of block opposite east side of plaza.

Chapter XX

1. B/C, V, 515.
2. *S. F. Californian,* Mar. 12, 1868.
3. McKittrick, *Vallejo, Son of California,* 302; also Alley, Bowen, *op. cit.,* 445.
4. Finley, *op. cit.,* 231.
5. Later the Blue Wing Tavern. S.V.H.S. *Saga of Sonoma,* The Blue Wing Inn; also Cross, *The Early Inns of California,* Chapt. 13, Sonoma's Blue Wing Hotel.

Chapter XXI

1. *CHSQ,* XLIX, No. 3, 202-15.
2. *CHSQ,* XXIV, No. 1, 58-62; also Sonoma Valley Hist., Soc., *op. cit.,* 10.
3. *Ibid.,* 28-9. (Toscano Hotel)
4. Thompson Co.,, *Historical Atlas of Sonoma County,* 20.
5. Hoover & Rensch, *Historic Spots of California,* 521.
6. Thompson Co., *op. cit.,* 20½.
7. Murphy, *op. cit.,* 205-7.
8. Finley, *op. cit.,* 261; also Thompson Co., *op. cit.,* 19.

Chapter XXII

1. Book - Deeds No. 7, 711-12, Sonoma Co. Records 11/24/1858.
2. U.S. Surveyor General Plats 1859.

3. *S. F. Bulletin,* Nov. 5, 1859; also Treganza, *op. cit.,* note p.6, F.A. Bridewell, 1960, Curator, added "Witnesses who saw remnants of the church (adobe) walls in the 40's said they were 30 ft. high." Also note p. 4, "adobe church was deliberately torn down in order to remove the valuable timbers for use in privately owned buildings. Rain was not responsible for the demolition. Portions of the walls 30' high remained in the 50's."
4. Kneiss, *Redwood Railroads,* 2.
5. Suscol Rancho, Land Grant Case, extensive records.
6. U.S. Land Office, May 31, 1862.

Chapter XXIII

1. Cerruti, *"Ramblings in California,"* ms. in B/L.
2. Egenhoff, *Fabricas,* 112.
3. Cerruti, *op. cit.*
4. *Ibid.*
5. *Ibid.*

Chapter XXIV

1. Newspapers - *Index-Tribune.*
2. Murphy, *op. cit.,* 244-5
3. Alley, Bowen, *op. cit.,* 88.
4. Leases, Book C, 142, Sonoma County Records.
5. Deeds, Book No. 76, 101-2-3, Sonoma County Records, 7/11/1881.

Chapter XXV

1. Grants, Sonoma City, Book A2, 38, Sonoma County Records; also Chapter XI, Note 13.
2. Deeds, Book No. 96, 219-25, 4/20/1885, Sonoma County Records.
3. Deeds, Book No. 155, 171-4, 9/13/1894, Sonoma County Records.
4. *San Francisco Chronicle,* September 28, 1902, 8.

Chapter XXVI

1. Deeds, Book No. 206, 520, 613, Sonoma County Records.
2. Deeds, Book No. 252, 511-12, Item 2, Sonoma County Records.
3. Knowland, *California Landmark History,* 61; also *Index-Tribune,* 9/30/1911, 4/19/1913.
4. Walsh, *op. cit.,* 144-150.
5. Deeds, Book No., 378, 458-9, Sonoma County Records.
6. Deeds, Book No. 370, 478, Sonoma County Records.
7. Deeds, Book No. 479, 346-7, Sonoma County Records.
8. Deeds, Book No. 1569, 86-8, Sonoma County Records.

Bibliography

Archives

Archbishop's Archives, San Francisco
Bancroft Library, Berkeley (B/L)
Bishop's Archives, Santa Rosa
California Historical Society, San Francisco (CHS)
California State Library, Sacramento
Community Archives, S.J., U. of Santa Clara, Santa Clara
Huntington Library and Art Gallery, San Marino
Mission San Francsco Solano, Sonoma
Mission San Rafael Arcangel Archives, San Rafael
St. Francis Solano Church Archives, Sonoma
St. Vincent de Paul Church Archives, Petaluma
Santa Barbara Mission Archives, Santa Barbara (SBMA)
Society of California Pioneers, San Francisco (SC Pioneers)
Sonoma County Recorder's Office, Santa Rosa
Sonoma (City and County) Library

Printed Works

Alley, Bowen & Co. *History of Sonoma County.* (San Francisco, 1880)

Bancroft, Hubert H. *History of California.* (San Francisco, 1886-1890). 7 vols. (B/C)

——————————. *California Pastoral.* (San Francisco, 1888).

Berger, John. *The Franciscan Missions of California.* (New York, 1941).

Bryant, Edwin. *What I Saw in California.* (New York, 1849).

Chapman, Charles E. *A History of California, The Spanish Period.* (Copyright 1921 by The Macmillan Co., renewed 1949 by Aimee F. Chapman)

Cross, Ralph Herbert. *The Early Inns of California 1844-1869.* (San Francisco, 1954).

Dakin, Susanna B. *The Lives of William Hartnell.* (Stanford 1949).

Dana, Julian. *Sutter of California.* (New York, 1934).

Davis, William Heath. *Sixty Years in California.* (San Francisco, 1889).

Egenhoff, Elisabeth L. *Fabricas.* California Division of Mines. (San Francisco, 1952).

Eldridge, Zoeth S. *The Beginnings of San Francisco.* (San Francisco, 1912). 2 vol.

Engelhardt, Zephyrin, O.F.M. *Missions and Missionaries of California.* (San Francisco. 1908-1915). 4 vols. (M and M)

——————————. *San Francisco or Mission Dolores.* (Chicago, 1924).

——————————. *Mission San Buenaventura.* (Santa Barbara, 1930).

Finley, E.L. *History of Sonoma County.* (Santa Rosa Press Democrat, Santa Rosa, 1937).

Forbes, Mrs. A.S.C. *California Missions and Landmarks.* (Los Angeles, 1915).

Geiger, Maynard, O.F.M. *Calendar of Documents in the Santa Barbara Mission Archives.* (Washington, D.C., 1947).

——————————. *Mission Santa Barbara, 1782-1965.* (Santa Barbara, 1965).

——————————. *Franciscan Missionaries in Hispanic California, 1769-1848.* (Huntington Library Publications, San Marino, 1969). Reprints with the permission of the Henry E. Huntington Library and Art Gallery, San Marino, California, 10/20/71.

Gregory, T. *History of Sonoma County.* (Los Angeles, California, 1911).

Gudde, Erwin G. *California Place Names.* (Berkeley and Los Angeles, 1960).

Hoover, Mildred B. and Rensch, H.E. and E.G. *Historic Spots in California.* 3rd Edition. Revised by Wm. N. Abeloe. (Stanford 1966).

Kneiss, A.H. *Redwood Railroads.* (Berkeley, 1956).

Printed Works *continued*

Knowland, Hon. Joseph R. *California, A Landmark History.* (Oakland, 1941).

Kroeber, A.L. *Handbook of the Indians of California, Smithsonian Institution, Bureau of American Ethnology, Bulletin 78.* (Washington, D.C., 1925).

McCarthy, Francis Florence. *History of Mission San Jose California, 1797-1835.* (Fresno, 1958).

McKittrick, Myrtle M. *Vallejo, Son of California.* (Portland, Ore., 1944).

Murphy, Celeste G. *People of the Pueblo.* (Sonoma, 1937-41).

Parmelee, Robert D. *Pioneer Sonoma.* (Sonoma, 1972).

Simpson, Sir George. *An Overland Journey Round the World During the Years 1841 and 1842.* (Philadelphia, 1847).

Sonoma Valley Historical Society. *Saga of Sonoma.* (Sonoma, 1954).

Spearman, Arthur Dunning, S.J. *The Five Franciscan Churches of Mission Santa Clara, 1777-1825.* (Palo Alto, 1963).

Thompson, R.A. *The Russian Settlement.* (Santa Rosa, 1896).

Thompson, Thos. H. & Co. *Historical Atlas of Sonoma County.* (Oakland, 1877).

Walsh, Marie T. *The Mission Bells of California.* (San Francisco, 1934).

Wilbur, Marguerite Eyer, (tr.). *Duflot de Mofras' Travels on the Pacific Coast.* (Santa Ana, 1937). 2 vols.

Periodical Literature

Gudde, Erwin G. (tr.). "Edward Vischer's First Visit to California." *California Historical Society Quarterly.* XIX, No. 3, 6-8. (CHSQ).

Index-Tribune, Newspaper, Weekly, Sonoma.

Lothrop, Marion L. "The Indian Campaigns of General M.G. Vallejo." *Quarterly, the Society of California Pioneers.* IX, No. 3, 161-205. (QSC Pioneers.)

Tays, George. "Mariano Guadalupe Vallejo and Sonoma." *California Historical Society Quarterly,* XVI and XVII. (Number of page as noted). (Tays, CHSQ).

Wilkes, Lt. Charles, USN. "Narrative of the United States Exploring Expedition, 1838-42." *Quarterly, the Society of California Pioneers.* IX, 180.

INDEX

147

El Camino Real

CIRCA

1830

M. San Rafael

M. San Francisco Solano

M. San Jose

Santa Clara

M. San Francisco de Assis

M. de Santa Cruz

M. San Juan Bautista

M. Carmelo

M. de la Soledad

M. de San Antonio

M. de San Miguel

M. de San Lu

N